Activists beyond Borders

Activists beyond Borders

ADVOCACY NETWORKS IN INTERNATIONAL POLITICS

MARGARET E. KECK

and

KATHRYN SIKKINK

CORNELL UNIVERSITY PRESS

Ithaca and London

For Douglas Johnson and Larry Wright

First published 1998 by Cornell University Press
First Printing, Cornell Paperbacks, 1998

Library of Congress Cataloging-in-Publication Data

Keck, Margaret E.
  Activists beyond borders : advocacy networks in international politics / Margaret E. Keck and Kathryn Sikkink.
    p. cm.
  Includes bibliographical references (p.) and index.
  ISBN-13: 978-0-8014-8456-8 (pbk. : alk. paper)
  ISBN-10: 0-8014-8456-1 (pbk. : alk. paper)
    1. Pressure groups. 2. World politics. 3. Human rights—Societies, etc. 4. Environmental protection—Societies, etc.
    5. Women's rights—Societies, etc. I. Sikkink, Kathryn, 1955–
  II. Title.
  JF529.K43 1997
  322.4'3—dc21

                                                        97-33165

Printed in the United States of America

Cornell University Press strives to use environmentally responsible suppliers and materials to the fullest extent possible in the publishing of its books. Such materials include vegetable-based, low-VOC inks and acid-free papers that are recycled, totally chlorine-free, or partly composed of nonwood fibers. For further information, visit our website at www.cornellpress.cornell.edu.

Paperback printing   10 9 8

Contents

Preface

One of the most haunting passages in Gabriel García Márquez' classic novel *One Hundred Years of Solitude*, describes the army arriving to quell striking banana workers in the mythical town of Macondo. When a crowd refuses to disperse, the soldiers fire on the men, women, and children gathered in the central plaza next to the train station. The sole survivor of the massacre, José Arcadio Segundo, awakens in a ghostly train filled with the corpses "who would be thrown into the sea like rejected bananas." Jumping off the train, he finds his way back to Macondo, where everyone assures him "there haven't been any dead here." "The military denied it even to the relatives of the victims who crowded the commandants' offices in search of news. 'You must have been dreaming,' the officers insisted. 'Nothing has happened in Macondo. . . .'"[1]

The novel was first published in Argentina in 1967, a year before the massacre of students in the Tlatelolco Plaza in Mexico City, and a decade before the "death flights" in Argentina, where victims were indeed thrown into the sea—but alive and sedated, with weights on their feet. Real life in Argentina and Mexico quickly began to bear a startling resemblance to the hallucinatory scenario traced by García Márquez. Officials denied any responsibility for the events or even (in the Argentine case) that anything had occurred. Fearful citizens professed that no one had actually been killed. Family members went from office to office, only to be told that no one knew anything about the whereabouts of their children.

Yet the people of Mexico and Argentina did create the "second opportunity on earth" denied to the citizens of Macondo in the last pages of the

---

[1] Gabriel García Márquez, *One Hundred Years of Solitude* (New York: Harper and Row, 1970), pp. 307–16.

novel.[2] In one of the more surprising human rights events of the mid-1990s, former military officers in Argentina confessed to direct involvement in the repression in the late 1970s. They gave details to journalists about their participation in the death flights. The commander-in-chief of the Argentine army, General Martin Balza, accepted responsibility for "errors" and "illegitimate methods" including executions, offered condolences to the family members, and committed himself "to a future that does not repeat the past."[3]

Why was the ending so different in real life? A key part of the explanation is the work of a network of domestic and international human rights activists who provided crucial information on events in Argentina and lobbied governments and international organizations to express concern, investigate, and bring pressure for change. Nongovernmental organizations (NGOs) were the first to publish information on human rights violations in Argentina, using testimony supplied by Argentine exiles, refugees, and human rights activists. Intergovernmental organizations such as the Inter-American Commission on Human Rights later corroborated and expanded this information. With the coming of democracy, Argentine researchers and prosecutors provided definitive evidence in trials of the military juntas for human rights abuses during the dictatorship. Whether General Balza's promise is prophetic or cynical remains to be seen. Human rights activists hope that by telling the truth about the past to the widest possible public they can prevent its repetition.

In Mexico, the truth took longer to come out. On 2 October 1968 the military fired machine guns into a student demonstration in the Tlatelolco Plaza, a large square where modern high-rise buildings, pre-Columbian ruins, and a sixteenth-century Spanish church coexist. The government officially admitted 43 deaths, but knowledgeable observers suggest that at least 300–500 people were killed, over 2,000 were wounded, and from 1,500 to 2,000 people were taken prisoner.[4]

Surprisingly, the massacre attracted very little international attention. The International Olympic Committee, which was to hold the Olympic Games in Mexico City only ten days later, confirmed that the games would go on as planned. Aside from student demonstrations of solidarity in a number of cities, a telegram to the Mexican government from PEN Club International protesting the arrest of various authors, and a

---

[2] Ibid., p. 422.

[3] Horacio Verbitsky, *El Vuelo* (Buenos Aires: Planeta Espejo de la Argentina, 1995); General Balza's comments from *Clarin*, 26 April 1995, as cited in *Microseminario*, "Primera Seccion, Informe Especial: Guerra Sucia Y Arrenpentidos," no. 193, 24–30 April 1995, pp. 3–7.

[4] Michael C. Meyer and William L. Sherman, *The Course of Mexican History* (Oxford: Oxford University Press, 1991), 4th ed., p. 669; Amnesty International *Annual Report 1968–69* (London, 1969), p. 12; and interviews with Mexican human rights activists.

telegram from a group of French intellectuals, there was no international condemnation of the massacre.[5] Why did this event, a 1968 version of China's 1989 Tiananmen Square massacre, not inspire an international response? One key part of the answer is that the international human rights network, and the human rights consciousness and practices that it created, did not exist in 1968. Because there was no credible independent source, the Mexican government was able to control information about the event, and its low casualty figures were almost universally accepted.[6]

For Mexican human rights activist Mariclaire Acosta, who was heading toward the Plaza when the massacre occurred, and whose friends were among the dead and arrested, the scene from the García Márquez novel was exactly like the scene in 1968 in Mexico City. Only weeks later it was as if the massacre had never happened. "I think that was one of the most devastating things about 1968. The world was totally indifferent. . . . It's very difficult to overcome that traumatic experience of this terrifying thing that is not happening officially."[7]

Twenty-five years later, on 2 October 1993, 100,000 people attended a commemoration. The survivors of the massacre decided to set up a nongovernmental truth commission, which would have as one of its first tasks to try to find out exactly how many people were killed in the plaza. The Mexican government refused to open its files, but many individual Mexicans have come forward to tell the commission their stories. The "magical realism" of García Márquez' train is yielding to the prosaic number counters and oral historians of the truth commission, in the hope that by making the facts known they can avoid a repetition of the past.

We argue in this book that the emergence of transnational advocacy networks helped instigate and sustain the change between 1968 and 1993. International activism around human rights finds historical echoes in past campaigns like those for the abolition of slavery and for woman suffrage, and foreshadows transnational campaigns in a multiplicity of other areas. We discuss these historical precursors to the modern networks, and then trace the emergence, evolution, and effectiveness of current transnational advocacy networks in three central issue areas: human rights, the environment, and women's rights. Approximately half of all international nongovernmental social change organizations work on these three issues.

---

[5] Ramon Ramirez, *El Movimiento Estudiantil de Mexico: Julio-Diciembre 1968*: vol. 2: *Documentos* (Mexico, D F.: Ediciones Era, 1969).

[6] The *New York Times*, 4 October 1968, p. A1, *Washington Post*, 14 October 1968, p. A3, and *Newsweek*, 14 October 1968, pp. 45–48, referred to casualties of 20–49 people, and to 100–500 wounded, which reflected the government figures.

[7] Interview with Mariclaire Acosta, Washington, D.C., 3 December 1993.

Although these networks often differ dramatically in the content of their demands, they share some crucial similarities. When they succeed, networks can break the cycles of history Gabriel García Márquez predicts for Macondo at the end of his book. Where the powerful impose forgetfulness, networks can provide alternative channels of communication. Voices that are suppressed in their own societies may find that networks can project and amplify their concerns into an international arena, which in turn can echo back into their own countries. Transnational networks multiply the voices that are heard in international and domestic policies. These voices argue, persuade, strategize, document, lobby, pressure, and complain. The multiplication of voices is imperfect and selective—for every voice that is amplified, many others are ignored—but in a world where the voices of states have predominated, networks open channels for bringing alternative visions and information into international debate. Political scientists have tended to ignore such nongovernmental actors because they are not "powerful" in the classic sense of the term. At the core of network activity is the production, exchange, and strategic use of information. This ability may seem inconsequential in the face of the economic, political, or military might of other global actors. But by overcoming the deliberate suppression of information that sustains many abuses of power, networks can help reframe international and domestic debates, changing their terms, their sites, and the configuration of participants. When they succeed, advocacy networks are among the most important sources of new ideas, norms, and identities in the international system. At the same time, participation in transnational networks can significantly enhance the political resources available to domestic actors.

The ideas and principles that participants in these networks espouse do not, all by themselves, produce these changes. Networks frequently fail to achieve their goals; in many instances, serious transnational problems exist but no network is formed. Our goal here goes beyond simply highlighting the presence of transnational advocacy networks in a variety of issue areas. By delving into the experience of particular transnational networks, we hope to generate a more powerful understanding of their origins, strategies, limits, and effectiveness, making it possible to situate them within the rapidly changing configuration of world politics.

We acknowledge the research support of the following institutions: the Howard Heinz Endowment/Center for Latin American Studies, University of Pittsburgh, Research Grant on Current Latin American Issues; the Joint Committee on Latin American Studies and the Advanced Fellowship in Foreign Policy Studies of the Social Science Research Council and the American Council of Learned Societies with funds provided by the Ford

Foundation; the John D. and Catherine T. MacArthur Foundation; and the McKnight Land Grant Professorship at the University of Minnesota.

We are grateful to John Bowen, Alison Brysk, Jan Herman Burgers, Douglas Chalmers, Marcus Colchester, Elizabeth Ann Donnelly, Raymond Duvall, Martha Finnemore, Norman Foster, Jonathan Fox, Arvonne Fraser, Marsha Freeman, Andrew Hurrell, Jane Jaquette, Elizabeth Jelin, Mary Katzenstein, Sally Kenney, Michael Kennedy, Sanjeev Khagram, Lisa Kois, Jeffrey Legro, David Lelyveld, Ellen Lutz, Andrew Moravcsik, Paul Nelson, Richard Price, James Riker, Thomas Risse-Kappen, Bruce Russett, James Scott, Gay Siedman, Anne-Marie Slaughter, Catalina Smulovitz, Daniel Thomas, David Trubek, Anna Tsing, Ann Waltner, David Weissbrodt, Christopher Welna, Alex Wendt, Mayer Zald; many of our students from Yale, Johns Hopkins, and the University of Minnesota, including Elizabeth Umlas, Karen Brown Thompson, Helen Kinsella, Petrice Flowers, and Michael Riley; and several anonymous reviewers for helpful comments on earlier versions. Kris Thalhammer, Amy Sanders, and Maria Florencia Belvedere provided superb research assistance. David Lumsdaine did an invaluable close reading of an early draft, and Marc Levy challenged us to make much more of it than we had planned. Jackie Smith generously allowed us to use some of her data in Table 1 in Chapter 1 and shared her coding program for our data collection. Robert Keohane and Sidney Tarrow encouraged us, made sharp comments and suggestions, and assigned our work—what more could anyone ask?

We have also had the opportunity to present portions of this work to panels and seminars at the American Political Science Association, the Law and Society Association, the American Society for International Law, the Latin American Studies Association, Columbia University, Duke University, the Catholic Academy in Weingarten, Germany, the University of Michigan, the University of Notre Dame, the University of Wisconsin, and Harvard University, and the various meetings of the research network on Collective Actors in Transnational Space of the MacArthur Consortium. We have benefited from the comments and suggestions of participants in these diverse settings.

We owe our deepest debt to the transnational activists with whom we have interacted over the years. Their generosity of spirit and sheer doggedness in pursuit of what they deeply believe is right have continued to influence the shape of world politics, in spite of the fact that prevailing theories failed to remark their existence. They have been generous in sharing time, ideas, and documents with us, and if we have been able to tell only a few of their stories, it is not because the others did not merit telling; all of them contributed to our understanding and inspired us in our work.

Roger Haydon has encouraged this project from the beginning, urged us to get it finished, got reviews back when he said he would, and continues to be both a fine editor and a terrific human being. May his sense of humor never fail him.

It is hard for us to imagine how people co-authored projects before the existence of the Internet. The ability to send formatted text back and forth (again and again) has meant that for very large parts of this manuscript, it is no longer possible for us to be sure who wrote which sentences, or originated or developed which ideas. The result, we believe, is genuine synergy; neither of us could have done this alone, and despite the occasional rough patch, we had a wonderful time doing it together.

Our families, Doug, Daniel, and Matthew and Larry, Melissa, and Laura, have suffered long and not always silently, but have hung in there nonetheless. We dedicate this book to our husbands, Larry Wright and Douglas Johnson, both longtime activists beyond borders, and thank them for what they have taught us about connection.

MARGARET E. KECK *and* KATHRYN SIKKINK

Baltimore and Minneapolis

CHAPTER 1

Transnational Advocacy Networks
in International Politics: Introduction

World politics at the end of the twentieth century involves, alongside states, many nonstate actors that interact with each other, with states, and with international organizations. These interactions are structured in terms of networks, and transnational networks are increasingly visible in international politics. Some involve economic actors and firms. Some are networks of scientists and experts whose professional ties and shared causal ideas underpin their efforts to influence policy.[1] Others are networks of activists, distinguishable largely by the centrality of principled ideas or values in motivating their formation.[2] We will call these *transnational advocacy networks*.

Advocacy networks are significant transnationally and domestically. By building new links among actors in civil societies, states, and international organizations, they multiply the channels of access to the international system. In such issue areas as the environment and human rights, they also make international resources available to new actors in domestic political and social struggles. By thus blurring the boundaries between a state's relations with its own nationals and the recourse both citizens

[1] Peter Haas has called these "knowledge-based" or "epistemic communities." See Peter Haas, "Introduction: Epistemic Communities and International Policy Coordination," *Knowledge, Power and International Policy Coordination*, special issue, *International Organization* 46 (Winter 1992), pp. 1–36.

[2] Ideas that specify criteria for determining whether actions are right and wrong and whether outcomes are just or unjust are shared principled beliefs or values. Beliefs about cause-effect relationships are shared casual beliefs. Judith Goldstein and Robert Keohane, eds., *Ideas and Foreign Policy: Beliefs, Institutions, and Political Change* (Ithaca: Cornell University Press, 1993), pp. 8–10.

1

and states have to the international system, advocacy networks are helping to transform the practice of national sovereignty.

To explore these issues, we first look at four historical forerunners to
modern advocacy networks, including the antislavery movement and the
campaign for woman suffrage, and we examine in depth three contemporary cases in which transnational organizations are very prominent:
human rights, environment, and women's rights. We also refer to
transnational campaigns around indigenous rights, labor rights, and infant formula. Despite their differences, these networks are similar in several important respects: the centrality of values or principled ideas, the
belief that individuals can make a difference, the creative use of information, and the employment by nongovernmental actors of sophisticated
political strategies in targeting their campaigns.

Scholars have been slow to recognize either the rationality or the significance of activist networks. Motivated by values rather than by material concerns or professional norms, these networks fall outside our
accustomed categories. More than other kinds of transnational actors,
advocacy networks often reach beyond policy change to advocate and
instigate changes in the institutional and principled basis of international interactions. When they succeed, they are an important part of
an explanation for changes in world politics. A transnational advocacy
network includes those relevant actors working internationally on an
issue, who are bound together by shared values, a common discourse,
and dense exchanges of information and services.[3] Such networks are
most prevalent in issue areas characterized by high value content and
informational uncertainty. At the core of the relationship is information
exchange. What is novel in these networks is the ability of nontradi-
tional international actors to mobilize information strategically to help
create new issues and categories and to persuade, pressure, and gain
leverage over much more powerful organizations and governments.
Activists in networks try not only to influence policy outcomes, but to
transform the terms and nature of the debate. They are not always successful in their efforts, but they are increasingly relevant players in policy debates.

Transnational advocacy networks are proliferating, and their goal is to
change the behavior of states and of international organizations. Simultaneously principled and strategic actors, they "frame" issues to make
them comprehensible to target audiences, to attract attention and encour-

---

[3] See also J. Clyde Mitchell, "Networks, Norms, and Institutions," in *Network Analysis*,
ed. Jeremy Boissevain and J. Clyde Mitchell (The Hague: Mouton, 1973), p. 23. A "common discourse" was suggested by Stewart Lawrence in "The Role of International 'Issue
Networks' in Refugee Repatriation: The Case of El Salvador" (Columbia University,
mimeo).

age action, and to "fit" with favorable institutional venues.[4] Network actors bring new ideas, norms, and discourses into policy debates, and serve as sources of information and testimony. Norms, here, follows the usage given by Peter Katzenstein,

> to describe collective expectations for the proper behavior of actors with a given identity. In some situations norms operate like rules that define the identity of an actor, thus having "constitutive effects" that specify what actions will cause relevant others to recognize a particular identity.[5]

They also promote norm implementation, by pressuring target actors to adopt new policies, and by monitoring compliance with international standards. Insofar as is possible, they seek to maximize their influence or leverage over the target of their actions. In doing so they contribute to changing perceptions that both state and societal actors may have of their identities, interests, and preferences, to transforming their discursive positions, and ultimately to changing procedures, policies, and behavior.[6]

Networks are communicative structures. To influence discourse, procedures, and policy, activists may engage and become part of larger policy communities that group actors working on an issue from a variety of institutional and value perspectives. Transnational advocacy networks must also be understood as political spaces, in which differently situated actors negotiate—formally or informally—the social, cultural, and political meanings of their joint enterprise.

---

[4] David Snow and his colleagues have adapted Erving Goffman's concept of framing. We use it to mean "conscious strategic efforts by groups of people to fashion shared understandings of the world and of themselves that legitimate and motivate collective action." Definition from Doug McAdam, John D. McCarthy, and Mayer N. Zald, "Introduction," *Comparative Perspectives on Social Movements: Political Opportunities, Mobilizing Structures, and Cultural Framings,* ed. McAdam, McCarthy, and Zald (New York: Cambridge University Press, 1996), p. 6. See also Frank Baumgartner and Bryan Jones, "Agenda Dynamics and Policy Subsystems," *Journal of Politics* 53:4 (1991): 1044–74.

[5] Peter J. Katzenstein, "Introduction," in *The Culture of National Security: Norms and Identity in World Politics,* ed. Katzenstein (New York: Columbia University Press, 1966), p. 5. See also Friedrich Kratochwil, *Rules, Norms, and Decisions: On the Conditions of Practical and Legal Reasoning in International Relations and Domestic Affairs* (Cambridge: Cambridge University Press, 1989); David H. Lumsdaine, *Moral Vision in International Politics: The Foreign Aid Regime, 1949–1989* (Princeton: Princeton University Press, 1993); Audie Klotz, *Norms in International Relations: The Struggle against Apartheid* (Ithaca: Cornell University Press, 1995); Janice E. Thomson, "State Practices, International Norms, and the Decline of Mercenarism," *International Studies Quarterly* 34 (1990): 23–47; and Martha Finnemore, "International Organizations as Teachers of Norms," *International Organization* 47 (August 1993): 565–97.

[6] With the "constructivists" in international relations theory, we take actors and interests to be constituted in interaction. See Martha Finnemore, *National Interests in International Society* (Ithaca: Cornell University Press, 1996), who argues that "states are embedded in dense networks of transnational and international social relations that shape their perceptions of the world and their role in that world. States are *socialized* to want certain things by the international society in which they and the people in them live" (p. 2).

We refer to transnational networks (rather than coalitions, movements, or civil society) to evoke the structured and structuring dimension in the actions of these complex agents, who not only participate in new areas of politics but also shape them. By importing the network concept from sociology and applying it transnationally, we bridge the increasingly artificial divide between international and national realms. Still, social science theories did not dictate our choice of "network" as the name to be given to the phenomena we are studying. The actors themselves did: over the last two decades, individuals and organizations have consciously formed and named transnational networks, developed and shared networking strategies and techniques, and assessed the advantages and limits of this kind of activity. Scholars have come late to the party.

Given our enterprise, it should be clear that we reject the separation common in our discipline between international relations and comparative politics. Moreover, even liberal theories of international relations that recognize that domestic interests shape states' actions internationally, and that states are embedded in an interdependent world where nonstate actors are consequential, cannot explain the phenomena we describe.[7] Robert Putnam's "two-level game" metaphor has taken liberal theorists some distance toward seeing international relations as a two-way street, in which political entrepreneurs bring international influence to bear on domestic politics at the same time that domestic politics shapes their international positions.[8] But however valuable its insights, even this two-way street is too narrow, implying a limited access to the international system that no longer holds true in many issue areas.

Instead, we draw upon sociological traditions that focus on complex interactions among actors, on the intersubjective construction of frames of meaning, and on the negotiation and malleability of identities and interests. These have been concerns of constructivists in international relations theory and of social movement theorists in comparative politics, and we draw from both traditions. The networks we describe in this book participate in domestic and international politics simultaneously, drawing upon a variety of resources, as if they were part of an international society. However, they use these resources strategically to affect a world of states and international organizations constructed by states. Both these dimensions are essential. Rationalists will recognize the language of incentives and constraints, strategies, institutions, and rules, whereas con-

[7] For an impressive effort to systematize liberal international relations theory, see Andrew Moravcsik, "Liberalism and International Relations Theory," Harvard University, Center for International Affairs, Working Paper no. 92-6, revised April 1993. Liberal institutionalists since Robert O. Keohane and Joseph S. Nye, *Power and Interdependence: World Politics in Transition* (Boston: Little, Brown, 1977), have taken complex interdependence as axiomatic in the development of regime theory.

[8] Robert Putnam, "Diplomacy and Domestic Politics: The Logic of Two-Level Games," *International Organization* 42 (Summer 1988): 427–60.

structivists and social constructionists will be more comfortable with our stress on norms, social relations, and intersubjective understandings. We are convinced that both sets of concerns matter, and that recognizing that goals and interests are not exogenously given, we can think about the strategic activity of actors in an intersubjectively structured political universe. The key to doing so is remembering that the social and political contexts within which networks operate at any particular point contain contested understandings as well as stable and shared ones. Network activists can operate strategically within the more stable universe of shared understandings at the same time that they try to reshape certain contested meanings.

Part of what is so elusive about networks is how they seem to embody elements of agent and structure simultaneously. When we ask who creates networks and how, we are inquiring about them as structures—as patterns of interactions among organizations and individuals. When we talk about them as actors, however, we are attributing to these structures an agency that is not reducible to the agency of their components. Nonetheless, when we sometimes refer to networks as actors in this book, we do not lose sight of the fact that activists act on behalf of networks.

Our approach to these transnational interactions must therefore be both structural and actor-centered. We address four main questions: (1) What is a transnational advocacy network? (2) Why and how do they emerge? (3) How do advocacy networks work? (4) Under what conditions can they be effective—that is, when are they most likely to achieve their goals?[9]

When we started this book, the realm of transnational social movements and networks was still an almost uncharted area of scholarship, both theoretically and empirically, and thus required a style of research aimed at the discovery of new theory and patterns. Because few existing theories attempt to explain the transnational phenomena we are studying, we could not rely on standard social science methods for hypothesis testing. Social scientists recognize that generating theory and formulating hypotheses require different methods from those for testing theory. Our approach thus resembles what sociologists call "grounded theory," which is the most systematic attempt to specify how theoretical insights are generated through qualitative research.[10] While doing the research for

---

[9] On the problem of measuring effectiveness, see William A. Gamson, *The Strategy of Social Protest* (Chicago: Dorsey Press, 1975); and J. Craig Jenkins and Bert Klandermans, eds., *The Politics of Social Protest* (Minneapolis: University of Minnesota Press, 1995).

[10] See Gary King, Robert O. Keohane, and Sidney Verba, *Designing Social Inquiry: Scientific Inference in Qualitative Research* (Princeton: Princeton University Press, 1994), p. 38; Barney G. Glaser and Anselm L. Strauss, *The Discovery of Grounded Theory: Strategies for Qualitative Research* (Chicago: Aldine, 1967); Barney G. Glaser, *Theoretical Sensitivity* (Mill Valley, Calif.: Sociological Press, 1978); and Anselm Strauss and Juliet Corbin, "Grounded Theory Methodology: An Overview," in *Handbook of Qualitative Research*, ed. Norman Denzin and Yvonna Lincoln (Thousand Oaks, Calif.: Sage, 1994), pp. 273–85.

this book, we first explored these new patterns of interaction inductively, by studying the histories of particular networks involved in transnational campaigns. Because cross-national and cross-cultural activism are intensely context-sensitive, we cast a wide net in our search for intervening variables between values and advocacy and between advocacy and its (apparent) effect. Nevertheless, looking comparatively across regions and issue areas, we found striking commonalities in how and why networks emerged, and in the strategies they adopted. Although we eventually found that theoretical work on domestic social movements has a great deal to say about how transnational advocacy networks function, we did not begin with this assumption. Out of our observed commonalities we generated some initial arguments about why networks emerge and under what conditions they can be effective. In the tradition of grounded theory, we used additional comparative cases to further explore and refine our initial arguments. In each of our cases we refer to issues where networks exist and where networks do not exist, and we explore both successful and unsuccessful networks and campaigns.

International and domestic nongovernmental organizations (NGOs) play a prominent role in these networks, in some cases inspired by an international voluntarism that is largely unaccounted for in international relations theory. Social scientists have barely addressed the political role of activist NGOs as simultaneously domestic and international actors. Much of the existing literature on NGOs comes from development studies, and either ignores interactions with states or is remarkably thin on political analysis.[11] Examining their role in advocacy networks helps both to distinguish NGOs from, and to see their connections with, social movements, state agencies, and international organizations.

We examine transnational advocacy networks and what they do by analyzing campaigns networks have waged. For our purposes, campaigns are sets of strategically linked activities in which members of a diffuse principled network (what social movement theorists would call a "mobilization potential") develop explicit, visible ties and mutually recognized roles in pursuit of a common goal (and generally against a common target). In a campaign, core network actors mobilize others and initiate the tasks of structural integration and cultural negotiation among the groups in the network. Just as in domestic campaigns, they connect groups to each other, seek out resources, propose and prepare

---

[11] Although development journals (especially *World Development*) routinely include articles discussing the role of NGOs, political science journals do not, nor have many political scientists been a part of such discussions in the development community. See David Korten, *Getting to the 21st Century: Voluntary Action and the Global Agenda* (Hartford, Conn.: Kumarian Press, 1990).

activities, and conduct public relations. They must also consciously seek to develop a "common frame of meaning"—a task complicated by cultural diversity within transnational networks.[12] Activist groups have long used the language of campaigning to talk about focused, strategically planned efforts. International campaigns by environmental and conservation organizations, for example, have traditionally had a topical focus (saving furry animals, whales, tropical forests), whereas human rights campaigns have focused on either a country (the Argentina campaign) or an issue (torture).[13]

Analysis of campaigns provides a window on transnational relations as an arena of struggle in ways that a focus on networks themselves or on the institutions they try to affect does not. In most chapters we also consider noncampaigns—issues that activists identified as problematic, but around which networks did not campaign. This focus on campaigns highlights *relationships*—how connections are established and maintained among network actors, and between activists and their allies and opponents. We can identify the kinds of *resources* that make a campaign possible, such as information, leadership, and symbolic or material capital.[14] And we must consider the kinds of *institutional structures*, both domestic and international, that encourage or impede particular kinds of transnational activism. Here we draw from several traditions. Thomas Risse-Kappen's recent work argues that domestic structures mediate transnational interactions. By domestic structures he means state structure (centralized vs. fragmented), societal structure (weak vs. strong), and policy networks (consensual vs. polarized).[15] Similarly, social movement theorists agree that understanding the political context or "opportunity structure" is key both to understanding a movement's emergence and to gauging its success. Assessing opportunity structure can be an exercise in comparative statics—looking at differential access by citizens to political institutions like legislatures, bureaucracies, and courts—or it can be viewed dynamically, as in changes in formal or informal political power relations over time. We agree with Sidney Tarrow on the need to combine the more narrowly institutional version

[12] See Jürgen Gerhards and Dieter Rucht, "Mesomobilization: Organizing and Framing in Two Protest Campaigns in West Germany," *American Journal of Sociology* 98:3 (November 1992): 558–59.

[13] For a discussion of World Wildlife Fund campaigns, see Arne Schiotz, "A Campaign is Born," *IUCN Bulletin* 14:10–12 (1983): 120–22.

[14] The classic statement on resource mobilization and social movements is John D. McCarthy and Mayer N. Zald, "Resource Mobilization and Social Movements: A Partial Theory," *American Journal of Sociology* 82:6 (1977): 1212–41.

[15] Thomas Risse-Kappen, "Bringing Transnational Relations Back In: Introduction," in *Bringing Transnational Relations Back In: Non-State Actors, Domestic Structures, and International Institutions*, ed. Risse-Kappen (Cambridge: Cambridge University Press, 1995), p. 22.

with a dynamic approach.[16] Finally, a focus on campaigning lets us explore negotiation of meaning while we look at the evolution of tactics; we can recognize that cultural differences, different conceptions of the stakes in a campaign, and resource inequalities among network actors exist, at the same time that we identify critical roles that different actors fill. Campaigns are processes of issue construction constrained by the action context in which they are to be carried out: activists identify a problem, specify a cause, and propose a solution, all with an eye toward producing procedural, substantive, and normative change in their area of concern. In networked campaigns this process of "strategic portrayal"[17] must work for the different actors in the network and also for target audiences.

What Is a Transnational Advocacy Network?

Networks are forms of organization characterized by voluntary, reciprocal, and horizontal patterns of communication and exchange. The organizational theorist Walter Powell calls them a third mode of economic organization, distinctly different from markets and hierarchy (the firm). "Networks are 'lighter on their feet' than hierarchy" and are "particularly apt for circumstances in which there is a need for efficient, reliable information," and "for the exchange of commodities whose value is not easily measured."[18] His insights about economic networks are extraordinarily suggestive for an understanding of political networks, which also form around issues where information plays a key role, and around issues where the value of the "commodity" is not easily measured.

In spite of the differences between domestic and international realms, the network concept travels well because it stresses fluid and open relations among committed and knowledgeable actors working in specialized issue areas. We call them advocacy networks because advocates plead the causes of others or defend a cause or proposition. Advocacy captures what is unique about these transnational networks: they are organized to promote causes, principled ideas, and norms, and they often

[16] Sidney Tarrow, "States and Opportunities: The Political Structuring of Social Movements," in *Comparative Perspectives on Social Movements*, pp. 41–61. By political opportunity structure he means "*consistent—but not necessarily formal, permanent, or national—signals to social or political actors which either encourage or discourage them to use their internal resources to form social movements* . . . The most salient kinds of signals are four: the opening up of access to power, shifting alignments, the availability of influential allies, and cleavages within and among elites" (p. 54, italic in original).

[17] Deborah A. Stone, *Policy Paradox and Political Reason* (New York: HarperCollins, 1988), p. 6.

[18] Walter W. Powell, "Neither Market nor Hierarchy: Network Forms of Organization," *Research in Organizational Behavior* 12 (1990): 295–96, 303–4.

involve Individuals advocating policy changes that cannot be easily linked to a rationalist understanding of their "interests."

Some issue areas reproduce transnationally the webs of personal relationships that are crucial in the formation of domestic networks.[19] Advocacy networks have been particularly important in value-laden debates over human rights, the environment, women, infant health, and indigenous peoples, where large numbers of differently situated individuals have become acquainted over a considerable period and developed similar world views. When the more visionary among them have proposed strategies for political action around apparently intractable problems, this potential has been transformed into an action network.

Major actors in advocacy networks may include the following: (1) international and domestic nongovernmental research and advocacy organizations; (2) local social movements; (3) foundations; (4) the media; (5) churches, trade unions, consumer organizations, and intellectuals; (6) parts of regional and international intergovernmental organizations; and (7) parts of the executive and/or parliamentary branches of governments. Not all these will be present in each advocacy network. Initial research suggests, however, that international and domestic NGOs play a central role in all advocacy networks, usually initiating actions and pressuring more powerful actors to take positions. NGOs introduce new ideas, provide information, and lobby for policy changes.

Groups in a network share values and frequently exchange information and services. The flow of information among actors in the network reveals a dense web of connections among these groups, both formal and informal. The movement of funds and services is especially notable between foundations and NGOs, and some NGOs provide services such as training for other NGOs in the same and sometimes other advocacy networks. Personnel also circulate within and among networks, as relevant players move from one to another in a version of the "revolving door."

Relationships among networks, both within and between issue areas, are similar to what scholars of social movements have found for domestic activism.[20] Individuals and foundation funding have moved back and forth among them. Environmentalists and women's groups have looked at the history of human rights campaigns for models of effective international institution building. Refugee resettlement and indigenous people's rights are increasingly central components of international environmental

---

[19] See Doug McAdam and Dieter Rucht, "The Cross-National Diffusion of Movement Ideas," *Annals of the American Academy of Political and Social Science* 528 (July 1993): 56–74.

[20] See McCarthy and Zald, "Resource Mobilization and Social Movements"; Myra Marx Feree and Frederick D. Miller, "Mobilization and Meaning: Toward an Integration of Social Psychological and Resource Perspectives on Social Movements," *Sociological Inquiry* 55 (1985): 49–50; and David S. Meyer and Nancy Whittier, "Social Movement Spillover," *Social Problems* 41.2 (May 1994): 277–98.

activity, and vice versa; mainstream human rights organizations have joined the campaign for women's rights. Some activists consider themselves part of an "NGO community."

Besides sharing information, groups in networks create categories or frames within which to generate and organize information on which to base their campaigns. Their ability to generate information quickly and accurately, and deploy it effectively, is their most valuable currency; it is also central to their identity. Core campaign organizers must ensure that individuals and organizations with access to necessary information are incorporated into the network; different ways of framing an issue may require quite different kinds of information. Thus frame disputes can be a significant source of change within networks.

WHY AND HOW HAVE TRANSNATIONAL ADVOCACY NETWORKS EMERGED?

Advocacy networks are not new. We can find examples as far back as the nineteenth-century campaign for the abolition of slavery. But their number, size, and professionalism, and the speed, density, and complexity of international linkages among them has grown dramatically in the last three decades. As Hugh Heclo remarks about domestic issue networks, "if the current situation is a mere outgrowth of old tendencies, it is so in the same sense that a 16-lane spaghetti interchange is the mere elaboration of a country crossroads."[21]

We cannot accurately count transnational advocacy networks to measure their growth over time, but one proxy is the increase in the number of international NGOs committed to social change. Because international NGOs are key components of any advocacy network, this increase suggests broader trends in the number, size, and density of advocacy networks generally. Table 1 suggests that the number of international nongovernmental social change groups has increased across all issues, though to varying degrees in different issue areas. There are five times as many organizations working primarily on human rights as there were in 1950, but proportionally human rights groups have remained roughly a quarter of all such groups. Similarly, groups working on women's rights accounted for 9 percent of all groups in 1953 and in 1993. Transnational environmental organizations have grown most dramatically in absolute and relative terms, increasing from two groups in 1953 to ninety in 1993, and from 1.8 percent of total groups in 1953 to 14.3 percent in 1993. The

[21] Hugh Heclo, "Issue Networks and the Executive Establishment," in *The New American Political System*, ed. Anthony King (Washington, D.C.: American Enterprise Institute, 1978), p. 97.

Table 1. International nongovernmental social change organizations (categorized by the major issue focus of their work)

Issue area (N)	1953 (N=110)	1963 (N=141)	1973 (N=183)	1983 (N=348)	1993 (N=631)
Human rights	33 30.0%	38 27.0%	41 22.4%	79 22.7%	168 26.6%
World order	8 7.3	4 2.8	12 6.6	31 8.9	48 7.6
International law	14 12.7	19 13.4	25 13.7	26 7.4	26 4.1
Peace	11 10.0	20 14.2	14 7.7	22 6.3	59 9.4
Women's rights	10 9.1	14 9.9	16 8.7	25 7.2	61 9.7
Environment	2 1.8	5 3.5	10 5.5	26 7.5	90 14.3
Development	3 2.7	3 2.1	7 3.8	13 3.7	34 5.4
Ethnic unity / Group rts.	10 9.1	12 8.5	18 9.8	37 10.6	29 4.6
Esperanto	11 10.0	18 12.8	28 15.3	41 11.8	54 8.6

SOURCE: Union of International Associations, *Yearbook of International Organizations* (1953, 1963, 1973, 1983, 1993). We are indebted to Jackie Smith, University of Notre Dame, for the use of her data from 1983 and 1993, and the use of her coding form and codebook for our data collection for the period 1953–73.

percentage share of groups in such issue areas as international law, peace, ethnic unity, and Esperanto, has declined.[22]

Although the networks discussed in this book represent only a subset of the total number of networks, these include the issue area of human rights,

[22] Data from a collaborative research project with Jackie G. Smith. We thank her for the use of her data from the period 1983–93, whose results are presented in Jackie G. Smith, "Characteristics of the Modern Transnational Social Movement Sector," in Jackie G. Smith, et al., eds. *Transnational Social Movements and World Politics: Solidarity beyond the State* (Syracuse: Syracuse University Press, forthcoming 1997), and for permission to use her coding form and codebook for our data collection for the period 1953–73. All data were coded from Union of International Associations, *The Yearbook of International Organizations, 1948–95* (published annually).

around which the largest number of international nongovernmental social change organizations has organized. Together, groups working on human rights, environment, and women's rights account for over half the total number of international nongovernmental social change organizations.

International networking is costly. Geographic distance, the influence of nationalism, the multiplicity of languages and cultures, and the costs of fax, phone, mail, and air travel make the proliferation of international networks a puzzle that needs explanation. Under what conditions are networks possible and likely, and what triggers their emergence?

Transnational advocacy networks appear most likely to emerge around those issues where (1) channels between domestic groups and their governments are blocked or hampered or where such channels are ineffective for resolving a conflict, setting into motion the "boomerang" pattern of influence characteristic of these networks (see Figure 1); (2) activists or "political entrepreneurs" believe that networking will further their missions and campaigns, and actively promote networks; and (3) conferences and other forms of international contact create arenas for forming and strengthening networks. Where channels of participation are blocked, the international arena may be the only means that domestic activists have to gain attention to their issues. Boomerang strategies are most common in campaigns where the target is a state's domestic policies or behavior; where a campaign seeks broad procedural change involving dispersed actors, strategies are more diffuse.

The Boomerang Pattern

It is no accident that so many advocacy networks address claims about rights in their campaigns. Governments are the primary "guarantors" of rights, but also their primary violators. When a government violates or refuses to recognize rights, individuals and domestic groups often have no recourse within domestic political or judicial arenas. They may seek international connections finally to express their concerns and even to protect their lives.

When channels between the state and its domestic actors are blocked, the boomerang pattern of influence characteristic of transnational networks may occur: domestic NGOs bypass their state and directly search out international allies to try to bring pressure on their states from outside. This is most obviously the case in human rights campaigns. Similarly, indigenous rights campaigns and environmental campaigns that support the demands of local peoples for participation in development projects that would affect them frequently involve this kind of triangulation. Linkages are important for both sides: for the less powerful third world actors, networks provide access, leverage, and information (and

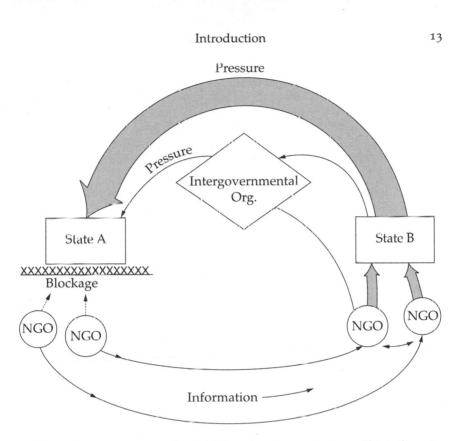

Figure 1 Boomerang pattern. State A blocks redress to organizations within it; they activate network, whose members pressure their own states and (if relevant) a third-party organization, which in turn pressure State A.

often money) they could not expect to have on their own; for northern groups, they make credible the assertion that they are struggling with, and not only for, their southern partners. Not surprisingly, such relationships can produce considerable tensions.

On other issues where governments are inaccessible or deaf to groups whose claims may nonetheless resonate elsewhere, international contacts can amplify the demands of domestic groups, pry open space for new issues, and then echo back these demands into the domestic arena. The cases of rubber tappers trying to stop encroachment by cattle ranchers in Brazil's western Amazon and of tribal populations threatened by the damming of the Narmada River in India are good examples of this.[23]

[23] On the former, see Margaret E. Keck, "Social Equity and Environmental Politics in Brazil: Lessons from the Rubber Tappers of Acre," *Comparative Politics* 27 (July 1995): 409–24; on the latter, see William F. Fisher, ed., *Toward Sustainable Development? Struggling over India's Narmada River* (Armonk, N.Y.: M. E. Sharpe, 1995).

Political Entrepreneurs

Just as oppression and injustice do not themselves produce movements or revolutions, claims around issues amenable to international action do not produce transnational networks. Activists —"people who care enough about some issue that they are prepared to incur significant costs and act to achieve their goals"[24]—do. They create them when they believe that transnational networking will further their organizational missions—by sharing information, attaining greater visibility, gaining access to wider publics, multiplying channels of institutional access, and so forth. For example, in the campaign to stop the promotion of infant formula to poor women in developing countries, organizers settled on a boycott of Nestlé, the largest producer, as its main tactic. Because Nestlé was a transnational actor, activists believed a transnational network was necessary to bring pressure on corporations and governments.[25] Over time, in such issue areas, participation in transnational networks has become an essential component of the collective identities of the activists involved, and networking a part of their common repertoire. The political entrepreneurs who become the core networkers for a new campaign have often gained experience in earlier ones.

The Growth of International Contact

Opportunities for network activities have increased over the last two decades. In addition to the efforts of pioneers, a proliferation of international organizations and conferences has provided foci for connections. Cheaper air travel and new electronic communication technologies speed information flows and simplify personal contact among activists.[26]

Underlying these trends is a broader cultural shift. The new networks have depended on the creation of a new kind of global public (or civil society), which grew as a cultural legacy of the 1960s.[27] Both the activism that swept Western Europe, the United States, and many parts of the third world during that decade, and the vastly increased opportunities for international contact, contributed to this shift. With a significant decline in air fares, foreign travel ceased to be the exclusive privilege of the

[24] Pamela E. Oliver and Gerald Marwell, "Mobilizing Technologies for Collective Action," in *Frontiers in Social Movement Theory*, ed. Aldon D. Morris and Carol McClurg Mueller (New Haven: Yale University Press, 1992), p. 252.

[25] See Kathryn Sikkink, "Codes of Conduct for Transnational Corporations: The Case of the WHO/UNICEF Code," *International Organization* 40 (Autumn 1986): 815–40.

[26] The constant dollar yield of airline tickets in 1995 was one half of what it was in 1966, while the number of international passengers enplaned increased more than four times during the same period. Air Transport Association home page, June 1997, http://www.air-transport.org/data/traffic.htm. See James Rosenau, *Turbulence in World Politics* (Princeton: Princeton University Press, 1990), pp. 12, 25.

[27] See Sidney Tarrow, "Mentalities, Political Cultures, and Collective Action Frames: Constructing Meanings through Action," in *Frontiers in Social Movement Theory*, p. 184.

wealthy. Students participated in exchange programs. The Peace Corps and lay missionary programs sent thousands of young people to live and work in the developing world. Political exiles from Latin America taught in U.S. and European universities. Churches opened their doors to refugees, and to new ideas and commitments.

Obviously, internationalism was not invented in the sixties. Religious and political traditions including missionary outreach, the solidarity traditions of labor and the left, and liberal internationalism have long stirred action by individuals or groups beyond the borders of their own state. While many activists working in advocacy networks come out of these traditions, they tend no longer to define themselves in terms of these traditions or the organizations that carried them. This is most true for activists on the left who suffered disillusionment from their groups' refusal to address seriously the concerns of women, the environment, or human rights violations in eastern bloc countries. Absent a range of options that in earlier decades would have competed for their commitments, advocacy and activism through either NGOs or grassroots movements became the most likely alternative for those seeking to "make a difference."

Although numerous solidarity committees and human rights groups campaigned against torture and disappearances under Latin American military regimes, even on behalf of the same individuals they employed different styles, strategies, and discourses, and understood their goals in the light of different principles. Solidarity organizations based their appeals on common ideological commitments—the notion that those being tortured or killed were defending a cause shared with the activists. Rights organizations, in principle, were committed to defending the rights of individuals regardless of their ideological affinity with the ideas of the victim. One exception to this ideal involved the use of violence. Amnesty International, for example, defended all prisoners against torture, summary execution, or the death penalty, but it would adopt as its more visible and symbolic "prisoners of conscience" only those individuals who had not advocated violence.

Although labor internationalism has survived the decline of the left, it is based mainly on large membership organizations representing (however imperfectly) bounded constituencies. Where advocacy networks have formed around labor issues, they have been transitory, responding to repression of domestic labor movements (as in labor support networks formed around Brazil, South Africa, and Central America in the early 1980s).[28]

---

[28] Brazil Labor Information and Resource Center, an advocacy group that functioned in the early 1980s, won the support of a large number of unions in the U.S., Canada, and Western Europe in a campaign protesting prosecution of Brazilian labor leaders for leading strikes and addressing rallies; the Labor Committee on South Africa brought together union leaders and intellectuals to disseminate information on labor organizing and repression among South Africa's newly militant industrial unions; the Labor Committee on Central America was composed of labor leaders who built alternative channels of contact and collaboration with Central American (especially Salvadoran and Guatemalan) labor activists in the face of the AFL-CIO's support for Ronald Reagan's policies in the region.

Advocacy networks in the north function in a cultural milieu of internationalism that is generally optimistic about the promise and possibilitites of international networking. For network members in developing countries, however, justifying external intervention or pressure in domestic affairs is a much trickier business, except when lives are at stake. Linkages with northern networks require high levels of trust, as arguments justifying intervention on ethical grounds confront the ingrained nationalism common to many political groups in the developing world, as well as memories of colonial and neocolonial relations.

How Do Transnational Advocacy Networks Work?

Transnational advocacy networks seek influence in many of the same ways that other political groups or social movements do. Since they are not powerful in a traditional sense of the word, they must use the power of their information, ideas, and strategies to alter the information and value contexts within which states make policies. The bulk of what networks do might be termed persuasion or socialization, but neither process is devoid of conflict. Persuasion and socialization often involve not just reasoning with opponents, but also bringing pressure, arm-twisting, encouraging sanctions, and shaming. Audie Klotz's work on norms and apartheid discusses coercion, incentive, and legitimation effects that are often part of a socialization process.[29]

Our typology of tactics that networks use in their efforts at persuasion, socialization, and pressure includes (1) *information politics,* or the ability to quickly and credibly generate politically usable information and move it to where it will have the most impact; (2) *symbolic politics,* or the ability to call upon symbols, actions, or stories that make sense of a situation for an audience that is frequently far away;[30] (3) *leverage politics,* or the ability to call upon powerful actors to affect a situation where weaker members of a network are unlikely to have influence; and (4) *accountability politics,* or the effort to hold powerful actors to their previously stated policies or principles.

A single campaign may contain many of these elements simultaneously. For example, the human rights network disseminated information about human rights abuses in Argentina in the period 1976–83. The

[29] Klotz, *Norms in International Relations,* pp. 152–64.
[30] Alison Brysk uses the categories "information politics" and "symbolic politics" to discuss strategies of transnational actors, especially networks around Indian rights. See "Acting Globally: Indian Rights and International Politics in Latin America," in *Indigenous Peoples and Democracy in Latin America,* ed. Donna Lee Van Cott (New York: St. Martin's Press/Inter-American Dialogue, 1994), pp. 29–51; and "Hearts and Minds: Bringing Symbolic Politics Back In," *Polity* 27 (Summer 1995): 559–85.

Mothers of the Plaza de Mayo marched in circles in the central square in Buenos Aires wearing white handkerchiefs to draw symbolic attention to the plight of their missing children. The network also tried to use both material and moral leverage against the Argentine regime, by pressuring the United States and other governments to cut off military and economic aid, and by efforts to get the UN and the Inter-American Commission on Human Rights to condemn Argentina's human rights practices. Monitoring is a variation on information politics, in which activists use information strategically to ensure accountability with public statements, existing legislation and international standards.

The construction of cognitive frames is an essential component of net works' political strategies. David Snow has called this strategic activity "frame alignment": "by rendering events or occurrences meaningful, frames function to organize experience and guide action, whether individual or collective."[31] "Frame resonance" concerns the relationship between a movement organization's interpretive work and its ability to influence broader public understandings. The latter involve both the frame's internal coherence and its experiential fit with a broader political culture.[32] In recent work, Snow and his colleagues and Sidney Tarrow, in turn, have given frame resonance a historical dimension by joining it to Tarrow's notion of protest cycles.[33] Struggles over meaning and the creation of new frames of meaning occur early in a protest cycle, but over time "a given collective action frame becomes part of the political culture—which is to say, part of the reservoir of symbols from which future movement entrepreneurs can choose."[34]

Network members actively seek ways to bring issues to the public agenda by framing them in innovative ways and by seeking hospitable venues. Sometimes they create issues by framing old problems in new ways; occasionally they help transform other actors' understandings of their identities and their interests. Land use rights in the Amazon, for example, took on an entirely different character and gained quite different allies viewed in a deforestation frame than they did in either social justice or regional development frames. In the 1970s and 1980s many states decided for the first time that promotion of human rights in other countries was a legitimate foreign policy goal and an authentic expression of national interest.

[31] David A. Snow et al., "Frame Alignment Processes, Micromobilization, and Movement Participation," *American Socilogocial Review* 51 (1986): 464.

[32] David A. Snow and Robert D. Benford, "Ideology, Frame Resonance, and Participant Mobilization," in *From Structure to Action: Comparing Social Movement Research across Cultures,* ed. Bert Klandermans, Hanspeter Kriesi, and Sidney Tarrow (Greenwich, Conn.: JAI Press, 1988), pp. 197–217.

[33] David A. Snow and Robert D. Benford, "Master Frames and Cycles of Protest," in *Frontiers in Social Movement Theory,* pp. 133–55.

[34] Tarrow, "Mentalities," p. 197.

This decision came in part from interaction with an emerging global human rights network. We argue that this represents not the victory of morality over self-interest, but a transformed understanding of national interest, possible in part because of structured interactions between state components and networks. This changed understanding cannot be derived solely from changing global and economic conditions, although these are relevant.

Transnational networks normally involve a small number of activists from the organizations and institutions involved in a given campaign or advocacy role. The kinds of pressure and agenda politics in which advocacy networks engage rarely involve mass mobilization, except at key moments, although the peoples whose cause they espouse may engage in mass protest (for example, those ousted from their land in the Narmada dam case).[35] Boycott strategies are a partial exception. Instead of mass mobilization, network activists engage in what Baumgartner and Jones, borrowing from law, call "venue shopping," which relies "more on the dual strategy of the presentation of an image and the search for a more receptive political venue."[36] The recent coupling of indigenous rights and environmental issues is a good example of a strategic venue shift by indigenous activists, who found the environmental arena more receptive to their claims than human rights venues had been.

Information Politics

Information binds network members together and is essential for network effectiveness. Many information exchanges are informal—telephone calls, E-mail and fax communications, and the circulation of newsletters, pamphlets and bulletins. They provide information that would not otherwise be available, from sources that might not otherwise be heard, and they must make this information comprehensible and useful to activists and publics who may be geographically and/or socially distant.[37]

[35] Gerhards and Rucht, "Mesomobilization," details the organizational efforts to prepare demonstrations and parallel meetings to coincide with the 1988 meeting of the World Bank and International Monetary Fund in Berlin. This was by far the largest mass action in conjunction with the multilateral development bank campaign, which began holding meetings and demonstrations parallel to the banks' annual meetings in 1986. Interestingly, the authors seem not to have been aware of the existence of a transnational campaign of which this action was a part. On Narmada, see Medha Patkar, "The Struggle for Participation and Justice: A Historical Narrative," pp. 157–78; Anil Patel, "What Do the Narmada Tribals Want?," pp. 179–200; and Lori Udall, "The International Narmada Campaign: A Case of Sustained Advocacy," pp. 201–30, in *Toward Sustainable Development?* ed. Fisher.
[36] Baumgartner and Jones, "Agenda Dynamics," 1050.
[37] Rosenau, *Turbulence,* p. 199, argues that "as the adequacy of information and the very nature of knowledge have emerged as central issues, what were once regarded as the petty quarrels of scholars over the adequacy of evidence and the metaphysics of proof have become prominent activities in international relations."

Nonstate actors gain influence by serving as alternate sources of information. Information flows in advocacy networks provide not only facts
but testimony—stories told by people whose lives have been affected.
Moreover, activists interpret facts and testimony, usually framing issues
simply, in terms of right and wrong, because their purpose is to persuade
people and stimulate them to act. How does this process of persuasion
occur? An effective frame must show that a given state of affairs is neither natural nor accidental, identify the responsible party or parties, and
propose credible solutions. These aims require clear, powerful messages
that appeal to shared principles, which often have more impact on state
policy than advice of technical experts. An important part of the political
struggle over information is precisely whether an issue is defined primarily as technical—and thus subject to consideration by "qualified" experts—or as something that concerns a broader global constituency.

Even as we highlight the importance of testimony, however, we have to
recognize the mediations involved. The process by which testimony is
discovered and presented normally involves several layers of prior translation. Transnational actors may identify what kinds of testimony would
be valuable, then ask an NGO in the area to seek out people who could
tell those stories. They may filter the testimony through expatriates,
through traveling scholars like ourselves, or through the media. There is
frequently a huge gap between the story's original telling and the
retellings—in its sociocultural context, its instrumental meaning, and
even in its language. Local people, in other words, sometimes lose control over their stories in a transnational campaign. How this process of
mediation/translation occurs is a particularly interesting facet of network politics.[38]

Networks strive to uncover and investigate problems, and alert the
press and policymakers. One activist described this as the "human rights
methodology"—"promoting change by reporting facts."[39] To be credible,
the information produced by networks must be reliable and well documented. To gain attention, the information must be timely and dramatic.
Sometimes these multiple goals of information politics conflict, but both
credibility and drama seem to be essential components of a strategy
aimed at persuading publics and policymakers to change their minds.

The notion of "reporting facts" does not fully express the way networks strategically use information to frame issues. Networks call attention to issues, or even create issues by using language that dramatizes

[38] We are grateful to Anna Lowenhaupt Tsing for this point.
[39] Dorothy Q. Thomas, "Holding Governments Accountable by Public Pressure," in
Ours by Right: Women's Rights as Human Rights, ed. Joanna Kerr (London: Zed Books,
1993), p. 83. This methodology is not new. See, for example, Lumsdaine, *Moral Vision*, pp.
187–88, 211–13.

and draws attention to their concerns. A good example is the recent campaign against the practice of female genital mutilation. Before 1976 the widespread practice of female circumcision in many African and a few Asian and Middle Eastern countries was known outside these regions mainly among medical experts and anthropologists.[40] A controversial campaign, initiated in 1974 by a network of women's and human rights organizations, began to draw wider attention to the issues by renaming the problem. Previously the practice was referred to by technically "neutral" terms such as female circumcision, clitoridectomy, or infibulation. The campaign around female genital "mutilation" raised its salience, literally creating the issue as a matter of public international concern. By renaming the practice the network broke the linkage with male circumcision (seen as a personal medical or cultural decision), implied a linkage with the more feared procedure of castration, and reframed the issue as one of violence against women. It thus resituated the practice as a human rights violation. The campaign generated action in many countries, including France and the United Kingdom, and the UN studied the problem and made a series of recommendations for eradicating certain traditional practices.[41]

Uncertainty is one of the most frequently cited dimensions of environmental issues. Not only is hard information scarce (although this is changing), but any given data may be open to a variety of interpretations. The tropical forest issue is fraught with scientific uncertainty about the role of forests in climate regulation, their regenerative capacity, and the value of undiscovered or untapped biological resources. Environmentalists are unlikely to resolve these questions, and what they have done in some recent campaigns is reframe the issue, calling attention to the impact of deforestation on particular human populations. By doing so, they called for action independent of the scientific data. Human rights activists, baby food campaigners, and women's groups play similar roles, dramatizing the situations of the victims and turning the cold facts into human stories, intended to move people to action. The baby food cam-

[40] Female genital mutilation is most widely practiced in Africa, where it is reported to occur in at least twenty-six countries. Between 85 and 114 million women in the world today are estimated to have experienced genital mutilation. *World Bank Development Report 1993: Investing in Health* (New York: Oxford University Press, 1993), p. 50.

[41] See Leonard J. Kouba and Judith Muasher, "Female Circumcision in Africa: An Overview," *African Studies Review* 28:1 (March 1985): 95–110; Alison T. Slack, "Female Circumcision: A Critical Appraisal," *Human Rights Quarterly* 10:4 (November 1988): 437–86; and Elise A. Sochart, "Agenda Setting, The Role of Groups and the Legislative Process: The Prohibition of Female Circumcision in Britain," *Parliamentary Affairs* 41:4 (October 1988): 508–26. On France, see Marlise Simons, "Mutilation of Girls' Genitals: Ethnic Gulf in French Court," *New York Times*, 23 November 1993, p. 13. For UN recommendations, see the "Report of the Working Group on Traditional Practices Affecting the Health of Women and Children," UN Document E/CN.4/1986/42 at 26 (1986).

paign, for example, relied heavily on public health studies that proved that improper bottle feeding contributed to infant malnutrition and mortality, and that corporate sales promotion was leading to a decline in breast feeding.[42] Network activists repackaged and interpreted this information in dramatic ways designed to promote action: the British development organization War on Want published a pamphlet entitled "The Baby Killers," which the Swiss Third World Action Group translated into German and retitled "Nestlé Kills Babies." Nestlé inadvertently gave activists a prominent public forum when it sued the Third World Action Group for defamation and libel.

Nongovernmental networks have helped legitimize the use of testimonial information along with technical and statistical information. Linkage of the two is crucial, for without the individual cases activists cannot motivate people to seek changed policies. Increasingly, international campaigns by networks take this two-level approach to information. In the 1980s even Greenpeace, which initially had eschewed rigorous research in favor of splashy media events, began to pay more attention to getting the facts right. Both technical information and dramatic testimony help to make the need for action more real for ordinary citizens.

A dense web of north-south exchange, aided by computer and fax communication, means that governments can no longer monopolize information flows as they could a mere half-decade ago. These technologies have had an enormous impact on moving information to and from third world countries, where mail service has often been slow and precarious; they also give special advantages of course, to organizations that have access to them. A good example of the new informational role of networks occurred when U.S. environmentalists pressured President George Bush to raise the issue of gold miners' ongoing invasions of the Yanomami indigenous reserve when Brazilian president Fernando Collor de Mello was in Washington in 1991. Collor believed that he had squelched protest over the Yanomami question by creating major media events out of the dynamiting of airstrips used by gold miners, but network members had current information faxed from Brazil, and they countered his claims with evidence that miners had rebuilt the airstrips and were still invading the Yanomami area.

The central role of information in these issues helps explain the drive to create networks. Information in these issue areas is both essential and dispersed. Nongovernmental actors depend on their access to information to help make them legitimate players. Contact with like-minded groups at home and abroad provides access to information necessary to their work,

---

[42] See D. B. Jellife and E. F. P. Jellife, *Human Milk in the Modern World* (Oxford: Oxford University Press, 1978).

broadens their legitimacy, and helps to mobilize information around particular policy targets. Most nongovernmental organizations cannot afford to maintain staff people in a variety of countries. In exceptional cases they send staff members on investigation missions, but this is not practical for keeping informed on routine developments. Forging links with local organizations allows groups to receive and monitor information from many countries at a low cost. Local groups, in turn, depend on international contacts to get their information out and to help protect them in their work.

The media is an essential partner in network information politics. To reach a broader audience, networks strive to attract press attention. Sympathetic journalists may become part of the network, but more often network activists cultivate a reputation for credibility with the press, and package their information in a timely and dramatic way to draw press attention.[43]

Symbolic Politics

Activists frame issues by identifying and providing convincing explanations for powerful symbolic events, which in turn become catalysts for the growth of networks. Symbolic interpretation is part of the process of persuasion by which networks create awareness and expand their constituencies. Awarding the 1992 Nobel Peace Prize to Maya activist Rigoberta Menchú and the UN's designation of 1993 as the Year of Indigenous Peoples heightened public awareness of the situation of indigenous peoples in the Americas. Indigenous people's use of 1992, the 500th anniversary of the voyage of Columbus to the Americas, to raise a host of issues well illustrates the use of symbolic events to reshape understandings.[44]

The 1973 coup in Chile played this kind of catalytic role for the human rights community. Because Chile was the symbol of democracy in Latin America, the fact that such a brutal coup could happen there suggested that it could happen anywhere. For activists in the United States, the role of their government in undermining the Allende government intensified the need to take action. Often it is not one event but the juxtaposition of disparate events that makes people change their minds and act. For many people in the United States it was the juxtaposition of the coup in Chile, the war in Vietnam, Watergate, and the Civil Rights Movement that gave birth to the human rights movement. Likewise, dramatic footage of the Brazilian rainforest burning during the hot summer of 1988 in the

---

[43] See on social movements and media, see Todd Gitlin, *The Whole World Is Watching* (Berkeley: University of California Press, 1980). For a report on recent research, see William A. Gamson and Gadi Wolfsfeld, "Movements and Media As Interacting Systems," *Annals of the American Association of Political and Social Science* 528 (July 1993): 114–25.

[44] Brysk, "Acting Globally."

United States may have convinced many people that global warming and tropical deforestation were serious and linked issues. The assassination of Brazilian rubber tapper leader Chico Mendes at the end of that year crystallized the belief that something was profoundly wrong in the Amazon.

Leverage Politics

Activists in advocacy networks are concerned with political effectiveness. Their definition of effectiveness often includes some policy change by "target actors" such as governments, international financial institutions like the World Bank, or private actors like transnational corporations. In order to bring about policy change, networks need to pressure and persuade more powerful actors. To gain influence the networks seek leverage (the word appears often in the discourse of advocacy organizations) over more powerful actors. By leveraging more powerful institutions, weak groups gain influence far beyond their ability to influence state practices directly. The identification of material or moral leverage is a crucial strategic step in network campaigns.

Material leverage usually links the issue to money or goods (but potentially also to votes in international organizations, prestigious offices, or other benefits). The human rights issue became negotiable because governments or financial institutions connected human rights practices to military and economic aid, or to bilateral diplomatic relations. In the United States, human rights groups got leverage by providing policymakers with information that convinced them to cut off military and economic aid. To make the issue negotiable, NGOs first had to raise its profile or salience, using information and symbolic politics. Then more powerful members of the network had to link cooperation to something else of value: money, trade, or prestige. Similarly, in the environmentalists' multilateral development bank campaign, linkage of environmental protection with access to loans was very powerful.

Although NGO influence often depends on securing powerful allies, their credibility still depends in part on their ability to mobilize their own members and affect public opinion via the media. In democracies the potential to influence votes gives large membership organizations an advantage over nonmembership organizations in lobbying for policy change; environmental organizations, several of whose memberships number in the millions, are more likely to have this added clout than are human rights organizations.

Moral leverage involves what some commentators have called the "mobilization of shame," where the behavior of target actors is held up to the light of international scrutiny. Network activists exert moral leverage on the assumption that governments value the good opinion of others;

insofar as networks can demonstrate that a state is violating international obligations or is not living up to its own claims, they hope to jeopardize its credit enough to motivate a change in policy or behavior. The degree to which states are vulnerable to this kind of pressure varies, and will be discussed further below.

Accountability Politics

Networks devote considerable energy to convincing governments and other actors to publicly change their positions on issues. This is often dismissed as inconsequential change, since talk is cheap and governments sometimes change discursive positions hoping to divert network and public attention. Network activists, however, try to make such statements into opportunities for accountability politics. Once a government has publicly committed itself to a principle—for example, in favor of human rights or democracy—networks can use those positions, and their command of information, to expose the distance between discourse and practice. This is embarrassing to many governments, which may try to save face by closing that distance.

Perhaps the best example of network accountability politics was the ability of the human rights network to use the human rights provisions of the 1975 Helsinki Accords to pressure the Soviet Union and the governments of Eastern Europe for change. The Helsinki Accords helped revive the human rights movement in the Soviet Union, spawned new organizations like the Moscow Helsinki Group and the Helsinki Watch Committee in the United States, and helped protect activists from repression.[45] The human rights network referred to Moscow's obligations under the Helsinki Final Act and juxtaposed these with examples of abuses. In an illustration of the boomerang effect, human rights activist Yuri Orlov said, "We do not have the means to reach our government. My appeal to Brezhnev probably got as far as the regional KGB office. . . . The crucial question is what means are there for a Soviet citizen to approach his own government, other than indirectly through the governments of other countries."[46]

Domestic structures through which states and private actors can be held accountable to their pronouncements, to the law, or to contracts vary considerably from one nation to another, even among democracies. The centrality of the courts in U.S. politics creates a venue for the representation of diffuse interests that is not available in most European democra-

[45] Discussion of the Helsinki Accords is based on Daniel Thomas, "Norms and Change in World Politics: Human Rights, the Helsinki Accords, and the Demise of Communism, 1975–1990," Ph.D. diss., Cornell University, 1997.

[46] Walter Parchomenko, *Soviet Images of Dissidents and Nonconformists* (New York: Praeger, 1986), p. 156, as cited in Thomas, p. 219.

cies.[47] It also explains the large number of U.S. advocacy organizations that specialize in litigation. The existence of legal mechanisms does not necessarily make them feasible instruments, however; Brazil has had a diffuse interests law granting standing to environmental and consumer advocacy organizations since 1985, but the sluggishness of Brazil's judiciary makes it largely ineffective.

UNDER WHAT CONDITIONS DO ADVOCACY NETWORKS HAVE INFLUENCE?

To assess the influence of advocacy networks we must look at goal achievement at several different levels. We identify the following types or stages of network influence: (1) issue creation and agenda setting; (2) influence on discursive positions of states and international organizations; (3) influence on institutional procedures; (4) influence on policy change in "target actors" which may be states, international organizations like the World Bank, or private actors like the Nestlé Corporation; and (5) influence on state behavior.

Networks generate attention to new issues and help set agendas when they provoke media attention, debates, hearings, and meetings on issues that previously had not been a matter of public debate. Because values are the essence of advocacy networks, this stage of influence may require a modification of the "value context" in which policy debates takes place. The UN's theme years and decades, such as International Women's Decade and the Year of Indigenous Peoples, were international events promoted by networks that heightened awareness of issues.

Networks influence discursive positions when they help persuade states and international organizations to support international declarations or to change stated domestic policy positions. The role environmental networks played in shaping state positions and conference declarations at the 1992 "Earth Summit" in Rio de Janeiro is an example of this kind of impact. They may also pressure states to make more binding commitments by signing conventions and codes of conduct.

The targets of network campaigns frequently respond to demands for policy change with changes in procedures (which may affect policies in the future). The multilateral bank campaign, discussed in Chapter 4, is largely responsible for a number of changes in internal bank directives mandating greater NGO and local participation in discussions of projects. It also opened access to formerly restricted information, and led to the establishment of an independent inspection panel for World Bank

---

[47] On access to the courts and citizen oversight of environmental policy in the U.S. and Germany, see Susan Rose Ackerman, *Controlling Environmental Policy: The Limits of Public Law in Germany and the United States* (New Haven: Yale University Press, 1995).

projects. Procedural changes can greatly increase the opportunity for advocacy organizations to develop regular contact with other key players on an issue, and they sometimes offer the opportunity to move from outside to inside pressure strategies.

A network's activities may produce changes in policies, not only of the target states, but also of other states and/or international institutions. Explicit policy shifts seem to denote success, but even here both their causes and meanings may be elusive. We can point with some confidence to network impact where human rights network pressures have achieved cutoffs of military aid to repressive regimes, or a curtailment of repressive practices. Sometimes human rights activity even affects regime stability. But we must take care to distinguish between policy change and change in behavior; official policies regarding timber extraction in Sarawak, Malaysia, for example, may say little about how timber companies behave on the ground in the absence of enforcement.

We speak of stages of impact, and not merely types of impact, because we believe that increased attention, followed by changes in discursive positions, make governments more vulnerable to the claims that networks raise. (Discursive changes can also have a powerfully divisive effect on networks themselves, splitting insiders from outsiders, reformers from radicals.[48]) A government that claims to be protecting indigenous areas or ecological reserves is potentially more vulnerable to charges that such areas are endangered than one that makes no such claim. At that point the effort is not to make governments change their position but to hold them to their word. Meaningful policy change is thus more likely when the first three types or stages of impact have occurred.

Both issue characteristics and actor characteristics are important parts of our explanation of how networks affect political outcomes and the conditions under which networks can be effective. Issue characteristics such as salience and resonance within existing national or institutional agendas can tell us something about where networks are likely to be able to insert new ideas and discourses into policy debates. Success in influencing policy also depends on the strength and density of the network and its ability to achieve leverage. Although many issue and actor characteristics are relevant here, we stress issue resonance, network density, and target vulnerability.

Issue Characteristics

Issues that involve ideas about right and wrong are amenable to advocacy networking because they arouse strong feelings, allow networks to recruit volunteers and activists, and infuse meaning into these volunteer activities. However, not all principled ideas lead to network formation,

---

[48] We thank Jonathan Fox for reminding us of this point.

and some issues can be framed more easily than others so as to resonate with policymakers and publics. In particular, problems whose causes can be assigned to the deliberate (intentional) actions of identifiable individuals are amenable to advocacy network strategies in ways that problems whose causes are irredeemably structural are not. The real creativity of advocacy networks has been in finding intentionalist frames within which to address some elements of structural problems. Though the frame of violence against women does not exhaust the structural issue of patriarchy, it may transform some of patriarchy's effects into problems amenable to solution. Reframing land use and tenure conflict as environmental issues does not exhaust the problems of poverty and inequality, but it may improve the odds against solving part of them. Network actors argue that in such reframing they are weakening the structural apparatus of patriarchy, poverty, and inequality and empowering new actors to address these problems better in the future. Whether or not they are right, with the decline almost everywhere of mass parties of the left, few alternative agendas remain on the table within which these issues can be addressed.

As we look at the issues around which transnational advocacy networks have organized most effectively, we find two issue characteristics that appear most frequently: (1) issues involving bodily harm to vulnerable individuals, especially when there is a short and clear causal chain (or story) assigning responsibility; and (2) issues involving legal equality of opportunity. The first respond to a normative logic, and the second to a juridical and institutional one.

Issues involving physical harm to vulnerable or innocent individuals appear particularly compelling. Of course, what constitutes bodily harm and who is vulnerable or innocent may be highly contested. As the early failed campaign against female circumcision shows, one person's harm is another's rite of passage. Still, campaigns against practices involving bodily harm to populations perceived as vulnerable or innocent are most likely to be effective transnationally. Torture and disappearance have been more tractable than some other human rights issues, and protesting torture of political prisoners more effective than protesting torture of common criminals or capital punishment. Environmental campaigns that have had the greatest transnational effect have stressed the connection between protecting environments and protecting the often vulnerable people who live in them.

We also argue that in order to campaign on an issue it must be converted into a "causal story" that establishes who bears responsibility or guilt.[49] But the causal chain needs to be sufficiently short and clear to make the case convincing. The responsibility of a torturer who places an electric prod to a prisoner's genitals is quite clear. Assigning blame to state leaders for the actions of soldiers or prison guards involves a longer

[49] Deborah A. Stone, "Causal Stories and the Formation of Policy Agendas," *Political Science Quarterly* 104:2 (1989): 281–300.

causal chain, but accords with common notions of the principle of strict chain of command in military regimes.

Activists have been able to convince people that the World Bank bears responsibility for the human and environmental impact of projects it directly funds, but have had a harder time convincingly making the International Monetary Fund (IMF) responsible for hunger or food riots in the developing world. In the latter case the causal chain is longer, more complex, and much less visible, since neither the IMF nor governments reveal the exact content of negotiations.

An example from the Nestlé Boycott helps to illustrate the point about causal chains. The boycott was successful in ending direct advertising and promotion of infant formula to mothers because activists could establish that the corporation directly influenced decisions about infant feeding, with negative effects on infant health. But the boycott failed to prevent corporations from donating infant formula supplies to hospitals. Although this was the single most successful marketing tool of the corporation, the campaign's longer and more complex story about responsibility failed here because publics believe that doctors and hospitals buffer patients from corporate influence.

The second issue around which transnational campaigns appear to be effective is increased legal equality of opportunity (as distinguished from outcome). Our discussions of slavery and woman suffrage in Chapter 2 address this issue characteristic, as does one of the most successful transnational campaigns we don't discuss—the antiapartheid campaign. What made apartheid such a clear target was the legal denial of the most basic aspects of equality of opportunity. Places where racial stratification is almost as severe as it is in South Africa, but where such stratification is not legally mandated, such as Brazil and some U.S. cities, have not generated the same concern.[50]

Actor Characteristics

However amenable particular issues may be to strong transnational and transcultural messages, there must be actors capable of transmitting those messages and targets who are vulnerable to persuasion or leverage. Networks operate best when they are dense, with many actors, strong connections among groups in the network, and reliable information flows. (Density refers both to regularity and diffusion of information exchange within networks and to coverage of key areas.) Effective networks must involve reciprocal information exchanges, and include activists from target countries as well as those able to get institutional

---

[50] See Douglas S. Massey and Nancy A. Denton, *American Apartheid: Segregation and the Making of the Underclass* (Cambridge: Harvard University Press, 1993).

leverage. Measuring network density is problematic; sufficient densities are likely to be campaign-specific, and not only numbers of "nodes" in the network but also their quality—access to and ability to disseminate information, credibility with targets, ability to speak to and for other social networks—are all important aspects of density as well.

Target actors must be vulnerable either to material incentives or to sanctions from outside actors, or they must be sensitive to pressure because of gaps between stated commitments and practice. Vulnerability arises both from the availability of leverage and the target's sensitivity to leverage; if either is missing, a campaign may fail. Countries that are most suceptible to network pressures are those that aspire to belong to a normative community of nations. This desire implies a view of state preferences that recognizes states' interactions as a social—and socializing—process.[51] Thus moral leverage may be especially relevant where states are actively trying to raise their status in the international system. Brazilian governments since 1988, for example, have been very concerned about the impact of the Amazon issue on Brazil's international image. President José Sarney's invitation to hold the 1992 United Nations Conference on Environment and Development in Brazil was an attempt to improve that image. Similarly, the concern of recent Mexican administrations with Mexico's international prestige has made it more vulnerable to pressure from the human rights network. In the baby food campaign, network activists used moral leverage to convince states to vote in favor of the WHO/UNICEF codes of conduct. As a result, even the Netherlands and Switzerland, both major exporters of infant formula, voted in favor of the code.

THINKING ABOUT TRANSNATIONAL POLITICS

By focusing on international interactions involving nonstate actors, we follow in the tradition of earlier work in transnational politics that signaled the emergence of multiple channels of contact among societies, and the resultant blurring of domestic and international politics.[52] The network concept offers a further refinement of that work. Both the Keohane and Nye collection and the various analysts of the "new transnationalism" lump together relations among quite distinct kinds of transnational actors: multinational corporations, the Catholic church, international scientific organizations, and activist groups.[53] All

[51] See Finnemore, *National Interests in International Society.*

[52] Robert Keohane and Joseph Nye, eds., *Transnational Relations and World Politics* (Cambridge: Harvard University Press, 1971).

[53] The only factor that many of these transnational relations share is that all operate across national borders, and all are characterized by purposeful actors (at least one of which is a nonstate agent). See Risse-Kappen, "Introduction," *Bringing Transnational Relations Back In,* p. 8.

these relations can be characterized as forms of transnational networks, but we distinguish three different categories based on their motivations: (1) those with essentially *instrumental goals,* especially
transnational corporations and banks; (2) those motivated primarily by
shared causal ideas, such as scientific groups or epistemic communities;[54] and (3) those motivated primarily by *shared principled ideas or values* (transnational advocacy networks).

These different categories of transnational networks correspond to different endowments of political resources and patterns of influence. In transnational relations among actors with instrumental goals, we would expect
economic resources to carry the most weight; in epistemic communities,
technical expertise and the ability to convince policymakers of its importance counts most. Like epistemic communities, transnational advocacy networks rely on information, but for them it is the interpretation and strategic
use of information that is most important. Influence is possible because the
actors in these networks are simultaneously helping to define the issue area
itself, convince target audiences that the problems thus defined are soluble,
prescribe solutions, and monitor their implementation. Thus transnational
advocacy networks are distinctive in the centrality of principled ideas; their
strategies aim to use information and beliefs to motivate political action and
to use leverage to gain the support of more powerful institutions.

Without assuming that political interactions in the international system are reducible to domestic politics writ large, we have drawn extensively on insights developed in studies of domestic politics. American
political science has been especially attentive to theories of group formation and behavior. However, both pluralist and elitist theories clas-
sify issue areas narrowly either by economic sector or by government
policy clusters.[55] By extending the use of issue area to principled issues

[54] See Haas, ed., *Knowledge, Power, and International Policy Coordination.* Theorists of epistemic communities exclude activist groups from their definition, seeing epistemic communities mainly as groups of scientists, limited to more technical issues in international relations.
M. J. Peterson, in "Whalers, Cetologists, Environmentalists, and the International Management of Whaling," *International Organization* 46 (Winter 1992), pp. 149, 155, distinguishes actors
in epistemic communities from activists, who are "not constrained by canons of reasoning"
and who frame issues in simple terms, dividing the world into "bad guys" and "good guys."
[55] Andrew S. McFarland, "Interest Groups and Political Time: Cycles in America," *British
Journal of Political Science* 21 (July 1991): 261. Attempts to characterize patterns of influence
have included explanations highlighting group characteristics, issue characteristics, and,
more recently, patterns of interaction—policy committees and issue networks. See, e.g.,
Heclo, "Issue Networks"; Jack Hayward, "The Policy Community Approach to Industrial
Policy," in *Comparative Political Dynamics: Global Research Perspectives,* ed. Dankwart Rustow
and Kenneth Paul Erickson (New York: HarperCollins, 1991), pp. 381–407; and Howard
Aldrich and David A. Whetten, "Organization-sets, Action-sets, and Networks: Making the
Most of Simplicity," in *Handbook of Organizational Design,* ed. Paul Nystrom and William
Starbuck (New York: Oxford University Press, 1981). This organization literature has occa-
sionally been applied to international relations. See Gayl D. Ness and Steven R. Brechin,
"Bridging the Gap: International Organizations as Organizations," *International Organization*
42 (Spring 1988): 245–73.

as well, we are rejecting an economically reductionist notion of interests, adopting instead a more interactive approach to how interests are shaped within networks. The network literature in sociology has developed formal mechanisms for identifying and mapping networks, and exploring their attributes and relations—such as the network's density or the strength of links within it.[56]

As the notion of a policy community as a patterned interaction within an issue area gained currency, it led to greater interaction with European social scientists, who thought most interest group theory was too closely patterned on U.S. politics. Europeans brought to the debate a concern with group boundaries and relations among members, and with ideas and the intellectuals who frame and spread them. This focus dovetailed with a growing interest, inspired by the work of John Kingdon, in the dynamics of the public agenda.[57] Research on public interest advocacy groups and citizens groups blur the boundaries between social movement and interest group theories. Public interest advocacy groups "thrive on controversy" and are created by political entrepreneurs and supported by private foundations. Like our own, this work highlights the interactive context in which political claims are conceived and negotiated.[58]

Similar concerns have become important in studies of social movements over the last decade. Organizations and individuals within advocacy networks are political entrepreneurs who mobilize resources like information and membership and show a sophisticated awareness of the political opportunity structures within which they are operating.[59] Our stress on the role of values in networks is consistent with some arguments

[56] Methodologies and software for analyzing networks are discussed in David Knoke and James H. Kuklinski, *Network Analysis,* Sage university papers series, Quantitative applications in the social sciences, no. 28 (Beverly Hills and London: Sage, 1982). It is unclear whether the high investment of time and money of using these methodologies to analyze more far-flung international networks can be justified by the theoretical payoffs generated. Although network sampling is possible, "no completely satisfactory strategy currently exists" (p. 27).

[57] Stephen Brooks, "Introduction: Policy Communities and the Social Sciences," in *The Political Influence of Ideas,* ed. Stephen Brooks and Alain-G. Gagnon (Westport, Conn.: Praeger, 1994), p. 5; and John W. Kingdon, *Agendas, Alternatives, and Public Policies* (Boston: Little, Brown, 1984).

[58] Jack L. Walker, *Mobilizing Interest Groups in America: Patrons, Professions, and Social Movements* (Ann Arbor: University of Michigan Press, 1991), p. 12. On the expansion of citizen action, see especially Michael W. McCann, *Taking Reform Seriously: Perspectives on Public Interest Liberalism* (Ithaca: Cornell University Press, 1986); and Jeffrey Berry, "Citizen Groups and the Changing Nature of Interest Group Politics in America," *Annals of the American Academy of Political and Social Science* 528 (July 1993): 30–41.

[59] See, inter alia, David A. Snow, Louis A. Zurcher, and Sheldon Ekland-Olsen, "Social Networks and Social Movements: A Microstructural Approach to Differential Recruitment," *American Sociological Review* 45 (1980): 787–801; Snow et al., "Frame Alignment Processes"; Snow and Benford, "Ideology, Frame Resonance, and Participant Mobilization"; Sidney Tarrow, *Power in Movement: Social Movements, Collective Action, and Mass Politics in the Modern State* (Cambridge: Cambridge University Press, 1994); and McAdam, McCarthy, and Zald, "Introduction," in *Comparative Perspectives on Social Movements,* pp. 1–20.

contained in the literature on "new social movements."[60] Most important, however, over the last decade social movement theory has increasingly focused on the interaction between social structural conditions and action, on the social context of mobilization, and on the transformation of meanings among activists and among mass publics that make people believe they can have an impact on an issue.

As cognitive and relational aspects of these theoretical approaches have come to the fore, their potential utility for studying transnational group activities becomes much greater. By disaggregating national states into component—sometimes competing—parts that interact differently with different kinds of groups, we gain a much more multidimensional view of how groups and individuals enter the political arena. Focusing on interactive contexts lets us explore the roles of values, ideas, and different kinds of information and knowledge. As Heclo argues, "network members reinforce each other's sense of issues as their interests, rather than (as standard political or economic models would have it) interests defining positions on issues."[61] These theoretical approaches travel well from domestic to transnational relations precisely because to do so, they do not have to travel at all. Instead, many transnational actors have simply thrown off the fiction of the unitary state as seen from outside.[62]

TOWARD A GLOBAL CIVIL SOCIETY?

Many other scholars now recognize that "the state does not monopolize the public sphere,"[63] and are seeking, as we are, ways to describe the sphere of international interactions under a variety of names: transnational relations, international civil society, and global civil society.[64] In these views, states no longer look unitary from the outside. Increasingly

[60] See Russell J. Dalton, Manfred Kuechler, and Wilheim Burklin, "The Challenge of New Movements," in *Challenging the Political Order: New Social and Political Movements in Western Democracies*, ed. Dalton and Kuechler (Cambridge: Polity Press, 1990), pp. 10–16.

[61] Heclo, "Issue Networks," p. 102.

[62] Douglas Chalmers takes this idea the furthest, arguing that many of these international actors should now be viewed simply as "internationalized domestic actors," and their international resources as political resources like any other. See "Internationalized Domestic Politics in Latin America: The Institutional Role of Internationally Based Actors," unpublished paper, Columbia University, 1993.

[63] M. J. Peterson, "Transnational Activity, International Society, and World Politics," *Millennium* 21:3 (1992): 375–76.

[64] See, for example, Ronnie Lipschutz, "Reconstructing World Politics: The Emergence of Global Civil Society," *Millennium* 21:3 (1992): 389–420; Paul Wapner, "Politics beyond the State: Environmental Activism and World Civic Politics," *World Politics* 47 (April 1995): 311–40; and the special issue of *Millennium* on social movements and world politics, 23: 3 (Winter 1994).

dense interactions among individuals, groups, actors from states, and international institutions appear to involve much more than re-presenting interests on a world stage.

We contend that the advocacy network concept cannot be subsumed under notions of transnational social movements or global civil society. In particular, theorists who suggest that a global civil society will inevitably emerge from economic globalization or from revolutions in communication and transportation technologies ignore the issues of agency and political opportunity that we find central for understanding the evolution of new international institutions and relationships.

One strong globalization thesis is "world polity theory" associated with the sociologist John Meyer and his colleagues. For Meyer world cultural forces play a key causal role in constituting the state's characteristics and action.[65] World polity researchers have shown conclusively that states with very different histories, cultures, and social and political structures all came to adopt similar conceptions of what it means to be a state and what it means to be a citizen, regardless of patterns of institutional development. Yet in attributing so much to transnational diffusion, they remain silent on the sources of world culture except to argue that it originates from the modern Western tradition. In their view, international NGOs are not actors, but "enactors" of world cultural norms; the role of the International Olympic Committee is functionally the same as that of Greenpeace or Amnesty International.[66]

We lack convincing studies of the sustained and specific processes through which individuals and organizations create (or resist the creation of) something resembling a global civil society. Our research leads us to believe that these interactions involve much more agency than a pure diffusionist perspective suggests. Even though the implications of our findings are much broader than most political scientists would admit, the findings themselves do not yet support the strong claims about an emerging global civil society.[67] We are much more comfortable with a conception of transnational civil society as an arena of struggle, a fragmented and contested area where "the politics of transnational civil society is centrally

[65] For examples see John W. Meyer and Michael T. Hannan, eds., *National Development and the World System* (Chicago: University of Chicago Press, 1979); and George Thomas, John Meyer, Francisco Ramirez, John Boli, eds., *Institutional Structure: Constituting State, Society, and Individual* (Newbury Park, Calif.: Sage, 1987).

[66] John Boli and George M. Thomas, "Introduction: World Polity Formation since 1875," in *World Polity Formation since 1875: World Culture and International Non-Governmental Organizations* (Stanford University Press, forthcoming).

[67] Sidney Tarrow, *Power in Movement: Social Movements and Contentious Politics*, rev. ed. (Cambridge: Cambridge University Press, forthcoming 1998), Chapter 11. An earlier version appeared as "Fishnets, Internets and Catnets: Globalization and Transnational Collective Action," Instituto Juan March de Estudios e Investigaciones, Madrid: Working Papers 1996/78, March 1996; and Peterson, "Transnational Activity."

about the way in which certain groups emerge and are legitimized (by governments, institutions, and other groups)."[68]

PRINCIPLES, NORMS, AND PRACTICES

In his classic work *The Anarchical Society*, Hedley Bull made no bones about the fact that in talking about international society he was talking about a society of states. Such a society of states exists, he believed, "when a group of states, conscious of certain common interests and common values, form a society in the sense that they conceive themselves to be bound by a common set of rules in their relations with one another, and share in the working of common institutions."[69] Bull resisted the notion of an international society made up of individuals, believing that developments in that direction (the Nuremberg and Tokyo war crimes tribunals and the Universal Declaration of Human Rights) added confusion to the international scene, in that "there is no agreement as to the relative importance of these different kinds of legal and moral agents, or on any general scheme of rules that would relate them one to another."[70] Bull would have recognized the advocacy networks we discuss in this book as contributors to such uncertainty. However, he also believed in the existence of a set of basic values without which international society was inconceivable—consisting in the protection of life and bodily integrity, observance of agreements, and reasonable consistency of property relations.[71] Understanding the importance of the actors and/or the rules of interaction among them requires attention to the place of values or norms in theorizing about relations.

Interpretivist theories have highlighted the independent role of norms in international relations, and have seen identities, norms, and interests as mutually constitutive.[72] Norms constrain because they are embedded in social structures that partially demarcate valued communities. Nevertheless, systemic explanations need to be grounded in process tracing if they are to show the mechanisms by which norms constrain.[73] That

[68] Andrew Hurrell and Ngaire Woods, "Globalisation and Inequality," *Millennium* 24:3 (1995), p. 468.

[69] Hedley Bull, *The Anarchical Society: A Study of Order in World Politics*, 2d ed. (New York: Columbia University Press, 1995), p. 13.

[70] Ibid., p. 37.

[71] Ibid., p. 4.

[72] See, e.g., Katzenstein, *The Culture of National Security*, pp. 22–25; Klotz, *Norms in International Relations*, p. 26.

[73] See Klotz's discussion in *Norms in International Relations* of U.S. activists' successful reframing of apartheid as an issue of racial equality, which linked domestic civil rights activity with their campaign around South Africa.

means, to see norms in action we have to examine the actions of indi
viduals and groups in historical contexts. Norms and practices are mutually constitutive—norms have power in, and because of, what people
do.

We use the term "practice" here not only as "that which is done," but
as "the act of doing something repeatedly." This allows us to consider
the intensity of norms as well as normative change. Playing music requires practice—so much practice that in the end hands can move
without the conscious mediation of thought telling them where to go.
Similarly, we can imagine norms whose practice over time has become
so automatic that they gain a taken-for-granted quality, in which practices and standards become so routinized as to be taken almost as laws
of nature. Normative change is inherently disruptive or difficult because it requires actors to question this routinized practice and con-
template new practices.[74]

What distinguishes principled activists of the kind we discuss in this
volume is the intensely self-conscious and self-reflective nature of their
normative awareness. No mere automatic "enactors," these are people
who seek to amplify the generative power of norms, broaden the scope of
practices those norms engender, and sometimes even renegotiate or
transform the norms themselves. They do this in an intersubjective context with a wide range of interlocutors, both individual and corporate. Finally, thinking about norms in relation to practices eliminates the duality
between principled and strategic actions. Practices do not simply echo
norms—they make them real. Without the disruptive activity of these actors neither normative change nor change in practices is likely to occur.
States and other targets of network activity resist making explicit definitions of "right" and "wrong," and overcoming this resistance is central to
network strategies.

This general point about the relationship between norms and practices
can be illustrated by a discussion of the changing nature of sovereignty.
All of our networks challenge traditional notions of sovereignty. Most
views of sovereignty in international relations focus almost exclusively
on the understandings and practices of states as the sole determinants of
sovereignty, seen as a series of claims about the nature and scope of state
authority.[75] Claims about sovereignty are forceful, however, because
they represent *shared* norms, understandings, and expectations that are

---

[74] See Pierre Bourdieu, *Outline of a Theory of Practice* (Cambridge: Cambridge University
Press, 1977), pp. 17–19.

[75] See, e.g., Kenneth Waltz, *Theory of International Politics* (Reading, Mass: Addison-Wes-
ley, 1979), pp. 95–96; F. H. Hinsley, *Sovereignty*, 2d ed. (Cambridge: Cambridge University
Press, 1986); and Stephen Krasner, "Westphalia and All That," in *Ideas and Foreign Policy*, ed.
Goldstein and Keohane, pp. 235–64.

constantly reinforced through the practices of states,[76] and by the practices of nonstate actors.

Traditionally, as stated by the World Court, the doctrine of state sovereignty has meant that the state "is subject to no other state, and has full and exclusive powers within its jurisdiction"[77] It is a core premise that "how a state behaved toward its own citizens in its own territory was a matter of domestic jurisdiction, i.e., not anyone else's business and therefore not any business for international law."[78] Similarly, how states disposed of the resources within their territories or regulated the development of their economies were at least theoretically sovereign affairs. Much international network activity presumes the contrary: that it is both legitimate and necessary for states or nonstate actors to be concerned about the treatment of the inhabitants of another state. Once granted that cross-border and global environmental problems mean that economic activities within one nation's borders are of legitimate interest to another or others, the frontiers of legitimate interest have been fuzzy—and contested. Transnational advocacy networks seek to redefine these understandings; we ask whether and when they succeed.

Because many of these campaigns challenge traditional notions of state sovereignty, we might expect states to cooperate to block network activities. The ideas that environmental, indigenous, women's and human rights networks bring to the international arena impinge on sovereignty in several ways. First, the underlying logics of the "boomerang" effect and of networks—which imply that a domestic group should reach out to international allies to bring pressure on its government to change its domestic practices—undermine absolute claims to sovereignty. Second, by producing information that contradicts information provided by states, networks imply that states sometimes lie. NGOs often provide more reliable sources of information to international organizations, but by acting on that information, especially when it explicitly contradicts state posi-

[76] Alexander Wendt stresses that sovereignty is an institution that exists "only in virtue of certain intersubjective understandings and expectations; there is no sovereignty without an other." He argues that sovereignty norms are now so taken for granted that "it is easy to overlook the extent to which they are both presupposed by and an ongoing artifact of practice." "Anarchy Is What States Make of It," pp. 412–13. Still, even critics of standard views of sovereignty are so concerned with exposing how the discourse of sovereignty is constructed and maintained that they often ignore how conceptions of the state are evolving. See also Richard Ashley, "Untying the Sovereign State: A Double Reading of the Anarchy Problematique," *Millennium* 17:2 (1988): 227–61.
[77] See Stanley Hoffmann, "International Systems and International Law," in *The Strategy of World Order*, vol. II: *International*, ed. Richard A. Falk and Saul H. Mendlovitz (New York: World Law Fund, 1966), p. 164.
[78] Louis Henkin, *How Nations Behave: Law and Foreign Policy*, 2d ed. (New York: Columbia University Press, 1979), p. 228. See also James Mayall, *Nationalism and International Society* (Cambridge: Cambridge University Press, 1990), p. 20.

tions, international institutions implicitly undermine their foundation as organizations of sovereign states.

If sovereignty is a shared set of understandings and expectations about state authority that is reinforced by practices, then changes in these practices and understandings should in turn transform sovereignty. The expansion of human rights law and policy in the postwar period is an example of a conscious, collective attempt to modify this set of shared norms and practices.[79] To this end, the human rights network employed two approaches. Activists pressured governments and international organizations to develop formal procedures to investigate the human rights situation in member states. The work of NGOs exposed state repressive practices, causing other states to respond by demanding explanations, and repressive states in turn produced justifications. The combination of changing international norms, compelling information, institutional procedures for action, and targeted lobbying and pressure campaigns created awareness and often caused states to modify their human rights practices. When a state recognizes the legitimacy of international interventions and changes its domestic behavior in response to international pressure, it reconstitutes the relationship between the state, its citizens, and international actors. This pattern, by which network practices instantiate new norms, is a common one among the transnational advocacy networks we will discuss.

ORGANIZATION OF THE BOOK

The case studies that follow, which examine different kinds of advocacy network structures, strategies, and goals, were chosen to highlight the variety of transnational interactions. Chapter 2 asks whether these networks are really a new phenomenon, examining four campaigns that occurred between the 1830s and 1930s. Although not all of them involve transnational networks, all involved transnational actors in the kinds of principled and strategic actions that characterize modern networks. Chapter 3 considers the largest and best-known network, whose practices since the Second World War have promoted changes in norms and institutions around human rights. Comparison of how human rights activists responded to egregious human rights abuses in Argentina during the 1970s and to endemic abuses over the last several decades in Mexico helps to pinpoint the scope, impact, and strategies of the human rights network.

[79] See Paul Sieghart, *The Lawful Rights of Mankind: An Introduction to the International Legal Code of Human Rights* (Oxford: Oxford University Press, 1985), pp. 67–68.

Chapter 4 looks at the development of advocacy networks around third world environmental issues, focusing particularly on the issue of tropical deforestation. It looks at two concrete instances of deforestation, in Rondônia in the Brazilian Amazon and in Sarawak, Malaysia, each of which was inserted into a different global campaign (the multilateral development bank campaign and tropical timber campaign, respectively). In both cases, how the ideas and practices of transnational actors fit into domestic political contexts is key to the analysis. These cases illustrate the difficulty of frame negotiation, where networks bring together actors with different normative and political agendas. Chapter 5 looks at a comparatively new network, the international network on violence against women, and focuses especially on the negotiations of meaning that were part of the network's emergence. Finally, in the conclusions, we turn to the question of impact: how effective have these networks been in meeting the goals they set for themselves, and what are the effects of their practices in international society?

CHAPTER 2

Historical Precursors to Modern Transnational Advocacy Networks

When we suggest that transnational advocacy networks have become politically significant forces in international relations over the last several decades, we immediately face a series of challenges. First, where we see links among activists from different nationalities and cultures, others may see cultural imperialism—attempts to impose Western values and culture upon societies that neither desire nor benefit from them. Are "moral" campaigns just thinly disguised efforts by one group to gain its interest and impose its will on another? Next, some question the novelty of these phenomena. After all, internationalism in various forms has been around for a long time. Finally, still others ask about significance—have these campaigns ever produced any important social, political, or cultural changes? On what basis do we attribute such changes to network activists' work, rather than to deeper structural causes?

A look at history can give us greater purchase on these questions. In this chapter we examine several campaigns that cast light on the work of modern transnational advocacy networks. They include the 1833–65 Anglo-American campaign to end slavery in the United States, the efforts of the international suffrage movement to secure the vote for women between 1888 and 1928, the campaign from 1874 to 1911 by Western missionaries and Chinese reformers to eradicate footbinding in China, and efforts by Western missionaries and British colonial authorities to end the practice of female circumcision among the Kikuyu of Kenya in 1920–31. For each of these campaigns, we pay attention to comparable "noncampaigns" or related issues around which activists did not organize. In the case of footbinding these included the issues of female infanticide and concubinage in China. In Kenya, the absence of a campaign among other cultural groups like the Maasai that also practiced female circumcision was a puzzle even to reformers at the time. Likewise, activists sometimes criticized the antislavery movement for failing to concern itself with "wage slavery" and the woman suffrage movement with ignoring other issues related to women's subordination in society and in their homes.

We deliberately selected campaigns in which foreign linkages or actors were central to the organizing effort, though the degree and nature of international involvement vary significantly.[1] Besides being the obvious level of analysis for the international relations scholar, this focus offers potential theoretical payoffs by making distinctions between self-interested and principled motivations for action clearer. When foreign missionary women act to eradicate footbinding in China, the tenuous connection between actor and "beneficiary" suggests the action is "disinterested" or motivated by humanitarian rather than material concerns.

These historical cases provide wide variation in the domestic structures of the target state: the antislavery campaign and the woman suffrage movement demanded policy change in independent and democratic states; the footbinding campaign occurred in the final years of Imperial China and the female circumcision debate in a British colony.[2] We might expect transnational campaigns initiated primarily by British citizens to be most effective in a British colony, less so in another independent democratic state, and least effective in a foreign and culturally distant empire. The order of effectiveness in these cases, however, is exactly the reverse: the footbinding campaign led to the most rapid change; the international women's suffrage movement took over half a century to secure its goal in most countries of the world; the Anglo-American antislavery campaign succeeded only after sixty years of effort and a hugely destructive civil war; and the early campaign against female circumcision failed to change important attitudes or practices.

Each of these campaigns began with an idea that was almost unimaginable, even by its early proponents. That they could abolish slavery, gain the vote for women, or end footbinding hardly seemed possible. One of the main tasks that social movements undertake, however, is to make possible the previously unimaginable, by framing problems in such a

---

[1] Sidney Tarrow, skepticial that the world is now entering an "unheralded age of global movements," encourages "comparatively bold historical studies" of transnational movements in Sidney Tarrow, *Power in Movement: Social Movements and Contentious Politics*, rev. ed. (Cambridge: Cambridge University Press, 1998), chapter 11.

[2] Thomas Risse-Kappen stresses the importance of domestic structures for explaining the success of transnational networks in influencing state security policy, in "Ideas Do Not Float Freely: Transnational Coalitions, Domestic Structures, and the End of the Cold War," *International Organization* 48 (Spring 1994): 187.

way that their solution comes to appear inevitable. The case of female circumcision reminds us that such changes are neither obvious nor linear. They are the contingent result of contestations over meaning and resources waged by specific actors in a specific historical context.

INTERNATIONAL PRESSURES FOR THE ABOLITION OF SLAVERY IN THE UNITED STATES, 1833–1865

The antislavery movement, which began by demanding the abolition of the slave trade and then promoted the emancipation of slaves, spanned many countries over an entire century.[3] In its scope, methods, and sensibilities, it is the most obvious forerunner to the campaigns discussed in this book. It was also a notable success. "It is remarkable how rapidly, by historical standards, the institution of slavery gave way before the abolitionist onslaught, once the ideological campaign gained momentum. . . . [W]ithin the span of little more than a century, a system that had stood above criticism for 3,000 years was outlawed everywhere in the Western world."[4] We examine only one piece of this global campaign, the Anglo-American network in the period 1833–65, which focused primarily on the emancipation of slaves in the United States. A focus on foreign pressures to change practices within a single country, rather than campaigns leading to global prohibition regimes, provides a parallel to cases discussed in later chapters.[5]

British abolitionist sentiment in the late 1700s and early 1800s concentrated first on the abolition of the slave trade, in which British merchants and capital were heavily involved. After it was formally abolished in the United States and Britain in 1807, abolitionists sought legal prohibition on slavery in the territories controlled by the British, which was secured in 1833. After these "closer to home" issues were taken care of, the British abolitionists turned their attention to what they considered the most glaring instance of modern slavery, its practice in the United States. The Irish M.P. and antislavery leader Daniel O'Connell encouraged the movement to "enable us to begin the work with the vile and sanguinary slaveholders

---

[3] Quakers in Pennsylvania first protested slavery in the 1680s, but the real movement went from 1787, when British abolitionists launched a public campaign against the slave trade, to the emancipation of slaves in Brazil in the 1880s. See Robert William Fogel, *Without Consent or Contract: The Rise and Fall of American Slavery* (New York: W.W. Norton, 1989), p. 205. For surveys of the antislavery movement by political scientists, see Tarrow, *Power in Movement*; James Lee Ray, "The Abolition of Slavery and the End of International War," *International Organization* 43:3 (Summer 1989): 405–39; and Ethan A. Nadelmann, "Global Prohibition Regimes: The Evolution of Norms in International Society," *International Organization* 44:4 (Autumn 1990): 491–98.

[4] Fogel, *Without Consent or Contract*, pp. 204–5.

[5] Nadelmann, "Global Prohibition Regimes."

of Republican America. I want to be directly at them. No more side-wind attacks; firing directly at the hull, as the seaman says, is my plan."[6] One British antislavery publication urged Americans to "wipe out the shame which renders [you] a scorn among the nations of the world," while an address of the Irish Unitarian Christian Society to their brethren in America called slavery a "plague-spot in America, a cancer which must be boldly cut away," and a "compilation of the greatest crimes against God and men."[7]

Like their counterparts in target states of modern networks, many U.S. policymakers and citizens resented this British "intervention" in their affairs. One clergyman said, "we do not like the tone of English criticism upon us"; another complained of the British Anti-Slavery League meddling in American affairs and asked why there was not a league to oppose serfdom in Russia or polygamy in Turkey. A common complaint was that the British did not understand America's domestic institutions, and thus should stay out of its affairs.[8] Proslavery forces in the United States argued also that the condition of the lower classes in England was "far inferior" to that of American slaves. A congressman from South Carolina denounced British "exclamations and denunciations" on American slavery that filled "every public journal in Great Britain," despite poverty in Scotland and "enslaved subjects" in Ireland.[9]

Historians and political scientists have argued at great length over whether the end of slavery was the result of economic or moral pressures.[10] The most current and careful historical research argues that economics simply cannot explain the demise of slavery, and finds that the impetus behind abolition was primarily religious and humanitarian. Robert William Fogel concludes that a quarter century of research on the economics of slavery shows that slavery was "profitable, efficient, and economically viable in both the U.S. and the West Indies when it was destroyed. . . . Its death was an act of 'econocide,' a political execution of an immoral system at its peak of economic success, incited by men ablaze with moral fervor."[11]

[6] Quoted in Betty Fladeland, *Men and Brothers: Anglo-American Antislavery Cooperation* (Urbana: University of Illinois Press, 1972), p. 260.
[7] Douglas Charles Stange, *British Unitarians against American Slavery 1833–65* (Rutherford, N.J.: Fairleigh Dickinson University Press, 1984), pp. 59, 61.
[8] Ibid., pp. 63, 73, 84.
[9] As cited in Fladeland, *Men and Brothers*, p. 160.
[10] For an overview of the debate among historians, see David Brion Davis, "AHR Forum: Reflections on Abolitionism and Ideological Hegemony," John Ashworth, "The Relationship between Capitalism and Humanitarianism," and Thomas L. Haskell, "Convention and Hegemonic Interest in the Debate over Antislavery: A Reply to Davis and Ashworth," in *American Historical Review* 92 (October 1987): 797–878; for political scientists, see Ray, "Abolition of Slavery," and Nadelmann, "Global Prohibition Regimes."
[11] Fogel, *Without Consent or Contract*, p. 410.

Some historians, instead of seeing economics and morality as dichoto-
mous explanations, consider how the rise of capitalism and changes in
the market contributed to changing perceptions, conventions about
moral responsibility, and techniques of action that underlay the wave of
humanitarianism in the period 1750–1850.[12] Such approaches fit nicely
with Tarrow's argument that social movements emerged in the eigh-
teenth century from "structural changes that were associated with capitalism" such as "new forms of association, regular communication
linking center and periphery, and the spread of print and literacy."[13]

Technological and institutional change can alter the "moral universe"
in which action takes place, by changing how people think about responsibility and guilt, and by supplying them with new ways to act.[14] For
Thomas Haskell, humanitarianism requires not only the "ethical maxims
that make helping strangers the right thing to do" but also "a technique
or recipe for intervening—a specific sequence of steps that we know we
can take to alter the ordinary course of events," and which must be sufficiently routine to use easily.[15] Haskell shows how technological change
and the market facilitated the appearance of "recipes" that humanitarian
groups, especially the antislavery movement, later embraced. Tarrow reminds us that collective action repertoires like boycotts, mass petitioning,
or barricades were pioneered within particular struggles, and then were
diffused to or emulated by other social movements.[16] Eric Foner captures
this effect in the United States: "If anti-slavery promoted the hegemony
of middle class values, it also provided a language of politics, a training
in organization, for critics of the emerging order. The anti-slavery crusade was a central terminus, from which tracks led to every significant attempt to reform American society after the Civil War."[17]

The transnational antislavery campaign provided a "language of politics" and organizational and tactical recipes for other transnational campaigns as well. The woman suffrage campaign initially drew many of its
activists and tactics from the antislavery movement. The movement
against footbinding in China set up antifootbinding societies similar to
the antislavery societies in Britain and the United States. The "society" itself was a prominent recipe. The modern versions of these societies are

[12] Thomas L. Haskell, "Capitalism and the Origins of the Humanitarian Sensibility,"
parts I and II, *American Historical Review* 90 (April 1985): 339–61, and 90 (June 1985): 547–66.

[13] Tarrow, *Power in Movement*, p. 48.

[14] Haskell, "Capitalism," part I, 356.

[15] Ibid., p. 358. See also Charles Tilly, "Contentious Repertoires in Great Britain,
1758–1834," in *Repertoires & Cycles of Collective Action*, ed. Mark Traugott (Durham: Duke
University Press, 1995); and Tarrow, *Power in Movement*, chapter 2.

[16] Tarrow, *Power in Movement*, pp. 40–45.

[17] Eric Foner, *Politics and Ideology in the Age of the Civil War* (Oxford: Oxford University
Press, 1980), p. 76.

NGOs, and they have become even more specialized and diverse, offering a wider selection of organizational and strategic recipes.

In Britain and the United States, activists set up local, regional, and national antislavery organizations that frequently exchanged letters, publications, and visits. In Britain approximately 400,000 persons signed petitions against the slave trade in 1791–92 (one out of every eleven adults); in 1814 abolitionists gathered 750,000 names (one out of every eight adults); by 1833 one of every seven adults, or twice the number of voters in the most recent elections, signed petitions in favor of the emancipation of slaves.[18] This was clearly a mass movement, not a small group of elites. In the United States the size of the movement matched or may have exceeded that in Britain at its peak. In 1838 authors estimate that there were 1,350 local antislavery societies in the United States, with between 120,000 and 250,000 members.[19] The movement's petitions overwhelmed the congressional machinery, and were so disruptive to the political and regional compromises in each party that the House voted first to table them and later not even to receive them.[20]

The backbone of the movement in both countries was formed by Quakers and the "dissenting denominations"—Methodists, Presbyterians, and Unitarians, who brought a deeply religious, evangelical and philanthropic spirit to the movement in both countries.[21] They also drew on a tradition of transatlantic networking and information exchange that had flourished among them during the last decades before American independence.[22] Some members of the antislavery movement, especially in the United States, were more influenced by enlightenment ideas of equality and liberty than by Christianity.[23] The British religious denominations were more unified in their antislavery sentiment than the American denominations, and tried to encourage their American counterparts to take more forceful positions against slavery. British Unitarians, for example, were horrified to learn that the American Unitarian Association had named a slaveholder to their honorary board of vice presidents, and agitated against it until the association abolished the board.[24]

Antislavery groups in the United States and Britain borrowed tactics, organizational forms, research, and language from each other. They used the

---

[18] Fogel, *Without Consent or Contract*, pp. 212, 217, 227.

[19] Herbert Aptheker, *Abolitionism: A Revolutionary Movement* (Boston: Twayne, 1989), p. 56.

[20] This debate is the subject of William Lee Miller's fascinating book, *Arguing about Slavery: The Great Battle in the United States Congress* (New York: Knopf, 1996).

[21] *A Side Light on Anglo-American Relations, 1839–58: Furnished by Correspondence of Lewis Tappan and Others with the British and Foreign Anti-Slavery Society*, ed. Annie Abel and Frank Klingberg (Lancaster, Penn.: Association for the Study of Negro Life and History, 1927), p. 2.

[22] Alison Gilbert Olson, *Making the Empire Work: London and American Interest Groups, 1690–1790* (Cambridge, Mass.: Harvard University Press, 1992).

[23] Foner, *Politics and Ideology*, p. 66.

[24] Stange, *British Unitarians*, p. 96.

tactics of the petition, boycotts of slave-produced goods, and hired itinerant speakers very successfully on both sides of the Atlantic. Many of these
tactics originated in Britain and the transnational network served as a vehicle for diffusing tactical recipes and collective action repertoires from
one domestic social movement to another. In some cases, the antislavery
network did more than transfer recipes, becoming a place for transnational political communication that mutually altered the tactics used on
both sides of the Atlantic. Despite internal divisions, British and American
groups often arrived at common positions, such as opposition to the colonization schemes proposed on both sides of the Atlantic by the 1830s. The
British abolitionist campaign for immediate emancipation of West Indian
slaves led the American movement to switch its main demand from gradual emancipation of slaves to immediate emancipation. As to mutual influence, the U.S. antislavery movement eventually may have encouraged
the British movement to include women on a more equal status. The
British movement, on the other hand, particularly encouraged U.S. church
establishments to take a strong stand against slavery.[25]

One of the most important tactics the abolitionists used was what we
call "information politics" and what human rights activists a century and
a half later would call the human rights methodology: "promoting
change by reporting facts."[26] The most influential example was the volume *American Slavery As It Is: Testimony of a Thousand Witnesses.* Abolitionist activists Theodore Weld and Angelina and Sarah Grimke
compiled the book from testimonials of individuals, and extensive clippings from Southern newspapers. *American Slavery As It Is* became the
handbook of the antislavery cause, selling over 100,000 copies in its first
year and continuing to sell year after year.[27] William Lee Miller's description of the book shows how it foreshadowed many of the modern publications of transnational networks, both in its scrupulous attention to
reporting facts and its use of dramatic personal testimony to give those
facts human meaning and to motivate action.

> "Although this book was loaded with, and shaped by, a quite explicit
> moral outlook and conclusion—no book was ever more so—its essence
> was something else: a careful assembling of attested facts, to make its
> point. . . . The author or compilers did not simply tell you the facts and let
> the facts speak for themselves; they told you repeatedly, what to think of
> these facts. Nevertheless. . . it tried to persuade you by assembling over-
> whelming piles of undeniable specifics.[28]

[25] Aptheker, *Abolitionism,* pp. 91, 150.
[26] Dorothy Q. Thomas, "Holding Governments Accountable by Public Pressure," in *Ours
By Right: Women's Rights as Human Rights,* ed. by Joanna Kerr (London: Zed Books, 1993), p.
83.
[27] Miller, *Arguing about Slavery,* pp. 332–33.
[28] Ibid., p. 325.

The diffusion of tactics through transnational networks could never have led, by itself, to the emergence of a full-fledged antislavery movement in the United States. As Fogel points out, "Although England provided the spark for a new American crusade, the fire would neither have been lit nor sustained without kindling and a large reserve of fuel." Both the kindling and the fuel were domestic; there were militant leaders to spread the idea, and "a public ready to receive it."

Fogel's fire metaphor serves for the types of interactions that we describe throughout this book. There must be an idea, advocates to spread the idea, and a public ready to receive it. But how do we know when a public is "ready" to receive an idea? Why do some ideas resonate and others do not? In the case of the antislavery movement, the "vast supply of religious zeal" created by the Protestant revival movements of the early nineteenth century heightened the receptiveness of religious communities in Britain and the northeastern United States to antislavery ideas.[29] Revival theology emphasized each individual's capacity and responsibility for salvation through good works and efforts to root out individual and social sin. In this worldview, not only was slavery a social sin, but also the slave was being denied the individuality essential for personal salvation. Temperance movements could also appeal to this sensibility, because alcohol was seen as a major example of personal sin that in turn led to social sin, and many antislavery activists were also active in the temperance movement. Yet some apparently congruent concerns, such as "wage slavery"—that is, low wages and poor working conditions for the working classes in the North—did not resonate with the Protestant sensibility. Workers, however poor, were free to strive both for salvation and to improve their lot in life; slaves were not.

The world antislavery conferences held in London in 1840 and 1843 solidified Anglo-American cooperation. But the 1840 conference also sharpened internal divisions within the Anglo-American antislavery movement when the English majority refused to seat several black and white women elected as American delegates. They seated the women in the balcony as spectators, where part of the U.S. male delegation, including the fiery abolitionist William Lloyd Garrison, joined them. This led to a split in the movement, and the Garrisonians were not invited to the 1843 conference.

The antislavery campaign meets our definition of the transnational advocacy network as a set of relevant organizations working internationally with shared values, a common discourse, and dense exchanges of information. Communication technology of the time, of course, imposed a different pace on these exchanges. British abolitionists argued

[29] Fogel, *Without Consent or Contract*, pp. 267, 269.

in the mid-1800s that "America was no longer a distant land: it was only two weeks away."[30] Despite the distance, British and American antislavery groups exchanged letters, publications, and speakers, and were honorary members of each other's antislavery societies. (American antislavery speakers in Britain attracted large audiences; some early British speakers in the United States barely escaped lynching.)

After having first appeared as a series in an antislavery newspaper, Harriet Beecher Stowe's novel *Uncle Tom's Cabin* sold 300,000 copies in the United States in the first year (about one copy for every eight families in the North) and over one million copies in Great Britain in eight months in 1852.[31] In writing her novel, Stowe relied on the abolitionist compendium of facts and testimony, *American Slavery As It Is: Testimony of a Thousand Witnesses*—even, she said, sleeping with it under her pillow. "In 1853, she published a 'key' to Uncle Tom's cabin—a defense of its authenticity, an answer to those who said such things do not happen, or are rare—which drew heavily and explicitly on the testimony in *American Slavery As It Is*."[32] Stowe made a triumphant speaking tour of Britain in 1853 from which she returned with more than £20,000 for the cause. Even Queen Victoria probably would have received Stowe had the American minister not objected that this would appear as a British government endorsement of the abolitionist movement.[33]

As in modern issue networks, the line between government and movement in Britain was sometimes fuzzy. Many leading antislavery crusaders of the early 1800s such as William Wilberforce were members of Parliament, and they could often count on the abolitionist sentiments of members of the government.[34] In the United States during this period the abolition movement had few sympathizers in government (in the late 1830s they gained champions such as John Quincy Adams in Congress).

The transnational dimension was most influential and decisive when government links with civil society were impaired. In antebellum U.S. politics, Southern dominance in political institutions and Northern fear of breaking up the Union kept abolitionist sentiment out of these institutions.[35] Ironically, it was the constitutional provision allowing a slave to count as three-fifths of a person in determining congressional districts and electoral votes that gave the South this control of political

---

[30] Stange, *British Unitarians*, p. 96.

[31] Fogel, *Without Consent or Contract*, p. 342; Stange, *British Unitarians*, p. 140.

[32] Miller, *Arguing about Slavery*, p. 334.

[33] Fladeland, *Men and Brothers*, pp. 354–56.

[34] Ibid., p. 52.

[35] Southerners had held the presidency for forty out of fifty-two years, the Speaker of the House for twenty-eight of thirty-five years, the majority of the Supreme Court and of the cabinet, and "every Senate President pro-tem since the ratification of the Constitution." Fogel, *Without Consent or Contract*, p. 339.

institutions.[36] The South used its dominant position to silence debate over slavery, first tabling and then refusing to receive antislavery petitions, even those raising issues clearly within congressional purview such as slavery in the District of Columbia.

These "gag" rules, prohibiting members from introducing antislavery petitions or resolutions, made transnational linkage politics an attractive strategy for American abolitionists; by joining with British activists and at times leveraging the power of the British government on behalf of the antislavery cause, they could amplify their own voices.

For years, John Quincy Adams and a small handful of antislavery representatives were virtually alone in defending the right to petition against slavery. Throughout his long battle against the gag rules Adams' strategy was to frame antislavery as an issue of civil liberty. When Congress tried twice to censure him for introducing petitions against slavery, Adams made a brilliant defense, accusing the supporters of the gag rule of suppressing the constitutional right of petition, and of interfering with the most basic of civil liberties—the right of legislators to speak their minds freely in Congress.[37]

By the Congress of 1841–42, however, Adams had more support, especially from Joshua Giddings of Ohio and a number of other antislavery advocates in Congress. The abolitionist activists set up what Giddings dubbed a "select committee on Slavery" to plan congressional strategy on abolition, do research and writing for congressional speeches on slavery, and to print and circulate the speeches around the country, since officially printed documents "would be far more valuable than abolitionist tracts and pamphlets."[38] In those days a congressman had no staff, so the members of the select committee made the unprecedented decision to use their own personal funds to rent rooms and hire a research assistant to do fact-finding for their speeches. The man they hired was Theodore Weld, one of the most prominent abolitionist agents and speakers. Weld was also the leading researcher of the antislavery movement, and had helped compile *American Slavery As It Is*. As an itinerant abolitionist speaker, Weld had helped convert three of the congressional members of the select committee to the cause, so he was a logical choice for staff. Weld agreed to do the work because "these men are in a position to do for the Anti-slavery cause by a single speech more than our best lecturers can do in a year."[39] The select committee was a strange hybrid, something in between the NGOs that lobby Congress today and the modern committee or congressional staff. It was a forerunner of a modern advocacy

[36] Ibid.
[37] Miller, *Arguing about Slavery*, pp. 351–52.
[38] Ibid., p. 405.
[39] Ibid., pp. 405–6.

network, where activists and policymakers collaborate on joint projects motivated by principled ideas.

With the rise of a new antislavery leadership in the U.S. Congress, British abolitionist influence in the United States waned.[40] Paradoxically, it was a transnational factor, immigration, that robbed the South of its historical dominance of political institutions. The "huge influx of foreigners into the North after 1820" affected the distribution of House seats and electoral votes, giving the North the possibility of gaining control of the federal government.[41]

The task that fell to the new political antislavery leadership was one that only domestic leaders could carry out—a reinterpretation of the meaning of the U.S. Constitution. Before 1842 politicians and abolitionists alike believed that the Constitution prohibited the federal government from interfering with the issue of slavery. It was this "federal consensus" that had to be undermined for the antislavery campaign to proceed.[42] This interpretive task fell to the new political leadership in the House. With Weld's help, and following in the footsteps of Adams, they brilliantly claimed for themselves the role of defenders of the Constitution. In an 1837 pamphlet, Weld first developed the theory that freedom was national and slavery local, so whenever an individual left a slave state's jurisdiction, in the territories, in the District of Columbia, or on the high seas, "freedom instantly broke out." In 1842 Congressman Giddings used such theory to turn the classic arguments of Southern slaveholders against them. In an argument that grew out of the work of the select committee, he claimed that "if the Federal Government had no Constitutional right to interfere with slavery in any way," then it followed that the federal government "had no constitutional right to support it."[43] This line of argument then allowed the antislavery members to challenge the fugitive slave laws and the legalization of slavery in Washington. With the population shift to the North and savvy coalition-building by antislavery forces, this reframing helped the new Republican party put together a fragile but winning coalition in the 1860 elections that brought Lincoln to power.[44]

The outbreak of the Civil War did not immediately unify the Anglo-American antislavery alliance around a strong common purpose. Many leaders in the antislavery campaign were pacifists and found it hard to support any war. The carnage and destruction on the battlefield appalled British humanitarians, some of whom were sympathetic to the South's claim that it was fighting for independence against an imperial North.

[40] Fladeland, *Men and Brothers*, p. 342.
[41] Fogel, *Without Consent or Contract*, p. 319.
[42] Ibid., p. 282.
[43] Miller, *Arguing about Slavery*, p. 445; Fogel, *Without Consent or Contract*, p. 336.
[44] Ibid., pp. 338, 205.

Particularly troubling was that the leaders of both South and North denied that slavery was a cause of the war. Although "the most explosive confrontations between North and South throughout the antebellum period related to slavery," political constraints prevented both Northern and Southern leaders from identifying slavery as the source of the conflict.[45] Lincoln understood that many Northerners were not willing to fight to free blacks, and that an antislavery campaign could even drive the border states out of the Union. Yet his refusal to make emancipation a war aim left an increasingly moribund abolitionist movement in Britain in disarray, and allowed the British government to focus on its commercial interests rather than on the moral issues.[46]

Southern leaders believed that the British textile mills' dependence on Southern cotton would force the British government to recognize and support the Confederacy. "Nobody but crazyheaded abolitionists ever supposed for a moment that England would not recognize the Southern Confederacy," the *Richmond Whig* said in early 1861.[47] Still, Confederate leaders understood that vocal support of slavery would not help them in gaining British support.

The Southern leaders were not just engaging in wishful thinking. By mid-1862 the three most powerful men in the British government, Prime Minister Palmerston, Foreign Minister Lord John Russell, and Chancellor William Gladstone, were all leaning toward offering to mediate the Civil War jointly with France. This would have favored the South, and most likely provoked a Northern refusal, followed by British recognition of the Confederacy. Spurred by Confederate military victories, which made Southern separation appear irrevocable, by economic distress in the British textile industry, where almost a third of the mills were closed, and by popular distress at the war's carnage, British leaders felt that public opinion would support the peacemaker.[48]

By early 1863, well before the decisive military victories at Gettysburg and Vicksburg that turned the tide of the war in the Union's favor, the British leaders had changed their minds, and instead maintained a policy of wait-and-see neutrality. What led to this shift in British policy?

One factor was Lincoln's September 1862 Emancipation Proclamation, which reinvigorated the antislavery movement and clarified the moral dimension of the conflict.[49] Initially the British press and public pointed to the

[45] Howard Jones, *Union in Peril: The Crisis over British Intervention in the Civil War* (Chapel Hill: University of North Carolina Press, 1992), p. 16.

[46] Ibid.

[47] Brian Jenkins, *Britain and the War for the Union* (Montreal: McGill-Queen's University Press, 1974), vol. 1, p. 5.

[48] Jones, *Union in Peril*, pp. 151, 165.

[49] John M. Owen, "How Liberalism Produces Democratic Peace," *International Security* 19 (Fall 1994): 111.

hypocrisy of freeing slaves in territories over which Lincoln had no control, and perceived the proclamation as an incitement to slave revolt in the South.[50] In the aftermath of the Indian Mutiny, British fear of "servile insurrection" played a role "in shaping and distorting" the initial response.[51]

Yet the Emancipation Proclamation also reinvigorated the antislavery movement, which organized a series of large meetings and rallies in support of the Union in December 1862 and January 1863. When the feared slave revolt in the South failed to materialize, British leaders began to understand the long-range implications of Lincoln's proclamation. It paved the way for the end of slavery, and it clarified the war aims of the North so that any British offer to mediate the conflict put them in the position of condoning slavery.[52]

In the end, antislavery sentiment in Britain was "one of a combination of influences" that helped keep the British from recognizing the Confederacy and extending aid to her, an act that most agree could have altered the outcome of the Civil War.[53] Considering how close the British came to recognizing the South, each factor weighing against intervention was important. William Seward, Lincoln's secretary of state, convinced the British that his government would perceive any intervention as a hostile move, with all the complications that entailed for the long unprotected border with Canada. Neutrality in the Civil War also left Britain's hands free to handle difficult diplomatic situations in Europe. But there was also a moral dimension to the debate. The Emancipation Society's campaign helped mobilize British public opinion in favor of the North, convincing leaders that any policy that appeared to favor the slave states would be divisive and unpopular.[54]

In the case of abolition a nascent transnational advocacy network, mobilizing around a moral issue, using some tactics similar to modern networks, succeeded first in helping create abolition as a pressing political issue in the United States, and then, when the issue ultimately contributed to war, became a crucial factor in preventing British recognition of the South.

THE INTERNATIONAL MOVEMENT FOR WOMAN SUFFRAGE

Historians and international relations scholars have paid remarkably little attention to the international dimensions of movements for woman suffrage. (Such indifference to the international processes through which

[50] Jenkins, *Britain and the War*, vol. 2, p. 176; Jones, *Union in Peril*, p. 225.

[51] Jenkins, *Britain and the War*, vol. 2, p. 158.

[52] Owen, "How Liberalism Produces Democratic Peace," pp. 113–14. Jenkins, *Britain and the War*, vol. 2, pp 153–55, 398; Jones, *Union in Peril*, pp. 171–93.

[53] Flademan, *Men and Brothers*, p. 386.

[54] Jenkins, *Britain and the War*, vol. 2, p. 269; Owen, "How Liberalism Produces Democratic Peace," p. 114.

half the world's population was granted the right to political participation underscores the conceptual and empirical silences in our discipline on gender issues.) Recent historical research, however, stresses the mutual influence and international cooperation among woman suffrage movements around the world.[55] Nancy Cott argues that "anyone investigating feminism at the turn of the twentieth century cannot fail to recognize that she or he is looking at an international movement, one in which ideas and tactics migrated from place to place as individuals in different countries traveled, looked for helpful models, and set up networks of reform."[56]

The international movement for woman suffrage began with women's involvement in antislavery organizations in Britain and the United States. Their experience at the World Anti-Slavery Conference in 1840, when the English majority refused to seat women, spurred Lucretia Mott and Elizabeth Cady Stanton to press forward the organized movement for women's rights that led to the historic 1848 meeting at Seneca Falls, New York. Likewise, an early split in the suffrage movement in the United States came when suffragists' Republican allies supported the ballot for freed male slaves but not for women. Parallel to the contribution that the civil rights movement and "freedom summer" made to the women's movement in the 1960s and 1970s, these early connections and evolutions remind us that besides diffusing repertoires, movements in their shortcomings sow the seeds of future movements.[57]

When Elizabeth Cady Stanton first suggested a suffrage resolution at the Seneca Falls meeting, even her most resolute supporters were afraid that it might make the movement "look ridiculous" and compromise their other goals.[58] Voting was considered the quintessential male domain of action. Other issues, such as equality before the law in matters of property, divorce, and children, better pay for working women, equal access to jobs and education, and application of the same moral codes to the behavior of men and women, were much less controversial than the proposal that women should vote. Resolutions regarding these issues passed unanimously, while the suffrage resolution carried by a small minority, and only after eloquent speeches by Stanton and abolitionist Frederick Douglass.[59]

[55] Ellen Carol DuBois, "Woman Suffrage around the World: Three Phases of Suffragist Internationalism," in *Suffrage and Beyond: International Feminist Perspectives*, ed. Caroline Daley and Melanie Nolan (New York: New York University Press, 1994), p. 254.

[56] Nancy F. Cott, "Early Twentieth Century Feminism in Political Context: A Comparative Look at Germany and the United States," in *Suffrage and Beyond*, p. 234.

[57] Doug McAdam, *Freedom Summer* (New York: Oxford University Press, 1988).

[58] Elisabeth Griffith, *In Her Own Right: The Life of Elizabeth Cady Stanton* (New York: Oxford University Press, 1984), p. 54.

[59] Mari Jo Buhle and Paul Buhle, eds., *The Concise History of Woman Suffrage: Selections from the Classic Work of Stanton, Anthony, Gage, and Harper* (Urbana: University of Illinois Press, 1978), pp. 96–98.

We might consider these other initially "less controversial" issues present in 1848 at Seneca Falls the "non-cases" with which to compare woman suffrage. Why did suffrage, originally perceived as more radical, become the basis of a successful global campaign, while some of the other issues are still unresolved? We argue that suffrage, like slavery, was a clear example of denial of the most basic legal equality of opportunity. The causal chain was short: the law (and the state behind the law) denied women the right to vote. The solution, a change in the law, was simple. The issue lent itself to framing and action that appealed to the most basic values of the liberal state—equality, liberty, and democracy.

Like the abolitionists, most early women's rights advocates were motivated by the religious revival movements. The slogan of Susan B. Anthony, for example, was "resistance to tyranny is obedience to God." Other early suffragists, instead of asserting that women were entitled to equal rights and citizenship by virtue of being human (the liberal human rights idea), framed their arguments in terms of women's differences from men, and the unique qualities such as morality and nurturing that they could bring to the public realm.[60] Opponents of woman suffrage also believed that women were different, claiming that if given the vote women would be too conservative, too tied to the church, or too supportive of banning alcoholic beverages. Nineteenth-century campaigns against prostitution and trafficking in women ("white slavery") and for special protective legislation for women workers were premised on the idea that women's vulnerability and fragile nature required special protection.[61]

Although many domestic suffrage organizations were active in the nineteenth century, it was not until 1904, when women's rights advocates founded the International Woman Suffrage Association (IWSA), that an international campaign for suffrage based on an Enlightenment frame of equal rights was launched.[62] In fact there were three or four overlapping campaigns with different degrees of coordination. Suffrage groups were often divided by political and personal differences, and disagreed over the same kinds of strategic choices that modern networks would face: single-issue focus vs. broader demands; lobbying and political tactics vs. grassroots organizing; radical civil disobedience vs. legal forms of opposition.

A number of particular characteristics mark the international woman suffrage campaign. First, unlike the antislavery movement, the campaign relied more on symbolic and pressure politics than on information politics.

[60] Nitza Berkovitch, "From Motherhood to Citizenship: The Worldwide Incorporation of Women into the Public Sphere in the Twentieth Century," Ph.D. diss., Stanford University, 1995, p. 21.
[61] Ibid., pp. 23–46.
[62] Ibid., pp 46–50.

The problem women faced was more about entrenched social attitudes and practices than lack of information or understanding. Also, we find no examples of the international woman suffrage campaign using the boomerang pattern of influence we discuss in our introduction, nor the leverage politics that are basic to this pattern. Nowhere did women find powerful foreign organizations or governments willing to use leverage or devote resources to promote woman suffrage beyond their borders, nor were suffrage organizations able to use accountability politics, for no governments accepted international obligations to which they could later be held accountable. As a result women used symbolic politics more than any other tactic, and when peaceful tactics produced meager results they sometimes turned to civil disobedience and provocation. More than any other of the campaigns we discuss in this book, suffrage activists were prepared to break the law to gain attention to their cause, and to go to jail defending their beliefs.

The first and often overlooked international organization promoting woman suffrage was the World's Women's Christian Temperance Union (WCTU). Because it believed that the vote would allow women to secure prohibition, and physical security for themselves and their children, the WCTU changed from a conventional Protestant women's organization to a politically aggressive organization fighting for a wide range of issues including suffrage.[63] One WCTU activist traveled all over the world, "leaving in her wake some 86 women's organizations dedicated to achieving woman's suffrage."[64] Everywhere that women gained the vote between 1890 and 1902—Australia and New Zealand, the states of Wyoming, Utah, Colorado, and Idaho—the "members of the WCTU were by far the most numerous among the suffragists."[65] The WCTU was especially important for the early enfranchisement of women in New Zealand and Australia; suffragists from those countries later traveled back to Europe and the United States to spread the story of how they had won the vote and what it meant to them.

The second strand of the international movement was the women's groups associated with the Second Socialist International. In 1900, the Socialist International passed the first woman suffrage resolution, but suffrage became a fundamental demand of socialist parties only in 1907.[66] Socialist women around the world were not supposed to cooperate with "bourgeois suffragists" but in practice socialist and nonsocialist advocates for woman suffrage cooperated extensively.

[63] DuBois, "Woman Suffrage around the World," p. 256.
[64] Melanie Nolan and Caroline Daley, "International Feminist Perspective on Suffrage: An Introduction," in *Suffrage and Beyond*, p. 13.
[65] Patricia Grimshaw, "Women's Suffrage in New Zealand Revisited: Writing from the Margins," in *Suffrage and Beyond*, p. 34.
[66] DuBois, "Woman Suffrage around the World," p. 262.

The third strand of the international movement for woman suffrage was the independent militant "suffragettes" (so called to distinguish them from the more moderate "suffragists"). The suffragettes advocated public agitation, civil disobedience, and eventually even violent tactics to further their demand for the vote. By confronting speakers at meetings, chaining themselves to fences in front of government buildings, throwing stones through windows, and participating in street demonstrations that often ended in clashes with police and hostile male spectators, the suffragettes invited imprisonment, and once in jail they engaged in hunger strikes and had to be fed by force. The best known suffragette organization was the Women's Social and Political Union (WSPU) in Great Britain, under the leadership of the Pankhurst family, whose tactics had tremendous international influence. Although it did not endorse the more militant tactics of the suffragettes, the International Woman Suffrage Association "provided a conduit for their influence."[67] In the regular international meetings of IWSA, suffragette militancy spread among members who brought it back to their home countries. American suffragists who participated with the WSPU in Great Britain later took the militant approach and tactics back to the United States to lead the more militant wing of the women's movement there.[68]

A fourth strand of the international movement included women gathered in the International Council of Women (ICW), founded in 1888. Although after 1904 it adopted a strong suffrage stand, the ICW was not prepared to give the issue priority over the other issues on its agenda, which included demands for equal pay for equal work, access to professions, maternity benefits, suppression of traffic in women and children, peace and arbitration, the protection of women and men workers, and "development of modern household machinery to relieve women from household drudgery."[69] Although not at the forefront of the movement, the ICW contributed by promoting communication among women's organizations in diverse countries. Furthermore, it worked actively with intergovernmental organizations and conferences, including the international peace conferences in the Hague and the League of Nations. In 1907 it was one of only two private international organizations whose delegations the president of the Second Peace Conference at the Hague consented to receive.[70] This may be the earliest example of the now established practice of granting nongovernmental organizations a special role in international conferences.

[67] Ibid., p. 267.

[68] Sandra Stanley Holton, *Suffrage Days: Stories from the Women's Suffrage Movement* (London: Routledge, 1996), pp. 109, 155.

[69] International Council of Women, *Women in a Changing World: The Dynamic Story of the International Council of Women since 1888* (London: Routledge, 1966), pp. 23, 27.

[70] Ibid., p. 141.

The focused and militant IWSA expanded more rapidly than the ICW did in the early twentieth century: eleven countries were represented at the IWSA's founding conference in 1904, and forty-two were there at its 10th congress in 1926.[71] International congresses took place approximately every two years, and between congresses suffrage leaders and activists kept in touch with each other through letters, exchanges of books and pamphlets, visits, and speaking tours.[72] Despite their different national backgrounds these women developed a common way of thinking. The correspondence of two leaders from the Netherlands and Hungary, for example, reveals that despite totally different social and political situations, "these two were able to describe all kinds of events in similar terms. The common language encouraged a feeling of solidarity."[73]

Suffrage activists testify that their international connections provided support, inspiration, and ideas for tactics and strategies. As with the antislavery movement, these ideas spread through travel of key activists, family connections, and exchanges of letters, pamphlets, and newspapers. Some of the main tactics involved using symbolic politics to highlight the conflict between the discourse of equality and democracy and the actual situation of women. When Elizabeth Cady Stanton and her colleagues composed the Seneca Falls Declaration of Sentiments in 1848, they used the language of the Declaration of Independence to frame the demands for women's rights. "Cady Stanton's appropriation . . . was a brilliant propagandistic stroke. She thereby connected her cause to a powerful American symbol of liberty."[74] Similarly, when a small handful of women's rights activists in the United States began tax protests, refusing to pay taxes on their property until they were permitted to vote, one activist explicitly drew on the Revolutionary War slogan of "no taxation without representation," and requested that the local tax authorities choose July 4th to auction off her property in payment.[75] Although the tactic did not catch on in New England, it was later adopted in England by radical suffragists in the early twentieth century.[76] American suffragists also took symbolic advantage of the 1876 centennial of the American Revolution to press their demands for women's rights.

[71] Arnold Whittick, *Woman into Citizen* (London: Athenaeum, 1979), pp. 32, 92; *Women in a Changing World*, pp. 53, 203, 350.

[72] Griffith, *In Her Own Right*, pp. 181, 193, 214; Mineke Bosch and Annemarie Kloosterman, eds., *Politics and Friendship: Letters from the International Woman Suffrage Alliance 1902–1942* (Columbus: Ohio State University Press, 1990).

[73] *Politics and Friendship*, p. 15.

[74] Lois W. Banner, *Elizabeth Cady Stanton: A Radical for Women's Rights* (Boston: Little, Brown, 1980), p. 40.

[75] Dorothy Sterling, *Ahead of Her Time: Abby Kelley and the Politics of Antislavery* (New York: W.W. Norton, 1991), pp. 367–72.

[76] Holton, *Suffrage Days*, pp. 11–12, 107, 155, 163, 167, 174.

Transnational linkages between U.S. and British suffragists played an important role in a crucial principled and tactical debate among British suffragists over how inclusive should be the demand for woman suffrage. Voting in Britain was still linked to property, and married women could not own property. Many suffragists believed that demanding the vote for married women was too extreme, and thus advocated a more limited suffrage for spinsters with property. British radical suffragists wanted to demand the vote for all women, and linked their demand to the need to further democratize British society and extend the vote to all men as well. Suffrage activists in the United States supported the position of advocating the vote for both married and single women. Elizabeth Cady Stanton, who visited England frequently, attempted to "strengthen the resolve" of her British allies on this issue. Her diary records that she tried to impress upon her colleagues that "to get the suffrage for spinsters is all very well, but their work is to elevate the position of women at all points. . . . That the married women of this movement in England consent to the assumption that they are through marriage, practically represented and protected, supported and sheltered from all the adverse winds of life, is the strongest evidence of their own need for emancipation."[77] Radical suffragists were more active in international networks than were the more moderate British leaders. Perhaps because "of their more marginal standing in their own country," the international connection served as a valued endorsement of their own distinct identity."[78] Stanton contributed to the formation of the first suffrage organization in Britain to "formulate its demand in terms which expressly included married women," and drew upon the "transnational network" formed by her and her friends and colleagues for its early support.[79] Although the radicals were a minority in the British suffragist movement, their inclusive position eventually became dominant in Britain and around the globe. So resounding was the success of this position that we usually forget that British suffragists initially failed to advocate the vote for married women.

Speaking tours were an especially effective way of spreading the suffrage movement internationally. In 1913 two leaders of IWSA traveled to Asia and the Middle East. Upon their return, one reported that "the tangible results of our trip are that we are connected with correspondents representing the most advanced development of the woman's movement in Egypt, Palestine, India, Burma, China, Japan, Sumatra, Java, and the Philippine and Hawaiian Islands, and also in Turkey and Persia, which

[77] Elizabeth Cady Stanton, Theodore Stanton, and Harriot Stanton Blatch, *Elizabeth Cady Stanton as Revealed in her Letters, Diary, and Reminiscences* (New York: Harper, 1922), as cited in Holton, *Suffrage Days*, p. 63.

[78] Holton, *Suffrage Days*, p. 65.

[79] Ibid., p. 76.

we did not visit."[80] National suffrage societies from four of the countries they visited became members of the IWSA over the next ten years. The formation of a woman suffrage organization did not always lead to winning the franchise, however. Women in Switzerland, for example, first demanded suffrage in 1868, but did not receive it in all cantons until after 1971. Most countries granted woman suffrage after a few decades of focused organization by women's groups.

Sometimes international congresses headlined the issue enough to promote national debates. In the Netherlands, host to the 1908 International Congress of the IWSA, the press gave the congress a great deal of favorable coverage. Membership in the national woman suffrage organization grew from about 2,500 to 6,000, and men set up the Men's League for Woman Suffrage. Dutch women won the franchise in 1919, and the 1908 Conference was viewed as "a decisive breakthrough to the Dutch public which until then had stood somewhat aloof."[81]

The United States, Canada, and many European countries granted women the right to vote in the years during and immediately following the First World War. Many woman suffragists joined in the patriotic war effort, but others used the war aims as yet another symbolic vehicle to press for suffrage. Militant activists in both the United States and Britain pointed to the hypocrisy of fighting a war to make the world safe for democracy while at the same time denying democratic rights to half of their own populations. Subsequently, international suffragism focused on Latin America, the Middle East, and Asia, in part through the activities of the same international organizations (for example IWSA, renamed the International Alliance for Women), and in part through larger working-class movements and revolutionary nationalism.[82]

The international campaign for woman suffrage led to surprisingly rapid results. Woman suffrage was almost "unimaginable" even for visionary advocates of women's rights in 1848. Though it took until 1904 to found the first international organization dedicated primarily to the promotion of woman suffrage, less than fifty years later almost all countries in the world had granted women the vote. As new countries formed in the wake of decolonization, they enfranchised women because of women's contribution to the independence struggle and also because woman suffrage was now one of the accepted attributes of a modern state. The international campaign is a key part of the explanation for how votes for women moved from unimaginable to imaginable, and then become standard state policy.

[80] Whittick, *Woman into Citizen*, p. 52.
[81] *Politics and Friendship*, p. 46.
[82] DuBois, "Woman Suffrage around the World," pp. 270–71.

EARLY CAMPAIGNS AGAINST FOOTBINDING AND FEMALE CIRCUMCISION

Female circumcision and footbinding were both practices with long-lasting impact on women's health and activity level, practices we would now call violence against women. Both practices were deeply embedded culturally. Both involved highly ritualized rites of passage from girlhood to womanhood, and both were often seen as prerequisites for marriage.

Although we do not fully understand the origins of female circumcision, there is evidence that it was practiced by the ancient Egyptians. A cultural rather than religious custom, it has been practiced by groups in Africa and parts of the Middle East, including Animists, Moslems, Christians, and Ethiopian Jews. No Islamic law mandates female circumcision and in many Islamic countries it is not practiced.[83]

Although the Chinese had admired small feet since antiquity, there is little verifiable proof that women bound their feet before the tenth century.[84] The practice became more widespread during the Sung dynasty (960–1279), and was widely practiced by all classes during the Ming (1368–1644) and Ch'ing (1644–1911) dynasties.[85] Its origins are rooted in traditional folklore and aesthetic appeal. Some have explained it as a symbol of conspicuous leisure, and as a means to control women's movement and protect chastity.[86] It was widely believed that women without bound feet would not find husbands.

Both of these practices were deeply embedded in domestic life. Both were socially mandated but never legally enforced or required, and mothers and other females performed the rituals on girl children. Both affected girls of diverse classes and backgrounds, and both have been linked to the control of female sexuality and reproductive power. Bound feet had erotic appeal to men, and helped keep women confined to the home. As a result of the connection to sexuality, reformers recognized that feet were "the most risqué subject of conversation in China" during the late 1800s.[87] Female circumcision was even more inherently linked to sexuality because it involved removal of the clitoris, the main female organ of sexual pleasure. After concerted campaigns against both practices, footbinding was eradicated in China in the early twentieth century, while

---

[83] Nahid Toubia, "Female Genital Mutilation," in *Women's Rights, Human Rights: International Feminist Perspectives*, ed. Julie Peters and Andrea Wolper (New York: Routledge, 1995), p. 230.

[84] Howard Levy, *The Lotus Lovers: The Complete History of the Curious Erotic Custom of Footbinding in China* (Buffalo: Prometheus Books, 1992), p. 38.

[85] Alison R. Drucker, "The Influence of Western Women on the Anti-Footbinding Movement 1840–1911," *Historical Reflections* 8:3 (Fall 1981): 179.

[86] Levy, *The Lotus Lovers*, pp. 41, 44; Drucker, "The Influence of Western Women," p. 179.

[87] Mrs. Archibald Little, *Intimate China. The Chinese As I Have Seen Them* (London: Hutchinson, 1899), pp. 147, 150.

female circumcision continues to be practiced extensively throughout parts of Africa.

Why did missionary reformers choose to focus campaigns on these issues in the first place? Neither practice had an obvious impact—positive or negative—on conversions, nor were missionaries convinced that their campaigns would bring in more converts. In both countries, the Catholic church avoided the campaigns, fearing a detrimental impact on conversions. That fear appeared to be borne out in Kenya, where the campaign against female circumcision led to a profound drop in church membership.

The morality of evangelical groups was involved in both these cases. The missionaries in Kenya "were puritan 'Victorians' in the fullest sense of the word: drinking, smoking, dancing, and the other worldly amusements were regarded as sinful, and in sexual matters premarital virginity, chastity within marriage and no divorce were absolute requirements."[88] Yet many other practices that they morally condemned—in Kenya, polygamy, witchcraft, and traditional medicine, and in China, female infanticide, concubinage, and opium smoking—did not lead to parallel campaigns, although they did preach against them to their converts.

THE CAMPAIGN AGAINST FOOTBINDING IN CHINA, 1874–1911

Footbinding was in some ways analogous to the Western practice of corseting, but it was much more painful. Surrounded by ritual preparations, including making elegant pairs of tiny embroidered shoes, girls had their feet tightly wrapped to prevent growth at between four and eight years old. After years of intense pain, the toes were broken and flesh fell off to produce a narrow foot three to five inches long. Today we would call this a human rights abuse; few forms of modern torture leave such permanent deformation. Yet narratives of women who experienced footbinding testify not only to the pain but to the pride women felt in their small feet. The ritual of footbinding played a central role in female life. Historians stress the functions that footbinding served in socialization, appropriation of female labor, defining nationhood and gender roles, and as a central event in women's domestic culture.[89] "Footbinding prepared a girl physically and psychologically for her future role as wife

[88] Jocelyn Margaret Murray, "The Kikuyu Female Circumcision Controversy, with Special Reference to the Church Missionary Society's 'Sphere of Influence,'" Ph.D. diss., University of California, Los Angeles, 1974, p. 48.

[89] Dorothy Ko, *Teachers of the Inner Chambers: Women and Culture in Seventeenth-Century China* (Stanford: Stanford University Press, 1994), pp. 148, 150; and C. Fred Blake, "Footbinding in Neo-Confucian China and the Appropriation of Female Labor," *Signs: Journal of Women and Society* 19 (Spring 1994): 78.

and a dependent family member. . . . Through footbinding, the doctrine of separate spheres was engraved onto the bodies of female children."[90]

Footbinding was widespread in China, but not universal. Certain ethnic groups did not practice it; upper-class women were more likely than lower-class women to have their feet bound; and footbinding was less common in rural areas and in the rice-growing regions of China than it was elsewhere. Yet one writer says that in 1835 it prevailed throughout the empire, and estimates that five to eight out of every ten women had bound feet, depending on the locality.[91]

Manchu women had never bound their feet, and in the mid-seventeenth century the Manchu imperial court issued edicts to prohibit footbinding. However, people evaded the edicts and the court was obliged to give tacit consent to the practice.[92] Resistance to the decrees may have been a way for the majority Han ethnic group to assert its identity in the face of Manchu conquest. Although the Manchu were able to force every man to change his hairstyle and wear the queue, they could not affect the practice of footbinding.[93]

A vigorous movement to abolish footbinding originated in the late nineteenth century among foreigners in China's treaty ports, later spreading among those Chinese most exposed to Western ideas.[94] Chinese intellectuals and politicians took over the campaign, which culminated in a decree banning footbinding after the 1911 revolution. The campaign was strongest at the turn of the century, well before the 1919–20 May Fourth Movement which is often seen as a peak period of political, cultural, and social innovation, and before the formation of the Chinese Communist party in 1921. After the turn of the century progressive literature by and about women moved on to other issues.[95] In other words, changes in footbinding preceded rather than followed the main wave of cultural and political reform.[96]

In 1842 China's defeat in the Opium War led to the opening of treaty ports to foreign nationals and to an influx of missionaries and Western ideas. Chinese intellectuals began to argue that China needed reforms in order to avoid further humiliating defeat. At first, they stressed technological innovations and modern weapons, which were introduced between

---

[90] Ko, *Teachers of the Inner Chambers*, p. 149.

[91] Levy, *The Lotus Lovers*, pp. 52, 53.

[92] Virginia Chui-tin Chau, "The Anti-footbinding Movement in China (1850–1912)," Master's thesis, Columbia University, 1966, p. 10.

[93] We are indebted to Ann Waltner for this observation.

[94] Jane Hunter, *The Gospel of Gentility: American Women Missionaries in Turn of the Century China* (New Haven: Yale University Press, 1984), pp. 23–24.

[95] Roxane Witke, "Transformation of Attitudes towards Women during the May Fourth Era of Modern China," Ph.D. diss., University of California, Berkeley, 1970, pp. 6, 42.

[96] Ibid., p. 27.

1860 and 1894. Following China's defeat by the Japanese in 1895, however, intellectuals began to call for social, cultural and political reforms as
well.[97] Goals of a national reform movement emerging in the late 1890s
included an end to footbinding and improvement of the status of
women. The reform movement spread its message mainly through peri-
odicals and study societies.[98] Male reformers argued that improvements
in women's status were a necessary part of their program for national
self-strengthening.[99]

In 1898, the imperial authorities repressed the reform movement, leaving
key reformers dead or in prison. But despite increased antiforeign sentiment during the Boxer Rebellion, the antifootbinding movement continued to grow.[100] After the Boxer Rebellion the Imperial Court saw the need
to implement gradual reforms. One of the first was an antifootbinding
edict in 1902.[101] Earlier imperial decrees had no effect, but the 1902 decree
was the beginning of the end. When the new republican and nationalist
government came into power in 1911, it banned footbinding altogether.

Three groups were involved in the initial campaigns against footbinding: (1) Western missionaries who focused on Chinese Christians; (2) Westerners who led a campaign focused on non-Christian Chinese elites; and
(3) Chinese reformers who focused their campaign on non-Christian Chinese elites. A missionary of the London Missionary Society founded
the first antifootbinding society in 1874. In 1895 ten women of different
nationalities, led by Mrs. Archibald Little, the wife of a British merchant,
founded the T'ien tsu hui (Natural Foot Society), a nondenominational
umbrella organization. The first Chinese-initiated antifootbinding societies were set up in 1883 and 1895, but local opposition led to their collapse. In 1897 Chinese reformers founded the Pu'ch'an-tsu hui
(Antifootbinding Society), China's largest non-Christian antifootbinding
organization, which later established many branches and had a membership of 300,000.[102]

Each of the three actors took a characteristic approach to the issue. The
missionary approach was the most aggressive and moralistic.[103] Missionary schools promoted "natural feet" first by offering scholarships only to
girls with unbound feet; later they refused entry to girls with bound feet
and would not employ teachers with bound feet. The missionary schools
focused their attention on Christian converts, usually not from the Chinese elite.

[97] Chau, "The Anti-footbinding Movement in China," p. 27.
[98] Ibid., p. 28.
[99] Hunter, The Gospel of Gentility, pp. 23–24.
[100] Chau, "The Anti-footbinding Movement in China," pp. 126–28.
[101] Hunter, The Gospel of Gentility, p. 24.
[102] Drucker, "Influence of Western Women," p. 194.
[103] Witke, "Transformation of Attitudes," p. 20.

Perhaps the most innovative technique of the antifootbinding societies was to take on directly one social issue at the core of footbinding. Chinese families feared that daughters with unbound feet were unmarriageable. So the members of antifootbinding societies pledged not to bind the feet of their daughters and to marry their sons only to women with unbound feet. When registering in the societies, families listed the ages of their children for more convenient matchmaking.[104]

In contrast to the missionaries, Mrs. Little's Natural Foot Society focused on influencing powerful officials and non-Christian Chinese women "of wealth and fashion," thus partially divorcing the issue from the Christian context. Perhaps because Little was not a missionary, she could recognize the campaign's social and cultural implications and take a less rigid, more strategic position on the issue. Her strategy was to work with the upper classes and on footbinding alone, rather than to mix views on the practice with religion.[105] In a country where Christians were less than one percent of the population, this strategy was probably essential to the success of the message.

One of the first activities of the Natural Foot Society was to send a petition to the dowager-empress, inscribed in gold letters on white satin, enclosed in a silver casket, and signed by "pretty well every foreign lady in the Far East at that time."[106] Although none of the original founders of the Natural Foot Society could read Chinese, they immediately began an outreach campaign, holding meetings and translating materials into Chinese. The Natural Foot Society had a policy of getting their Chinese advisors to approve all their literature prior to publication to avoid any cultural or linguistic mistakes.[107]

The Natural Foot Society meetings were social as well as political events. Mrs. Little described a drawing room meeting in Szechuan as "a most brilliant affair . . . all the Chinese ladies laughed so gaily and were so brilliant in their attire that the few missionary ladies among them looked like sober moths caught in a flight of broidered butterflies. . . . All present were agreed that footbinding was of no use but it could only be given up by degrees."[108]

The members of the Natural Foot Society did engage in some international networking although this was not the central part of their work. At one meeting in China the members decided to contact a U.S. envoy in China and discussed whether there was sufficient interest in footbinding

---

[104] Chau, "Anti-footbinding Movement," pp. 107, 108.
[105] "Anti-Footbinding Society Conference," *North China Herald*, 23 January 1901, pp. 159–60.
[106] "Summary of Work Done by the Tien Tsu Hui," *Chinese Recorder* 38 (January 1907): 32.
[107] Chau, "Anti-footbinding Movement," p. 80.
[108] Little, *Intimate China*, p. 151.

in the United States to pressure the U.S. government to send instructions to him on the issue.[109] This would have been a classic "boomerang" maneuver predating current network tactics by ninety years, but there is no evidence that there was sufficient interest in the United States, or that U.S. or other foreign governments ever got involved in the issue of footbinding. Although most of the initial financial support and labor came from foreigners, by 1908 the Natural Foot Society was operating entirely under the leadership of Chinese women, who continued to campaign with vigor.[110] The foreign leaders of the society argued in 1907 that it was "high time to trust the movement more to Chinese direction."[111] This transfer from foreign to domestic leadership was a mark of the campaign's success.

The Natural Foot Society attempted to turn the tide against footbinding among influential Chinese through lobbying, publications, and speaking engagements, collecting signatures on petitions, essay competitions, and articles in local newspapers. A letter in 1907 summarizing the society's work records 162 meetings in thirty-three different cities, some with as many as 2,000 people present. More than a million tracts, leaflets, and placards were printed and circulated from the Shanghai office alone, in addition to letters to the editor and prize competitions for the best essays against binding.[112]

Only sixteen years passed between the formation of the first umbrella organization and the 1911 ban against footbinding; this is very rapid progress in the history of such campaigns. A corresponding behavioral change evolved slowly but surely. A source in 1905 indicated that 70 percent of female children still had their feet bound.[113] But by 1912 a missionary described footbinding as "on the wane and destined in course of time to disappear."[114] A 1929 study of a region to the south of Peking shows very dramatic change over a short period: "99.2% of those born prior to 1890 had bound feet, only 59.7% of those born between 1905 and 1909, and 19.5% of those born from 1910 to 1914, had bound feet; no new cases at all were found among those born after 1919."[115]

The swift eradication of such a culturally embedded practice is surprising—a practice that had lasted for almost a thousand years gone in little more than a generation. No key economic change occurred around the turn of the century that suddenly rendered the practice additionally dys-

---

[109] "Anti-Footbinding Society Conference," pp. 160.
[110] Drucker, "Influence of Western Women," pp. 187–89.
[111] "Summary of the Work Done by the Tien Tsu Hui," p. 34.
[112] Ibid., pp. 32–33.
[113] Ibid., p. 135.
[114] Ibid., p. 149.
[115] Sidney Gamble, "The Disappearance of Footbinding in Tinghsien," *American Journal of Sociology* 49 (September 1943): 181–83.

functional from a material standpoint. Nor had industrial change in China yet reached the point where large numbers of women were needed to work outside the home at the time that footbinding began to end. Instead, footbinding ended, just as slavery had ended, because of a concerted moral and political campaign against it. Historians of China differ about the relative weight of international and domestic actors in the campaign; some have stressed the role of foreign missionary groups,[116] while others place more importance on Chinese intellectuals.[117] One Chinese scholar wrote in the 1930s:

> In my opinion, for all the wrongs that Western culture might have done in China, one thing alone would have redeemed them, and that is, the conviction that their early missionaries aroused in the Chinese mind that the practice of footbinding was absurd and wrong. Prior to this, scholars did sometimes criticize this absurd custom, but the criticism was always casual, and no serious thought was ever given nor effort made, for the abolishment of this custom until the end of the last century . . . the first rolling of the stone, so to speak, was started by our sisters from the west."[118]

The most thorough treatment of the antifootbinding movement interprets it as part of a reform movement carried on "as a result of contact with the west."[119] The campaign appeared to form a pattern characteristic of modern networks, where both foreign and domestic actors were crucial to the success of the campaign, with foreign actors instrumental in "first rolling the stone" and domestic actors framing the issue to resonate with domestic audiences and generating the broad-based support necessary for success.

Foreign women initiated the antifootbinding movement and nationalist intellectuals and reformers embraced it. In China opposition to footbinding became associated with reform sentiment that was both antifeudal and antiforeign. After military defeat by foreigners, improving the status of women and ending footbinding were seen as tools to modernize and strengthen China so it could resist future intervention. "Not until such efforts were perceived as Chinese phenomena in a nationalistic context did a majority of Chinese . . . espouse them. . . . [T]he foreign and Christian roots of the anti-footbinding campaign had to be renounced in order for victory to be achieved. Yet Western women laid many of the foundations for the eradication of footbinding."[120]

[116] See Drucker, "Influence of Western Women," and Chau, "The Anti-footbinding Movement."

[117] Witke, "Transformation of Attitudes," p. 22.

[118] Ch'en Heng-che, "Influences of Foreign Cultures on the Chinese Woman," 1934, reprinted in *Chinese Women through Chinese Eyes*, ed. Li Yu-ning (Armonk, N.Y.: M. E. Sharpe, 1992), p. 64.

[119] Chau, "The Anti-footbinding Movement," p. 26.

[120] Drucker, "Influence of Western Women," p. 199.

Every campaign to change practices of this sort is a struggle to redefine the meaning of the practice. Foreign or international actors alone rarely succeed in changing embedded practices because they do not understand how to frame debates in convincing and accessible ways for the domestic audience. The Chinese reformers at the forefront of the antifootbinding campaign used arguments that resonated better with discourse of the time in China than did those used by the missionaries. The Chinese message blended appeals to modernity and to tradition. For example, Chinese intellectuals stressed that footbinding was contrary to the ancient way of doing things, and that the Chinese classics did not even mention it.[121] Thus, to eradicate a traditional practice, intellectuals appealed to even more ancient tradition. They referred to issues of filial piety, stressing that footbinding damaged the body—a gift from one's parents—and that a "natural footed woman could buy medicine for a sick parent in less time than it took a bound foot woman."[122] Yet at the same time, they invoked modernity, either by claiming that the custom was "the laughing stock of foreigners" or by citing a pseudo-scientific argument that sons born of deformed women would be weaker.[123] Chinese nationalists argued that one needed to adopt some Western practices in order to better resist Western domination. In an antifootbinding tract a Chinese literati argued: "To learn what the foreigners excel at in order to fight against them doesn't mean to respect or admire them. . . . In fact women with bound feet, who are completely useless, include one half of the population. . . . Useless women are an obstacle to progress."[124] In military defeat, the connection that Chinese reformers made between footbinding and weakness, and between individual weakness and the collective weakness of the country, appears to have been a powerful rhetorical weapon against binding.

The successful articulation between antifootbinding and Chinese nationalism at the turn of the century allowed the antifootbinding campaign to succeed rapidly. Once the campaign was launched and embraced by Chinese intellectuals, no strong organized opposition emerged. The Imperial Court had never advocated or practiced footbinding, and thus would not spearhead opposition. The absence of opposition surely helps explain the speed with which the antifootbinding movement achieved its goals.

THE CAMPAIGN AGAINST FEMALE CIRCUMCISION IN KENYA, 1923–1931

The term "female circumcision" has been used to refer to a variety of operations "involving damage to the female sexual and/or reproductive

[121] Chau, "Anti-footbinding Movement," pp. 21, 26.
[122] Drucker, "Influence of Western Women," p. 182, and Witke, "Transformation of Attitudes," p. 27.
[123] Chau, "Anti-footbinding Movement," pp. 98, 101, 104.
[124] Ibid., pp. 60–61.

organs," almost always including the removal of part or all of the clitoris (clitoridectomy/excision), and sometimes also involving the removal of the labia minora, the inner walls of the labia majora, and the sewing together of the vulva (infibulation).[125] Calling these operations female circumcision likens them to male circumcision, to which they bear only superficial similarities.[126] Male circumcision leaves neither lasting pain nor health problems, nor does it lessen male sexual pleasure. Female circumcision, on the other hand, carries short-term risks and can lead to chronic infection, painful urination and menstrual difficulty, malformations and scarring, and vaginal abscesses; it also reduces a woman's sexual response and pleasure.[127]

Yet in the Kikuyu language and culture, the practice of and the ceremonies surrounding female circumcision were exact parallels of male circumcision. Both marked the transition from childhood to adulthood. The names for both practices were the same for men and women, and the initiation ceremonies often took place at the same time in villages, although the males and females were separated for the actual physical operations.[128]

The changing names given to this practice reveal the intense debate over its meaning. Some use more technical and "neutral" terms like female circumcision, clitoridectomy, or infibulation. Modern campaigns in the 1970s and 1980s drew attention to the issue by renaming the problem "female genital mutilation," thus reframing the issue as one of violence against women. Because female circumcision was the main term used in the period under study (1920s and 1930s) we use that term in this chapter.

Female circumcision was widely practiced in Kenya, among the Kikuyu and many other related cultural groups. In Kikuyu culture "only a circumcised girl could be considered a woman. It was widely believed that uncircumcised girls would not physically be able to bear children. . . . In Kikuyu eyes an uncircumcised girl of marriageable age was an object of derision, indeed almost of disgust."[129]

Concerted efforts against female circumcision in Kenya began in the 1920s when Protestant missionaries led by the Church of Scotland Missionary Society (CSM) prohibited the operation among their converts and campaigned against it. Unlike the footbinding history, there is no evidence of any internal opposition to female circumcision within the Kikuyu communities before the arrival of the missionaries. The leader of the campaign, Dr. John Arthur, threw all of his considerable energy into

[125] Leonard J. Kouba and Judith Muasher, "Female Circumcision in Africa: An Overview," *African Studies Review* 28:1 (March 1985): 96.

[126] The male equivalent of what is called female circumcision would be the removal of all or part of the penis. Nahid Toubia, "Female Genital Mutilation," p. 226.

[127] Alison T. Slack, "Female Circumcision: A Critical Appraisal," *Human Rights Quarterly* 10:4 (November 1988): 445, 450–55.

[128] Murray, "The Kikuyu Female Circumcision Controversy," pp. 19–20.

[129] Carl G. Fosberg, Jr. and John Nottingham, *The Myth of "Mau Mau": Nationalism in Kenya* (Stanford: Hoover Institution Press, 1966), p. 112.

the church's efforts to stamp out the practice. Arthur, like the abolitionists, grew up in a Protestant evangelical atmosphere and "his whole life was molded by it."[130] All four major Protestant church missions in Kenya opposed female circumcision, but the Church of Scotland, the most puritan in belief, campaigned most actively for its eradication.

Perhaps the most curious question is why the missionaries focused so much energy on eradicating the practice among the Kikuyu, and not among groups in other parts of Africa where it also existed. Female circumcision was common in Ethiopia, and in Sudan and Somalia a much more severe form of genital mutilation—involving both circumcision and infibulation—was practiced. Even in Kenya and Tanzania other groups that practiced circumcision, such as the Maasai, were not the objects of the kinds of missionary pressures placed on the Kikuyu.[131] So this single case contains multiple cases of noncampaigns—noncampaigns in Ethiopia, Sudan, and Somalia, and a noncampaign among the Maasai. European influence was weaker in Ethiopia (Abyssinia), but after 1898 Sudan was settled by the British, and Somaliland was divided among the French, the British, and the Italians.[132] More British missionaries and settlers lived and worked in Kenya than elsewhere. There were also more girls' schools and medical missions, exposing missionaries in Kenya to the medical problems confronted by circumcised girls and to the social pressure for circumcision.

Still, what about the Maasai and other cultural groups in Kenya? Jocelyn Murray, who has conducted the most complete research on the controversy, argues that the missionaries focused on the Kikuyu because they were more receptive to missionary teachings and had more converts to Christianity. "Neither missionaries nor administrators had any 'leverage' to implement change among the Maasai. With the Kikuyu the position was very different. Both missionaries and administrators had a great deal of leverage."[133] The campaign was possible in the first place because a small but consistent group of Kikuyu supported the missionaries. The missionaries overestimated this support, but without it "not even the most determined of Scottish missionary crusaders would have been able to carry the campaign through."[134] This suggests that transnational campaigns are possible when populations themselves are divided over a practice.

[130] Murray, "The Kikuyu Female Circumcision Controversy, pp. 46–47.
[131] Murray, "The Kikuyu Female Circumcision Controversy," p. 3.
[132] On British attempts to regulate female circumcision in Sudan in 1946, see Asma Mohammed A'Haleem, "Claiming Our Bodies and Our Rights: Exploring Female Circumcision as an Act of Violence in Africa," in *Freedom from Violence: Women's Strategies from Around the World*, ed. Margaret Schuler (New York: UNIFEM, 1992), p. 152.
[133] Murray, "The Kikuyu Female Circumcision Controversy," p. 4.
[134] Ibid., p. 7.

In Kenya, British colonial administrators and missionaries used tactics similar to those used during the antifootbinding campaign in China to try to discourage female circumcision. Missionary schools refused to admit circumcised girls, and church members could be suspended for requiring their girls to be circumcised. The missionaries argued that the operation was medically unnecessary and dangerous, and also that it was unchristian because the associated rituals were pagan and overtly sexual.[135] Many African members of the CSM chose to leave the church to protest its position on this issue. Some accused church leaders of adding "an eleventh commandment" that was not in the Bible. One leader said, "I was a Christian, but if the choice lay between God and circumcision, we choose circumcision. But it is a false European choice."[136] As the issue became more heated, the CSM and other missionary societies lost substantial numbers of their members.

Female missionaries in Kenya were not represented in the decision-making bodies of the mission, and men often disregarded the recommendations of the women's conferences.[137] Nor does the rather extensive literature on the controversy mention any key role played by Kikuyu women in internal Kikuyu debates. Also, no associations separate from the missionary churches were ever set up to discourage circumcision. The involvement of Kikuyu in the campaign came only through their involvement with missions, where they often worked.

The campaign took place in the context of increasing African opposition to British colonial practices, such as land alienation for European settlers, heavy hut and poll taxes, and an oppressive labor recruiting system.[138] The Kikuyu Central Association (KCA), set up by young, mainly mission-educated Kikuyu men, represented nascent Kikuyu nationalism. The female circumcision controversy exacerbated an internal Kikuyu political split between the younger, militant KCA and the older Kikuyu leadership represented by chiefs associated with the Christian missions.[139] The KCA embraced some Western values but also attempted to preserve some traditional cultural practices, especially female circumcision; a major conflict developed between the KCA and the missionaries over this issue.[140]

[135] Marshall S. Clough, *Fighting Two Sides: Kenyan Chiefs and Politicians, 1918–1940* (Niwot, Colo.: University Press of Colorado, 1990), pp. 138–39.
[136] Fosberg and Nottingham, *Myth of "Mau Mau,"* p. 119.
[137] Robert Strayer, *The Making of Mission Communities in East Africa: Anglicans and Africans in Colonial Kenya, 1875–1935* (Albany: State University of New York Press, 1978), p. 6.
[138] Bethwell A. Ogot, "Kenya under the British: 1895–1963," in *Zamani: A Survey of East African History*, ed. Ogot (Nairobi: East African Publishing House, 1974), pp. 266–68, 278; Clough, *Fighting Two Sides*, pp. 66–72.
[139] Clough, *Fighting Two Sides*, pp. 142–46.
[140] Fosberg and Nottingham, *The Myth of "Mau Mau"*, pp. 86–87.

The campaign against female circumcision became a symbol for colonial attempts to impose outside values and rules upon the population.
The Kikuyu nationalist elite defended the practice as necessary to the
preservation of traditional culture, and attacked foreign efforts to eradicate it.[141] Because the KCA was the leading voice of Kikuyu nationalism,
and because it had taken up the crusade in favor of circumcision, female
circumcision became associated with Kikuyu nationalism. Since many
Protestant leaders opposed the KCA, their opposition to circumcision
was viewed as a tool to oppose the association. John Arthur drew up a
petition opposing circumcision that asked teachers and other mission em-
ployees not only to renounce circumcision, but also to disown the KCA.[142]

Jomo Kenyatta, the general secretary of the KCA and later the main
leader of the anticolonial struggle, wrote a stirring defense of female circumcision in his study of Kikuyu culture, *Facing Mount Kenya*, when he
was a student of anthropology at the London School of Economics in
1935. "For the present it is impossible for a member of the tribe to imagine an initiation without clitoridectomy. Therefore the abolition of the
surgical element in this custom means to the Gikuyu the abolition of the
whole institution. . . . [C]litoridectomy, like Jewish circumcision, is a mere
bodily mutilation which, however, is regarded as the condition sine qua
non of the whole teaching of tribal law, religion, and morality."[143] Kenyatta's concerns reflect a synthesis of his traditional knowledge and his
training as an anthropologist. Berman and Lonsdale argue that "functional anthropology was tailor-made for the cultural nationalist, for
whom all his indigenous institutions fitted together in harmonious order
before the corruptions of colonialism."[144]

In 1929–30 Kenyatta traveled to Britain to meet with British officials
and church members. The debate over female circumcision was one of
the major themes of his talks. Because relations between the KCA and European settlers in Kenya were strained, Kenyatta sought out contacts in
London to present the KCA position directly. He met with committees of
the House of Commons, a member of the House of Lords, the undersec-
retary of state for the colonies, and with church officials to present the
concerns of his organization, stated in a formal petition.[145]

[141] Ann Beck, *A History of the British Medical Administration of East Africa, 1900–1950* (Cambridge: Harvard University Press, 1970), p. 103.

[142] Clough, *Fighting Two Sides*, p. 143.

[143] Cited in Fosberg, Jr. and Nottingham, *The Myth of "Mau Mau,"* p. 133.

[144] Bruce Berman and John Lonsdale, "Louis Leakey's Mau Mau: A Study in the Politics
of Knowledge," *History and Anthropology* 5:2 (1991): 172. But Kenyatta's ethnography was no
more politicized than that of fellow anthropologist Louis Leakey, who served as an advisor
to the colonial authorities on Kikuyu issues and whose intense rivalry with Kenyatta shaped
his own views. Both Kenyatta and Leakey engaged in "redemptive criticism—the present
employment of the past in the hopes of reshaping the future" (p. 193).

[145] Ann Beck, "Some Observations on Jomo Kenyatta in Britain 1929–1930," *Cahiers
d'Etudes Africaines* 6:22 (1966): 308, 313.

During his meeting with officials of the Scottish church Kenyatta tried to defuse tensions, stressing that the major difference was that he believed in a more gradual strategy for ending circumcision.[146] In a convincing letter to the *Times* he presented the KCA's positions on five other key issues, appealing to the fair-mindedness of Britons by arguing that the repression of native views was a "short-sighted tightening of the safety valve of free speech which must inevitably result in dangerous explosion—the one thing all men wish to avoid."[147]

What is most striking about this trip is that it represents a boomerang effect in reverse—an attempt to counter foreign pressures at home by going over the heads of church authorities in Kenya to their superiors in Britain. Kenyatta impressed people with his seriousness, persistence, and moderation, and presented to them a different version of the story they had heard from British missionaries in Kenya.

In late 1929 the controversy in Kenya became more heated. The pro-circumcision forces circulated a satirical song that ridiculed missionaries, chiefs, and officials, and praised Kenyatta. The government and missionaries, fearing a threat to public order, repressed the singers, flogging them, sentencing them to detention camps, and prohibiting public meetings.[148] In this context, colonial authorities backed off from the missionaries' campaign on female circumcision. Kenyatta and his organization had helped reframe the debate from one about health and Christianity to one over nationalism, land, and the integrity of traditional culture. Convinced that the issue was exacerbating relations between Kikuyu and Europeans, colonial authorities asked Arthur to resign his seat on the Governor's executive council. Some officials advocated more gradual policies stressing education rather than prohibition; one official recommended "masterly inactivity"; another counseled, "the less talked about the operation of circumcision the better."[149] One of the political results of the controversy was to delegitimize Kikuyu leaders associated with the missions and increase the influence and membership of the KCA. It was one of a series of controversies among Kikuyu and between the Kikuyu and the British that contributed to tensions that twenty years later found expression in the mass movement that Europeans called Mau Mau.

In contrast with the nationalism of Chinese reformers, by the mid-twentieth century African intellectuals like Kenyatta were holding up an idealized version of the traditional past as an alternative to Western lifestyles and "progress" that they feared were inappropriate for their countries. The anticircumcision campaign became associated with colonialism and interference, and the practice of female circumcision with independence,

---

[146] Ibid., p. 322.
[147] Ibid., p. 325.
[148] Clough, *Fighting Two Sides*, p. 145.
[149] Beck, *History of the British Medical Administration*, pp. 101–2.

nationalism, and tradition. Kenyan nationalists articulated a material vs. spiritual distinction similar to the one made by Indian nationalists in the nineteenth century, where the material corresponded to the outside world, and the spiritual realm to the home. In this paradigm the home and women were to be the main foci for preserving national culture.[150]

Research conducted in 1973 shows how slow changes in female circumcision have been in Kenya. At the time of the controversy it appears that 100 percent of Kikuyu girls were circumcised. Even among the missionaries' strongest supporters, the number of those who decided not to circumcise their daughters was very small.[151] Nevertheless, those religious groups that adopted the most intransigent position against female circumcision in the 1920s and 1930s did later see far fewer circumcised girls among their members. Jocelyn Murray estimates that up to 75 percent of adolescent Kikuyu girls were still circumcised in the mid-1970s.[152] By the 1990s, a comparison of female genital mutilation in Africa estimates that 50 percent of Kenyan girls and women have been circumcised, as compared to 80 percent in the Sudan, 90 percent in Ethiopia, and 98 percent in Somalia, where more severe forms of the operation are common.[153] These figures suggest that though the missionary campaign did have some effect, it was far more limited than the missionaries hoped for, and less successful than other similar campaigns.

CONCLUSIONS

The campaigns examined in this chapter are especially valuable for the insights they provide about the relationship between the ideas advocacy networks help to diffuse and the domestic contexts in which these ideas do or do not take hold. They confirm the importance of attention to dynamic as well as static elements of domestic political opportunity structures—the play of oppositions and the conflicting representations of core values around which domestic groups organize. The cases also lead us to consider what the ideas and organizations involved can tell us about generative aspects of transnational networks.

Domestic Structures and Domestic Politics

The case studies call into question the argument that domestic structures are the key explanation for the differing impact of networks. If do-

[150] Partha Chatterjee, "Colonialism, Nationalism, and Colonialized Women: The Contest in India," *American Ethnologist* 16:4 (November 1989): 625–26.

[151] Murray, "The Kikuyu Female Circumcision Controversy," p. 244.

[152] Ibid., p. 352. It is interesting, however, that the initiation ceremonies that surrounded circumcision were virtually abandoned over time, while the physical operation was maintained (Murray, p. 25).

[153] Fran P. Hosken, *The Hosken Report: Genital and Sexual Mutilation of Females*, 4th rev. ed. (Lexington, Mass.: Women's International Network News, 1993), pp. 43–44.

mestic political institutions, state-society relations, and political culture
are so central, surely a colonial administration would have offered more
access to the British missionaries than to the Kikuyu nationalists. Not
only did the British exercise political control in Kenya, but the Christian
churches in Africa had been much more successful in their conversion efforts than they had in India and China.[154] Yet the Kikuyu most successfully resisted pressures and reframed the debate to neutralize the
missionaries. Imperial China in turn should have been one of the least
permeable domestic structures for foreign women without substantial
support from their governments.

On the other hand, how the activists' messages carried and resonated
with domestic concerns, culture, and ideology at the particular historical
moment in which they campaigned was crucial. Here the footbinding
and female circumcision cases offer an especially powerful contrast. One
of the most important differences between the two campaigns has to do
with how the advocacy campaign articulated with nationalist discourse.
Nationalism in China at the turn of the century was quite different from
nationalism in colonial Kenya in the 1920s. Chinese nationalism involved
a critique of tradition as a source of weakness, and an embrace of modernity—if only to use the tools of modernity to fight off the external enemy.
Antifootbinding, once stripped of its missionary origins, thus articulated
well with the desire to discard remnants of a feudal past in order to take
control of the future. Kenyan nationalism of the 1920s and 1930s had a
quite different flavor; it appealed to tradition as a means of strengthening
unity and defeating the colonial other. During the Chinese campaign the
meanings of footbinding changed; what had been a source of pride for
women and a "central motif in her interaction with other women"[155] became a symbol of the past. In Kenya, the opposite occurred; the missionary campaign was associated with a waning colonialism, and the
circumcised girl was part of emergent Kenyan nationalism. Chinese
(mainly male) elites assumed leadership of the campaign against footbinding because they saw it it as part of the modernization project they
advocated. The ideas in the campaign were thus effectively nationalized;
their missionary origins mattered less than their contribution to the national project. In Kenya, on the contrary, the anticircumcision campaign
never acquired domestic sponsors. Because the missionary origins of the
ideas were so deeply associated with the colonial regime, the two could
not be dissociated; in fact, the missionaries' desire to intervene in the
most intimate practices of the home strengthened the identity between
home and nation.

Chinese nationalists did not exempt the home from the nationalist reforms. Especially through the activities of Mrs. Little's Natural Foot Society,

[154] Strayer, *The Making of Mission Communities*, p. 2.
[155] Ko, *Teachers of the Inner Chambers*, pp. 148, 150.

the practice of footbinding was singled out and separated from the religious message, and from a range of other cultural issues. Although part of a broader reform movement, natural foot advocates did not demand a comprehensive package of cultural change. In Kenya, on the other hand, where missionaries campaigned against female circumcision in the context of the colonial state, the missionary church demanded "total cultural transformation," excluding the possibility of "selective change, by which the Kikuyu might absorb some elements of Western culture while rejecting others as unacceptable to their values or social institutions."[156]

Strong and dense linkages between domestic and foreign actors do not alone guarantee success. Advocacy campaigns take place in organizational contexts; not only must their ideas resonate and create allies, their organizations must also overcome opposition. In the language of social movement theory, we must consider these campaigns as parts of "multi-organizational fields."[157] The antislavery campaign was a very strong transatlantic network that nevertheless confronted powerful entrenched economic interests that had a well-developed ideology, strong political representation, and institutional and legal support in the state's rights provisions of the U.S. Constitution. The early abolition movement in Britain faced a weaker and smaller opposition—mainly from the British West Indies planter class. The British woman suffrage groups were the best organized among the national members of international suffrage organizations, but suffrage was granted in New Zealand, Australia, Finland, Denmark, Norway, and the USSR, as well as a number of U.S. states, before women received the vote in Great Britain. In Kenya a group of missionaries with tepid support from colonial authorities confronted a politically weak but ideologically strong opposition in the KCA. In China a well-organized set of antifootbinding societies faced strongly entrenched cultural beliefs, but no effectively organized political opposition. When the societies gained the support of both the Imperial Court and the nationalist reformer politicians, the eventual success of their campaign was assured.

Ideas and Organizations

The cases described here are not strictly comparable in terms of the kinds of transnational linkages they portray. The anticircumcision campaign involved only missionaries, footbinding involved both missionaries and secular internationalists, the antislavery societies built linkages

---

[156] Fosberg and Nottingham, *The Myth of "Mau Mau,"* p. 105.

[157] Bert Klandermans, "The Social Construction of Protest and Multi-Organizational Fields," in *Frontiers in Social Movement Theory*, ed. Aldon D. Morris and Carol McClurg Mueller (New Haven: Yale University Press, 1992), pp. 77–103.

largely on the basis of corresponding religious organizations, and the woman suffrage movement involved international organizations. The women's organizations are also the only ones that organized transnationally on their own behalf, a difference that distances this campaign somewhat from an advocacy model.

The footbinding case involved a variety of transnational linkages. The missionaries who began the campaign were by definition part of a transnational project of conversion—where saving souls required, in their view, discouraging sinful practices. Mrs. Little, founder of the Natural Foot Society, was likewise linked, through her merchant husband and associates, to another transnational project, the opening up of China to international trade. Like religious organizations, British merchants had a long history of forming loose networks linking London and the overseas world, sharing and strategically using information and promoting lobbies.[158] Thus although no transnational network was activated in the footbinding case, the extraterritorial linkages of the advocates were important parts of their identities—and of how the Chinese perceived them. In the Kikuyu case the implicit transnational dimension of the missionary campaign was challenged and proved toothless; Kenyatta effectively undermined it by going directly to the heads of the Scottish Presbyterian church, who did not provide strong support for their field personnel. Compare this with the experience related in the next chapter, where Peter Bell's human rights positions in Brazil received firm support from his supervisors at the Ford Foundation.

The antislavery campaign, on the other hand, involved a fully activated network, whose dynamics were very similar to modern networks. They differed mainly in the speed of communication and the kinds of actors involved. The antislavery societies' connections to and pressures on actors in the state foreshadow the work of modern NGOs and networks, as does their stress on gathering facts and testimony. Intergovernmental organizations and private foundations that play a central role in modern networks were absent; their place was taken by private philanthropy.

All of these campaigns emerged from religious organizations. The size and duration of the antislavery campaign, of course, stimulated organizational diversification. Not all abolitionists were motivated by religious sentiment, but religious organizations remained important for transnational communications. Nevertheless, the networks thus created generated new networks; this process is most evident in the international woman suffrage movement, whose origins lie in social networks forged in the antislavery campaigns. A multigenerational view underlines the fact that although networks are motivated by values, they are values

[158] Olson, *Making the Empire Work*, esp. chapters 7–8.

acted upon in relation to concrete practices. Such practices are themselves repertoires, and successful ones generate successors; the cause-oriented antislavery and antifootbinding societies and international woman suffrage organizations are early examples.

What Kinds of Values?

Most of the antislavery activists and missionaries who took the lead in the campaigns discussed above believed that their actions were justified on the basis of religious belief. Their universalism had a humanitarian side—and, frequently, an intolerant side as well. Regardless of such ambiguities, religious belief has been one of the main sources of the idea that action outside the borders of one's home countries was not only licit, but necessary. From the evangelical missionary traditions of the antifootbinding and anticircumcision campaigners to the social solidarity of Witness for Peace and the sanctuary movement in the early 1980s was a distance to travel, but in both cases activists were propelled by a belief in a higher law that trumps the laws of nation-states.

The cases considered in this chapter suggest that concern with two core issues pervaded these campaigns. First, activists worked on issues that involved bodily harm to vulnerable or innocent individuals—slavery and mutilation of children generated more concern than class issues of wage slavery or the morally charged issues of concubinage in China or polygamy in Kenya. Second, antislavery and suffrage activists in particular were concerned with securing legal equality of opportunity for excluded groups. Slavery brought these two issues together: activists argued that slaves must be granted legal freedom, citizenship, and the right to vote, but their publications and talks also stressed that freedom was necessary to end the arbitrary and illegitimate physical violence that masters vented against their slaves. In this sense many of these issues connect traditional humanitarian concern for protecting the vulnerable to a rights frame focused on empowering individual citizens. This focus on individuals may be the result of a common evangelical Protestant background shared by many of the activists in the campaigns considered here, as well as the prevailing Enlightenment and post-Enlightenment discourses. This individualism drew upon the revivals of the Second Great Awakening, in the early nineteenth century, "which identified moral progress with each individual's capacity to act as an instrument of God."[159]

Woman suffrage was central to the liberal emphasis on the importance of individual legal equality of opportunity, but it did not involve bodily

---

[159] Foner, *Politics and Ideology*, p. 65.

integrity. Women often argued that other societal evils, such as drunkenness and wife beating, could be alleviated by allowing women to vote.[160] Unlike the other networks, suffragists sought a procedural change, which they believed would lead women to make substantive changes through the ballot box.

Even antislavery activism fits the individualist characterization. Most antislavery activists were not willing to extend their efforts to the cause of "wage slavery" in either country. Garrison, whose position in favor of women's rights helped divide his movement, was adamant on the issue of wage slavery. "'To say that it is worse for a man to be free, than to be a slave, worse to work for whom he pleases, when he pleases, and where he pleases,' was simply ridiculous, Garrison insisted. Moreover, it was 'an abuse of language to talk of the slavery of wages.'"[161] This position derived from the profoundly individualistic abolitionist conception of both slavery and freedom, which understood slavery not as a class relationship, but as exercise of illegitimate power by one individual over another.

By focusing on power only in this juridical form, however, as a system of restraints and restrictions, antislavery discourse naturalized or made unproblematic "free" labor, ignoring the role of power in market and labor relations.[162] In addition it preserved a rigid separation between advocate and the "other" on whose behalf advocacy took place.

What Kinds of Interests?

Finally, what about the argument that moral campaigns are thinly disguised efforts to further other interests? Some missionaries and colonial authorities in Kenya used their opposition to female circumcision to further their campaign against the Kikuyu Central Association. Some statements by reformers in the campaigns around abolition, suffrage, footbinding, and female circumcision smack of repugnant beliefs in moral and cultural superiority, racism, and paternalism. Neither the backgrounds nor education of these reformers, nor the prevailing European attitudes toward foreigners, provided them with "broad vision, imagination, or sympathy" toward non-Western cultures.[163] Abolitionists in Britain often combined antislavery principles with support for British imperialism. They believed that imperialism would spread Christianity, Westernization, and the benefits of trade, and ingenuously saw no contradiction among these principles.[164]

[160] Grimshaw, "Women's Suffrage in New Zealand," p. 36.

[161] Foner, Politics and Ideology, p. 70.

[162] Gyan Prakash, Bonded Histories: Genealogies of Labor Servitude in Colonial India (Cambridge: Cambridge University Press, 1990), p. 6.

[163] Strayer, Making of Mission Communities, p. 7.

[164] Michael Craton, Sinews of Empire: A Short History of British Slavery (Garden City, N.Y.: Anchor Books, 1974), p. 293; also Fogel, Without Consent or Contract, p. 388.

Suffragists sometimes argued that educated and cultured women had a better claim to the vote than uneducated, immigrant men or former slaves.

Activists saw the victim as an unproblematic "other" who needed their assistance, and the reformers rarely recognized their own paternalism. Although some freed blacks like Frederick Douglass played prominent roles in the transatlantic campaign, for the most part the "victims" of slavery were absent from the movement. The frequent inability of reformers to transcend their historical setting, however, does not undermine the significance of the challenges they made to dominant social and political orders or their contributions to political transformation.

This "pure" advocacy model breaks down at the point where the intended beneficiaries of advocacy campaigns play a significant role in carrying them out. When suffragists were confronted with their second-class status in the antislavery conferences, they began to adapt the advocacy model on their own behalf. The result superimposes many of the tactical advantages of an advocacy network on a solidarity model that assumes a community of fate. This conceptual boundary will prove throughout the cases we explore in the book to be one of the richest sites of negotiation between interest and identity.

CHAPTER 3

Human Rights Advocacy Networks in Latin America

We can trace the idea that states should protect the human rights of their citizens back to the French Revolution and the U.S. Bill of Rights, but the idea that human rights should be an integral part of foreign policy and international relations is new. As recently as 1970, the idea that the human rights of citizens of any country are legitimately the concern of people and governments everywhere was considered radical. Transnational advocacy networks played a key role in placing human rights on foreign policy agendas.

The doctrine of internationally protected human rights offers a powerful critique of traditional notions of sovereignty, and current legal and foreign policy practices regarding human rights show how understandings of the scope of sovereignty have shifted. As sovereignty is one of the central organizing principles of the international system, transnational advocacy networks that contribute to transforming sovereignty will be a significant source of change in international politics.

After the Second World War the transnational human rights advocacy network helped to create regional and international human rights regimes, and later contributed to the implementation and enforcement of human rights norms and policy. In this chapter we first examine the network's role in the emergence of those norms, and then explore its effectiveness by comparing the impact of the international human rights pressures on Argentina and Mexico in the 1970s and 1980s.[1] Both are

[1] For a related study that examines the impact of U.S. human rights policy using a "two-level game" approach, see Lisa L. Martin and Kathryn Sikkink, "U.S. Policy and Human Rights in Argentina and Guatemala, 1973–80," in *Double-edged Diplomacy: International Bargaining and Domestic Politics*, ed. Peter B. Evans, Harold K. Jacobson, and Robert D. Putnam (Berkeley: University of California Press, 1993), pp. 330–62.

large countries with traditions of jealously guarding sovereign preroga-
tives. Both have poor human rights records, although human rights violations in Argentina during the military government's 1976–80 "dirty war"
were much more serious than in Mexico. The international human rights
network worked intensively on Argentina, contributing to improved
practices by the early 1980s. The network did not focus on Mexico, however, and endemic abuses continued throughout the 1980s. Only after the
network concentrated international attention on Mexico after 1987 did
the Mexican government begin to address human rights violations.

Emergence of the Human Rights Idea and the Network

The history of the emergence of the human rights network is the story
of the founding, growth, and linking of the organizations in the network.
The values that bind the actors together are embodied in international
human rights law, especially in the 1948 Universal Declaration of Human
Rights. This body of law justifies actions and provides a common language to make arguments and sets of procedures to advance claims. How
these international human rights norms and regimes emerged in the UN
has been discussed at length elsewhere and does not need to be repeated
here.[2] What is often missed, however, is how nongovernmental organizations helped spur state action at each stage in the process.[3]

The entities that make up the current transnational human rights advocacy network include the following: (1) parts of intergovernmental organizations, at both the international and regional level; (2) international
NGOs; (3) domestic NGOs; (4) private foundations; and (5) parts of some
governments. The most important organizations for human rights in
Latin America include the UN Commission on Human Rights, the UN
Committee on Human Rights, the Inter-American Commission on Human Rights (IACHR), Amnesty International, Americas Watch, the Washington Office on Latin America, domestic NGOs like the Mothers of the
Plaza de Mayo in Argentina and the Academy of Human Rights in Mexico, and the Ford Foundation as well as the European foundations that
fund international and domestic human rights NGOs.

Before 1945 none of these organizations existed. In 1961, when
Amnesty International was founded, most still either did not exist, or, in

---

[2] Jack Donnelly, *Universal Human Rights in Theory and Practice* (Ithaca: Cornell University
Press, 1989). See esp. table on pp. 224–25.
[3] But see David Forsythe, *Human Rights and World Politics*, 2d ed. (Lincoln: University of
Nebraska Press, 1989), pp. 83–101, 127–59; and Lars Schoultz, *Human Rights and United States
Policy toward Latin America* (Princeton: Princeton University Press, 1981), pp. 74–93, 104–8,
373–74.

the case of the foundations, had not yet begun to pay attention to human rights. But even before the modern networks emerged, key individuals and NGOs advanced the idea that human rights should be an international concern.

In Chapter 1 we mentioned the different traditions justifying actions by individuals or groups outside the borders of their own state: religious beliefs, solidarity, and liberal internationalism. None of these is a homogeneous category, and in some of the cases we consider in this book, individuals and groups from each of these three traditions participate together in a single campaign. Nevertheless, the logic of each tradition is distinct, and certain issues will separate one form of internationalism from the others. The activists discussed in Chapter 2 were motivated primarily by their religious beliefs, but most modern human rights activists have had a more secular inspiration.

Inspired by liberal internationalism, Woodrow Wilson articulated some human rights concerns in his campaign for global democracy and the rights of national self-determination during 1917–20. But the Convention of the League of Nations contained no mention of human rights, although it does mention "fair and humane conditions of labor" and "just treatment" of native inhabitants of dependent territories.[4]

Lawyer-diplomats first introduced and promoted the idea of internationally recognized human rights in the interwar period, and lawyers have continued to play a central role (in contrast with precursor campaigns where religious leaders predominated). Chilean jurist Alejandro Alvarez, Russian jurist and diplomat André Mandelstam, and Greek jurist and diplomat Antoine Frangulis first drafted and publicized declarations on international rights of man as part of their work with non-governmental legal organizations—the American Institute of International Law, the International Law Institute, and the International Diplomatic Academy.[5]

At the same time, a Jewish lawyer from Poland named Raphael Lemkin began a personal struggle to develop international law against racial massacres. Until Lemkin came up with the word "genocide" after the

[4] Jan Herman Burgers, "The Road to San Francisco: The Revival of the Human Rights Idea in the Twentieth Century," *Human Rights Quarterly* 14 (1992): 449.

[5] Mandelstam drafted a text of a "Declaration of the International Rights of Man" which the plenary session of the International Law Institute adopted in October of 1929. He later published articles and a book on the subject, and taught human rights courses in Geneva and the Hague. Two networks of NGOs, the International Federation of Leagues for the Defense of the Rights of Man and of the Citizen, and the International Union of Associations for the League of Nations, endorsed the principles of the declaration in 1931 and 1933. Frangulis introduced an international human rights resolution in the League of Nations in 1933, but it received scant support from countries already in the midst of the crisis leading to German withdrawal from the League. This section draws heavily on Burgers, "The Road to San Francisco," pp. 450–59, as well as on an interview with Burgers in the Hague, Netherlands, 13 November 1993.

Second World War, there was no word for the phenomenon in any language. Influenced as a boy by the massacre of Armenians in Turkey, he became convinced that the Nazis would carry out parallel outrages against Jews.[6] In 1933, at a conference sponsored by the League of Nations in Madrid, Spain, Lemkin proposed that an international treaty should be negotiated making "destruction of national, religious, and ethnic groups" an international crime akin to piracy, slavery, and drug smuggling.[7] "Lemkin's proposal met with howls of derision in which the delegates of Nazi Germany took the lead."[8]

Although liberal internationalism animated much human rights work, it is noteworthy that the jurists responsible for inserting the idea into early twentieth-century global debates came from countries at the periphery of the European system rather than at its cultural core. Both Frangulis and Mandelstam were political refugees, the former from the Greek dictatorship, the latter from the Bolshevist regime, and they saw in human rights a means of protecting individuals from the repressive practices of their own governments.[9] Wilsonian idealism and the high hopes for the League of Nations died a crashing death, however, with the advance of fascism in the late 1930s. The desire to build a new mentality and create new legal mechanisms that could avert a new continental war could not counter resurgent nationalism in Europe.[10]

An alternative source of internationalism in the early twentieth century was the tradition of solidarity that developed in trade union and socialist movements. These movements began by denying the relevance of the nation-state for workers, espousing a simple cosmopolitanism that fell before the decisions by most socialist parties to support their governments in the First World War. Despite this setback, the idea of international working-class solidarity remained a core value of the left throughout most of the twentieth century. It inspired thousands of young Communists and a considerable number of others to risk (and lose) their lives in Spain in the 1930s.[11] The Spanish Civil War also inspired liberal intellec-

[6] William Korey, "Raphael Lemkin: The Unofficial Man," *Midstream* (June/July 1989): 45–46.

[7] The Fifth International Conference for the Unification of Penal Law, held in cooperation with the Fifth Committee of the League of Nations. Raphael Lemkin, *Axis Rule in Occupied Europe: Laws of Occupation, Analysis of Government, Proposals for Redress* (Washington, D.C.: Carnegie Endowment, 1944), p. xiii.

[8] Korey, "Raphael Lemkin," p. 46.

[9] Like Lemkin, Mandelstam was motivated by the massacre of Armenians in Turkey in 1915, where he had been posted as a Russian diplomat; Frangulis was concerned about the persecution of Jews in Germany. Burgers, "The Road to San Francisco," p. 455.

[10] See Michael Bess, *Realism, Utopia, and the Mushroom Cloud: Four Activist Intellectuals and Their Strategies for Peace, 1945–1989* (Chicago: University of Chicago Press, 1993), pp. 1–40.

[11] See Peter N. Carroll, *The Odyssey of the Abraham Lincoln Brigade: Americans in the Spanish Civil War* (Stanford: Stanford University Press, 1994).

tuals who were stunned by the collapse of democratic ideals and institutions in the face of the fascist advance.

Apart from these few examples, policymakers and intellectuals paid almost no attention to the concept of human rights before the Second World War. Although many were deeply concerned with democracy and freedom, they did not use the language of human rights to defend them.[12] British author Herbert George Wells was an exception. Almost singlehandedly he reinserted the idea of an international bill of rights into the international arena during the debate over war aims at the beginning of the Second World War. Breaking with the religious motivations of nineteenth-century reformers and campaigners, Wells, a socialist and student of T. H. Huxley, championed the rationalist and scientific ideas of the period. As early as 1897 Wells had called for a "rational code of morality," asking, "are we not at the present time on a level of intellectual and moral attainment sufficiently high to permit of the formulation of a moral code . . . on which educational people can agree?"[13]

In 1939, recognizing that war was coming, Wells wrote that "if many of us are to die for democracy we better know what we mean by the word."[14] He launched a spirited public debate and effort to draft a new declaration of the rights of man that would clarify the war aims of the Allies by expressing "the broad principles on which our public and social life is based."[15] Wells sent the declaration to many people, including President Roosevelt, Gandhi, and Nehru (all of whom sent him reactions), and Jan Christiaan Smuts, prime minister of South Africa, who later drafted the preamble of the UN Charter.

Franklin Roosevelt incorporated this concern with human rights as part of the postwar order into his "Four Freedoms" State of the Union speech in January 1941.[16] The concept of a world founded upon essential freedoms—freedom of speech and expression, freedom of worship, freedom from want, and freedom from fear—was in part an outgrowth of his New Deal beliefs. Yet Roosevelt's concern for the international dimension of human rights was stimulated by the war and by a need to articulate war and peace aims that would set the Allies apart from Nazi Germany and the Axis powers.[17] Roosevelt was a friend of H. G. Wells, and was a

[12] See Burgers, "The Road to San Francisco," pp. 459–64.

[13] David C. Smith, *H.G. Wells: Desperately Mortal: A Biography* (New Haven: Yale University Press, 1986), p. 46.

[14] Ibid., p. 428.

[15] H. G. Wells, *The Times*, 23 October 1939, as cited in Burgers, "The Road to San Francisco," p. 464.

[16] Samuel I. Rosenman, *Working with Roosevelt* (New York: Harper, 1952), pp. 262–64.

[17] M. Glen Johnson, "The Contributions of Eleanor and Franklin Roosevelt to the Development of International Protection for Human Rights," *Human Rights Quarterly* 9 (1987): 21–23.

member of the International Diplomatic Academy, which had actively studied and promoted the cause of international human rights under the leadership of Frangulis and Mandelstam.[18] It is likely that these were among the sources he turned to as he formulated his "Four Freedoms" speech.

An explosion of intellectual, governmental, and nongovernmental activity followed upon the Wells campaign and Roosevelt's speech. This was a crucial moment of collaboration in creating a new postwar order, one of the pillars of which was to be the international protection of human rights. The U.S. domestic campaign for postwar international organization and the intense cooperation between the State Department and citizens' groups in this period can only be understood in the light of the administration's fear of a repeat of the U.S. failure to ratify the Versailles Treaty. For this reason, congressional and nongovernmental leaders were well represented in the official U.S. delegation to the 1945 conference in San Francisco that established the United Nations, and in addition the U.S. government invited 42 nongovernmental organizations to serve as consultants to the U.S. delegation in San Francisco.

THE INTER-AMERICAN TRADITION OF SUPPORT FOR INTERNATIONAL HUMAN RIGHTS

In Latin America there was a strong tradition of support for international law as a means by which weaker countries might contest the interventions of the more powerful, especially the United States. But while legalism had primarily been used to support concepts of sovereignty and nonintervention, international law also supported the promotion of human rights and democracy, which involved recognizing limits to the doctrine of absolute sovereignty and nonintervention. Until the Second World War this tension was resolved in favor of nonintervention. Nevertheless, support for the idea of protecting human rights through international or regional mechanisms has a long history in the region.[19] After the First World War most Latin American states joined the League of Nations and accepted the jurisdiction of the International Court of Justice. The regional legalist tradition found expression in the American Institute of International Law, founded in 1915 by Alejandro Alvarez with the sponsorship and financial support of the Carnegie Endowment for Inter-

[18] Interview with Jan Herman Burgers, the Hague, Netherlands, 13 November 1993.
[19] Larman Curtis Wilson, "The Principle of Non-intervention in Recent Inter-American Relations: The Challenge of Anti-Democratic Regimes," Ph.D. diss., University of Maryland, 1964, pp. 85–89; G. Pope Atkins, *Latin America in the International Political System*, 2d ed. (Boulder: Westview Press, 1989), p. 228.

national Peace. Although the institute's main goals were codification of existing international law and promotion of principles of nonintervention, its members did not see a contradiction between nonintervention and the protection of individual liberties.[20]

Although after the Second World War Latin American states increasingly made commitments and paid lip service to human rights, nonintervention was still the "touchstone" of the inter-American system.[21] Nevertheless, this legal tradition led Latin American states to support human rights language in the UN Charter, and to draft and pass the American Declaration on the Rights and Duties of Man at the Bogotá Conference in 1948, months before the UN passed the Universal Declaration of Human Rights. The Latin American countries attended the San Francisco conference and became charter members of the new United Nations Organization. They participated in drafting the human rights language that became the normative underpinning of all future network activities. These normative commitments, however, did not lead to regional efforts to promote human rights until the 1970s, when the regional and international human rights network emerged.

The UN Charter and Beyond

At the San Francisco conference, NGOs played a pivotal role in securing the inclusion of human rights language in the final UN charter. NGOs representing churches, trade unions, ethnic groups, and peace movements, aided by the delegations of some of the smaller countries, "conducted a lobby in favor of human rights for which there is no parallel in the history of international relations, and which was largely responsible for the human rights provisions of the Charter."[22]

NGOs found allies for their efforts in a number of Latin American nations, especially Uruguay, Panama, and Mexico.[23] The Mexican delegation, known for its spirited defense of nonintervention, nevertheless

[20] See Alejandro Alvarez, "Declaración sobre Las Bases Fundamentales y los Grandes Principios del Derecho Internacional Moderno," in *La Reconstrucción del Derecho de Gentes* (Santiago de Chile: Editorial Nascimento, 1943), pp. 89–91; and Alejandro Alvarez, *International Law and Related Subjects from the Point of View of the American Continent* (Washington, D.C.: Carnegie Endowment, 1922), pp. 27, 37.

[21] Wilson, "The Principle of Non-intervention," p. 374.

[22] John P. Humphrey, *Human Rights and the United Nations: A Great Adventure* (Dobbs Ferry, N.Y.: Transnational Publishers, 1984), p. 13. Also see U.S. Department of State, *The United Nations Conference on International Organization, San Francisco, California, 25 April to 26 June 1945: Selected Documents* (Washington: U.S. Government Printing Office, 1946).

[23] *Documents of the United Nations Conference on International Organization, San Francisco 1945*, vol. III: *Dumbarton Oaks Proposals, Comments, and Proposed Amendments* (New York: UN Information Organizations, 1945), p. 34; "New Uruguayan Proposals on the Dumbarton Oaks Proposals," 5 May 1945.

86 Activists beyond Borders

argued that the Dumbarton Oaks proposals "contain a serious hiatus in regard to the International Rights and Duties of Man, respect for which constitutes one of the essential objectives of the present war."[24] What is striking about the legislative history of the human rights language in the UN charter and in the inter-American system is how much the key Latin American delegations participated in, embraced, and furthered the human rights cause.[25] This contribution later undermined Latin American dictators' claims that human rights policies and pressures were an intolerable intervention in their internal affairs.

The charter itself testifies to the success of efforts by NGO lobbyists and Latin American delegations. The original Dumbarton Oaks proposal had only one reference to human rights; the final UN Charter has seven, including the key amendments proposed by the NGO consultants and Latin American states. It lists promotion of human rights among the basic purposes of the organization, and calls upon the Economic and Social Council (ECOSOC) to set up a human rights commission, the only commission specifically mandated in the charter.

The U.S. record at San Francisco on human rights issues was mixed. It supported the effort to include human rights language in the charter, but opposed references to economic human rights. Together with the two other key governmental actors, the USSR and the United Kingdom, the United States also wanted to limit possible infringement on domestic jurisdiction.[26] Although the human rights provisions had no teeth at this early stage, states were wary of their sovereignty implications.

As a result, the charter mandate on human rights is weaker than many NGOs desired, calling only for promoting and encouraging respect for human rights, rather than assuring or protecting them.[27] Though NGO consultants and a handful of Latin American states spoke eloquently at San Francisco for a more far-reaching vision of international human rights, that alternative vision, which called upon the UN to actively protect rights and provide the institutional machinery to do so, would have to wait another forty years to materialize. Still, by assigning institutional responsibility for human rights to the General Assembly and ECOSOC and by specifically recommending the creation of a human rights commission, the charter paved the way for all subsequent human rights actions within the UN system.

[24] "Opinion of the Department of Foreign Relations of Mexico Concerning the Dumbarton Oaks Proposals for the Creation of a General International Organization," 23 April 1945, United Nations Conference on International Organization, pp. 63, 71–73.

[25] Ibid, pp. 71–73.

[26] Johnson, "Contributions of Eleanor and Franklin Roosevelt," p. 24.

[27] Report of Rapporteur, Subcommittee I/1/A (Farid Zeineddine, Syria), to Committee I/1, 1 June 1945, Documents of the United Nations Conference on International Organization, p. 705.

The very first human rights treaty adopted by the UN was the Convention on the Prevention and Punishment of the Crime of Genocide, passed on 9 December 1948, one day before the UN approved the comprehensive Universal Declaration of Human Rights. As with some later human rights treaties, the genocide convention owed a special debt to the work of one individual, Raphael Lemkin. Lemkin came as a refugee to the United States in 1941, carrying with him documentary evidence of the policies of racial massacre the Nazis were inflicting on the Jews. In 1944 he published a book in which he coined the word "genocide" by combining the Greek word for race or tribe with the Latin word for killing.[28] Lemkin later served on the staff of the chief American prosecutor at the Nuremberg war crimes tribunal, where he introduced the new word and helped conduct seminars for the staff on the principles and background of the Nazi party and the administration of the German government under the Nazis.[29] The authors of the indictment incorporated the new word into their document as part of their discussion of crimes against humanity, and it was used repeatedly during the trial.[30] Although the word was not included in the court's judgment and sentence, it had already begun to gain wide currency. On 20 October 1946, a week after the Allies executed ten high Nazi officials and generals, a *New York Times* story carried the headline "Genocide is the New Name for the Crime Fastened on the Nazi Leaders." The *Times* gave Lemkin full credit for coining and popularizing the term.[31]

While in Nuremburg, Lemkin learned that the Nazis had killed forty-nine members of his family in concentration camps, death marches, and the Warsaw ghetto. He channeled his despair into a single-minded campaign to "inscribe into international law the crime and punishment of genocide."[32] At the new UN he lobbied the ambassadors of the United States, France, Britain, Panama, Cuba, and India to sponsor and support a resolution declaring genocide an international crime. Because the ambassadors thought the resolution would be more effective if introduced by smaller powers, Panama, Cuba, and India sponsored the original resolution. Lemkin then researched and drafted supporting statements in several languages for thirty different ambassadors, and lobbied for its passage. The secretariat of the Human Rights Division consulted Lemkin when preparing the first draft of the treaty, and "the influence of his ideas

[28] Lemkin, *Axis Rule*, p. 79.
[29] Robert Storey, *The Final Judgment? Pearl Harbor to Nuremberg* (San Antonio: Naylor, 1968), p. 96.
[30] Victor H. Bernstein, *Final Judgment: The Story of Nuremberg* (New York: Boni and Gaer, 1947), p. 136.
[31] *New York Times*, 20 October 1946, section 4, p. 13.
[32] Korey, "Raphael Lemkin," p. 47.

is very marked."[33] When the UN approved the treaty unanimously, Lemkin referred to it as "an epitaph on my mother's grave." It was to be his great disappointment that the United States, the first government to sign the treaty, failed to ratify it.[34]

The Senate's failure to ratify the genocide treaty was a signal of troubled times ahead for human rights in U.S. foreign policy. In the United States liberal internationalism had peaked in the immediate postwar period, giving way to a generation of liberal realists who saw only the hope of balancing clashing interests.[35] International human rights norms were subordinated to anticommunism during the Cold War.

With the advent of détente in the early 1970s came a more propitious environment for taking human rights seriously.[36] The brutal 1973 coup in Chile, one of Latin America's oldest democracies, was a watershed event in the creation of the Latin American human rights network, but it had such an impact because some parts of the network were already in place to document, frame, publicize, and dramatize the events.

The first human rights organization to gain wide international recognition was Amnesty International. Formed in the 1960s, Amnesty International (AI) made some key tactical choices that served to frame and strategically portray human rights issues for its membership and eventually for policymakers and the public. By focusing on specific individuals whose rights were violated, rather than on abstract ideas, AI emphasized that victims of human rights abuses were individuals with names, histories, and families. This led to strong identification between the victim and the public. Second, AI chose to work on a small range of gross violations of human rights, including political imprisonment, torture, and summary execution. Although this focus emerged from the liberal ideological tradition of the Western countries where the human rights movement began, the rights were embodied also in international norms and treaties around which there was a broad international consensus. Third, to maintain balance, AI selected one urgent case from the first world, one from the second world, and one from the third world each month for a special postcard campaign.[37] It thus protected itself from accusations that it was using human rights to pursue a broader political or ideological agenda of the right or left. AI's tactical innovations, later adopted by many other

[33] Leo Kuper, *The Prevention of Genocide* (New Haven: Yale University Press, 1985), p. 10.

[34] Korey, "Raphael Lemkin," pp. 45, 47.

[35] David Steigerwald, *Wilsonian Idealism in America* (Ithaca: Cornell University Press, 1994), pp. 138–50, 169–71.

[36] This discussion is developed further in Kathryn Sikkink, "The Origins and Continuity of Human Rights Policies in the United States and Western Europe," in *Ideas and Foreign Policy*, ed. Judith Goldstein and Robert Keohane (Ithaca: Cornell University Press, 1993), pp. 139–70.

[37] Harry M. Scoble and Laurie S. Wiseberg, "Human Rights and Amnesty International," *Annals of the American Academy* 413 (May 1974): 17.

members in the network, heightened the network's ability to raise the salience of the issue, make it resonate with the public, and attract the widest possible support.

Amnesty served as a training ground for human rights activists around the world. Mexican activist Mariclaire Acosta recalls,

> Obviously, my whole training, my whole human rights perspective, everything comes from Amnesty. It seems like all of these first and second generation Amnesty International people are like a little mafia. We all knew each other and loved each other dearly. And now we are spread all over the world doing other human rights work. It was like a star that exploded. It became a galaxy in many ways. People are either doing academic work in human rights or moving on to start their own NGO, or working for indigenous people rights, land rights, children's rights, and women's rights. I think Amnesty was wonderful, because it really trained a whole set of people all over the world to become conscious of human rights.[38]

INTERNATIONAL NONGOVERNMENTAL ORGANIZATIONS (INGOs)

The nongovernmental actors that promoted the idea of internationally protected human rights in the 1940s did not constitute a transnational advocacy network. Few organizations specialized in human rights, and those that did lacked the dense and constant information flows that characterize modern networks. Although some organizations are much older,[39] in the 1970s and 1980s human rights NGOs proliferated and diversified (see Table 1 in Chapter 1). Human rights organizations also formed coalitions and communication networks.[40] They developed strong links to domestic organizations in countries experiencing human rights violations. As these actors consciously developed linkages with each other, the human rights advocacy network emerged.

Coups and repression in such countries as Greece, Chile, Uruguay, Uganda, and Argentina increased global awareness about human rights violations. Membership in organizations such as AI in Europe and the United States grew and new organizations were created. The U.S. section

---

[38] Interview with Mariclaire Acosta, Washington, D.C., 3 December 1993.

[39] David Weissbrodt, "The Contribution of International Nongovernmental Organizations to the Protection of Human Rights," in *Human Rights in International Law: Legal and Policy Issues*, ed. Theodor Meron (Oxford: Clarendon Press, 1984), pp. 403–38.

[40] Laurie S. Wiseberg and Harry M. Scoble, "Monitoring Human Rights Violations: The Role of Nongovernmental Organizations," in *Human Rights and American Foreign Policy*, ed. Donald P. Kommers and Gilbert D. Loescher (Notre Dame: University of Notre Dame Press, 1979), pp. 183–84. In interviews, directors and staff of nine key human rights INGOs also stressed these links.

of AI, for example, expanded from 3,000 to 50,000 members between 1974 and 1976.[41] (The experience of human rights organizations parallels a more general growth in international nongovernmental organizations in the postwar period.[42]) Between 1983 and 1993 the total number of international human rights NGOs doubled, and their budgets and staffs grew dramatically.[43] The organizations that focused explicitly on human rights violations under both right-wing and left-wing governments, such as AI and the Human Rights Watch committees, grew most rapidly, suggesting that the power of the human rights idea was partly the result of a certain principled neutrality.

The network grew in the south as well. In the 1970s and 1980s domestic human rights organizations appeared throughout Latin America, increasing from 220 to 550 between 1981 and 1990.[44] Chilean organizations that were formed to confront government repression, especially the Catholic church's human rights office, the Vicaria de Solidaridad, became models for human rights groups throughout Latin America and sources of information and inspiration for human rights activists in the United States and Europe. A handful of visionary leaders within the human rights movement—such as Pepe Zalaquette, the exiled Chilean lawyer who later became the chairman of the International Executive Committee of Amnesty International, and Aryeh Neier, the strategist and fundraiser behind the phenomenal growth of the Watch committees—sensed its potential, conceived strategies, and attracted a generation of exceptional young leaders to the network. The work of these "political entrepreneurs" was fundamental to the emergence and growth of the network in the early years.

Some attention should be given to the personal stories behind the dramatic growth of the human rights network on Latin America. Many Latin American activists got involved in international human rights work when they went into exile. Pepe Zalaquette, the son of Lebanese immigrants in Chile, had worked in the agrarian reform program of the Allende government. After the coup in 1973 he tried to help friends who

[41] "The Growing Lobby for Human Rights," *Washington Post*, 12 December 1976, p. B1. Also see Paul Heath Hoeffel and Peter Kornbluh, "The War at Home: Chile's Legacy in the United States," *NACLA Report on the Americas* 17 (September–October 1983), pp. 27–39.

[42] See Table 1 in Chapter 1, and also Kjell Skjelsbaek, "The Growth of International Nongovernmental Organizations in the Twentieth Century," *International Organization* 25 (Summer 1971): 420–42.

[43] Two separate coding efforts based on organizations listed in the *Yearbook of International Organizations* confirm this growth. See Table 1, Chapter 1. Information on staff and budget changes based on information from interviews with staff of U.S. human rights organizations.

[44] Human Rights Internet, *Human Rights Directory: Latin America, Africa, and Asia*, ed. by Laurie S. Wiseberg and Harry M. Scoble (Washington, D.C., 1981); "Human Rights Directory: Latin American and the Caribbean," *Human Rights Internet Reporter* 13: 2–3 (January 1990).

suffered from the repression, and eventually joined the Vicaría de Solidaridad. The Pinochet government imprisoned Zalaquette in 1975, and expelled him from Chile in 1976. When he settled in the United States, Amnesty International USA elected him to its board of directors, and later he was elected to the international executive committee of AI, eventually becoming its elected chair from 1979 to 1982. He stepped down from the board to serve as deputy executive director of the organization from 1983 to 1985, before he was allowed to return to Chile in 1986.[45] In these various incarnations Zalaquette inspired a generation of new activists, many of whom mention him as one of the individuals they most admired. Ann Blyberg, who served for many years on the board of directors of Amnesty USA, remembers Zalaquette as one of a group of people she met in AI who drew her to the issue.

> These are people who have a sense of life, and are drawn to human rights because it is a way to live life most fully. With these people, you get an incredible sense of how rich it is to be alive. It is a *joie de vivre*. They have an incredible sense of humor. . . . Pepe Zalaquette was so full of life, so interested, so engaged in many things. He personified why it was important to struggle for human rights. If you are not driven by formal religious commitment, or by ideological commitment, then what is it that drives you? I met people who were so extraordinarily alive, it was stunning. . . . And after [my son] Jonah was born, you think about how you would feel if you lost a child. How is it possible with all this pain the world hasn't stopped turning, and yet these people are so alive? Somehow they reaffirm that life is important.[46]

Citizens in the United States and Europe became involved with human rights because they spent time living and working in Latin America. Some, such as Joe Eldridge, came to the human rights movement through their involvement in the church. "My father always said that we were children of God. My motivation fundamentally emerges from a religious perspective. Having been given life, I believe we are called to do things that edify life. We are choosing a path that leads to death or life. We must make decisions that move in the direction of affirming life."[47]

Eldridge was sent by the Methodist church as a missionary to Chile. He arrived the week after Salvador Allende had been elected president. Although he received a political education in Chile, human rights was not yet part of his political vocabulary. "Human rights entered my vocabulary on September 11, 1973, when it was suddenly denied to one-third of the Chilean population. That was a watershed. That defining moment

[45] Telephone interview with José Zalaquette, September 1993.
[46] Interview with Ann Blyberg, Washington, D.C., 17 March 1992.
[47] Interview with Joseph Eldridge, Washington, D.C., 18 March 1992.

has sustained my vision of what abuses of human rights are about. It has driven me."

At the end of October 1973 Eldridge came back to the United States to try to explain to his compatriots what was happening in Chile. "I vented my fury. I went around on a soapbox. I honed the message." Around this time, concerned church people, academics, and activists had funded a small NGO office in Washington, D.C., called the Washington Office on Latin America (WOLA). When the first director left, the Methodist church offered to pay Eldridge's salary as director. He now had an institutional foothold in Washington. "I really learned the limits of indignation, and how to put it in a language that Washington can digest." He paired up with a former businessman, Bill Brown, and together they formed an "odd couple" on Capitol Hill lobbying for human rights in Latin America. Brown convinced Eldridge to give up the poncho and sandals and to wear a suit when he went to meet with people in Congress. Eldridge served as director of WOLA from 1974 until 1986, and saw human rights become an integral part of the policy debate in Washington.

Domestic NGOs

Unlike the international NGOs that work on human rights violations in other countries, domestic NGOs focus on violations in their home countries. The number and capability of such domestic organizations vary enormously by country and by region. Latin America has more domestic human rights NGOs than do other parts of the third world. A 1981 directory of organizations in the developing world concerned with human rights and social justice listed 220 such organizations in Latin America, compared to 145 in Asia and 123 in Africa and the Middle East. A 1990 directory lists over 550 human rights groups in Latin America; some countries have as many as sixty.[48] An international "demonstration effect" was at work in Latin America during the decade of the 1980s, as the activities and successes of early human rights organizations inspired others to follow their example.

Many Latin America human rights activists became involved in networks as a result of their personal experience living under repressive regimes. Estela Barnes de Carlotto, president of the Argentine organization called the Grandmothers of the Plaza de Mayo, first became in-

---

[48] Human Rights Internet, *Human Rights Directory: Latin America, Africa, and Asia*; "Human Rights Directory: Latin American and the Caribbean," *Human Rights Internet Reporter* 13: 2–3. The definition used by these directories is broader than that of many human rights groups in Latin America; still, comparing the 1981 and 1990 figures give an idea of the dramatic growth in the Latin American network.

volved in 1977 when Argentine security forces "disappeared" first her husband and later her daughter, Laura Carlotto.[49] Her husband reappeared twenty-five days later, after Estela had paid a ransom of $9,000 to a private individual with contacts to repressive groups, but her daughter never reappeared. Shortly before she disappeared, Laura had told her mother that she was two months pregnant. What made the case unusual was that the military returned Laura's bullet-ridden body to the family, claiming that she had been killed in a confrontation with the military after trying to run a road block. Two people later contacted Estela, however, and told her that they had been imprisoned with her daughter in one of the secret concentration camps, and that she had given birth to a baby boy before she was "transferred" (the Argentine military euphemism for murder). Hoping to locate her grandson, Estela joined the Grandmothers of the Plaza de Mayo, who were just beginning to make international contacts. The Grandmothers modeled themselves after another human rights group in Argentina, the Mothers of the Plaza de Mayo, made up of the mothers of disappeared people. The Grandmothers had all lost grandchildren or pregnant daughters to state repression. Both groups demonstrated weekly in the central plaza in Buenos Aires, the Plaza de Mayo, demanding the return of their loved ones.

> When they kidnapped my daughter, I didn't know anything about Amnesty International, or the Inter-American Commission on Human Rights, or the United Nations. We began to learn about these organizations through people in Argentina that had an international vision, like Emilio Mignone. He told us "you have to petition the OAS, you need to send letters to Amnesty." We didn't send letters directly to these places because we knew that they wouldn't arrive if they were addressed to Amnesty International, so we always took advantage when someone traveled abroad to send letters.

The Grandmothers traveled to Europe, the United States, and Canada to denounce human rights violations in Argentina and to seek international solidarity.

The Grandmothers were also searching for international scientific assistance to answer some burning questions. In some cases, like that of the Carlotto family, they did not have actual proof that their daughter had given birth. In addition, even if they thought they had located a grandchild in an orphanage or with another family, they had no way of establishing paternity. The Grandmothers believed that foreign scientists

---

[49] This section draws on two sources. Interview with Estela Barnes de Carlotto, Buenos Aires, Argentina, 28 October 1992, and Mauricio Cohen Salama, *Tumbas anónimas: informe sobre la identificación de restos de víctimas de la represión ilegal* (Buenos Aires: Catálogos Editora, 1992), pp. 169–74.

could help them. Through an Argentine activist in the United States they first made contact with Eric Stover, the staff person for the human rights program of the American Association for the Advancement of Science (AAAS). Stover helped put them in contact with Mary-Claire King of the University of California, who told them of a specific blood test that could be used to establish grandparent paternity even without information about the parents. Also through Eric Stover the Grandmothers learned about forensic techniques that, through the exhumation and analysis of cadavers, could determine whether their daughters had given birth.

The AAAS arranged a scientific delegation to Argentina in 1984, after redemocratization, formed by Stover, King, and Clyde Snow, a forensic anthropologist, as well as a forensic odontologist, a forensic pathologist, and two other doctors. This was the first time the team had applied their several skills to cases of human rights violations and mass murder. The task was Herculean because most of the bodies had either been dropped into the ocean or were buried in mass graves. Estela Carlotto asked Snow to exhume the body of her daughter Laura, one of the few cases where the body had been returned to the family. "After the exhumation, Clyde Snow came to me and said, 'Estela, you are a grandmother.'" He knew that Laura had given birth because there were distinctive marks in the bones of the pelvis. He was also able to tell Estela that her daughter had been assassinated at a distance of about thirty centimeters, which directly contradicted the military's story of a shootout at a roadblock. Given the direction of the bullets, it appeared that Laura had been shot in the back of the head at close range. Snow also told Estela that while it was clear her daughter had taken care of her teeth and they were in good shape, in the period before her death they had deteriorated, which suggested that she had been detained and could not take care of them. Combined with the testimony of witnesses who had seen Laura in secret prisons, Snow's information was sufficient for Estela to include the case of her daughter's murder in the request for the United States to extradite ex-general Carlos Guillermo Suarez Mason, who had been in charge of the region where Laura was held. Meanwhile, grandparents gave blood which was analyzed by Dr. King, and in some cases she was able to establish the grand-paternity of adopted children who were later returned to their grandparents.

None of the investigations happened without trauma and conflict. When the AAAS team first arrived, some of the human rights organizations refused to cooperate with them. Some were distrustful of any group from the United States because of the U.S. government's complicity with repression in Latin America.[50] Others, especially the Mothers of the Plaza de Mayo, believed that the Argentine government owed them an official

[50] Cohen Salama, *Tumbas anónimas*, p. 120.

explanation of the whereabouts of their children, and argued that to accept information from any unofficial source was to relieve the government of responsibility.

Political stances of organizations and political histories of activists affected the configuration of human rights networks. Despite considerable collaboration, human rights organizations had to capture political space in advocacy networks for an approach that many schooled in a leftist solidarity tradition condemned as apolitical. This was especially true for Latin America, where human rights violations came in the main (though not exclusively) from right-wing regimes. Clearly, not all the relationships forged between international or foreign organizations and domestic organizations protecting the rights of oppressed peoples originated within the human rights tradition; the solidarity framework was a second main pattern for international advocacy among NGOs. Although both involve relationships between oppressed peoples and those in a position to support them, there are important conceptual differences. Individuals are endowed with rights; communities are the repositories of solidarity. Solidarity involves a substantive dimension that rights-based activism does not, that is, support based on a conviction of defending a just cause. Human rights appeals, on the other hand, raise the more procedural claims that violations of personhood or of recognized civil or legal norms and procedures are *always* unacceptable, whatever the victim's beliefs.

As defined, these are ideal types; between the two positions are many who see the defense of human rights as the best way to protect the lives of the people whose ideas they defend. Outside of the core activists in these campaigns, moreover, few would have recognized such a distinction. Nonetheless, for the core activists, transnational solidarity campaigns presume an ideological affinity that transnational human rights advocacy explicitly does not. Solidarity and human rights groups have often worked together, and some groups have tried to incorporate both traditions. Thus the Chile solidarity committees and the Committee in Solidarity with the People of El Salvador (CISPES) could join Amnesty International to denounce human rights violations in Chile or El Salvador. On other issues, however, human rights groups and solidarity groups broke ranks. For example, when human rights organizations began to denounce violations in Cuba, in Nicaragua under the Sandinista government, or by the Frente Faribundo Marti in El Salvador, the solidarity movement remained silent.

Parts of Intergovernmental Organizations (IOs)

Before 1948 no intergovernmental organizations focused on human rights; by 1990 twenty-seven included human rights as a significant part of their work.[51] The larger INGOs have UN consultative status, which is the formal accrediting procedure allowing them to participate in UN debates and activities. Set up after the Second World War, both the UN Commission on Human Rights and the Subcommission on the Protection of Minorities became more dynamic in the 1970s under the influence of new rules giving them broader latitude to investigate complaints,[52] and under pressure from INGOs, the Carter administration, and some European governments. The Human Rights Committee began to function in 1976, providing yet another arena for human rights debate and activism in the UN system.[53] These three organs hold periodic meetings that facilitate contact among the groups and individuals that form the human rights network, and have become focal points for network activity. In Geneva, the government representatives of the "like-minded" countries of the Netherlands, Denmark, Sweden, Norway, and Canada meet with representatives of human rights NGOs, and with UN representatives of the Human Rights Center to develop and pursue common strategies for human rights work.

Theo C. Van Boven, a Dutch diplomat known for his strong support of human rights, was appointed director of the UN Center for Human Rights in 1976 and steered it to a higher-profile role. Van Boven worked very closely with NGOs—too closely, according to his critics, among whom the Argentine government was the most vehement. Van Boven defended his close relations with NGOs. "It was thanks to them, in fact, that we could carry on our work, because I've always claimed that 85 percent of our information came from NGOs. We did not have the resources or staff to collect information ourselves, so we were dependent. They did a lot of work which we should do at the UN"[54] For Van Boven, the personal testimonies he listened to week after week from victims, family members and human rights organizations left him feeling both "more radical" and sometimes "very hopeless." NGOs provided the UN Center with concrete information on human rights violations, and also helped draft language for UN declarations and treaties. Amnesty International, for example, was deeply involved in the drafting process for the UN Convention against Torture.

[51] Based on information coded from *Yearbook of International Organizations: 1948* (Brussels: Union of International Associations, 1948), and *Yearbook of International Organizations: 1990* (Munich: K. G. Saur, 1990).
[52] Economic and Social Council (ECOSOC) resolutions 1235, passed in 1967, and 1503, passed in 1970, authorized the commission to review communications and investigate complaints that appear to reveal a consistent pattern of gross violations of human rights.
[53] The Covenant for Civil and Political Rights, and the Covenant for Economic, Social, and Cultural Rights were substantially drafted by 1954, but not approved by the General Assembly and opened for signature until 1966. The two covenants reached the required number of adherents for entry into legal force in 1976.
[54] Interview with Theo C. Van Boven, Maastricht, the Netherlands, 8 November 1993.

In the early 1980s the Soviet Union, the U.S. government under Ronald Reagan, and the Guatemalan and Argentine governments all attacked Van Boven and the Human Rights Center. "They were fighting against you, not openly, but behind your back, when it came to staff issues, finance and so on, trying to hit you there or to cut off things here, which is difficult to find out where and how it's being done. When certain decisions are made to cut your budget or not to renew people whose work is important to you . . ." A week after Van Boven made a very strong statement against recent massacres in various countries including Guatemala and El Salvador, a telegram arrived terminating his contract. But this did not end the UN's growing involvement in promoting human rights. When the Commission on Human Rights was blocked from conducting a full investigation of Argentine practices, it created a special working group on disappearances. Through this group it could monitor the Argentine situation as well as work on Guatemala, El Salvador, and other countries where the practice of disappearances was widespread.

The Inter-American Commission on Human Rights (IACHR) of the Organization of American States (OAS), established in 1959, was reorganized and strengthened in 1979 when the American Convention on Human Rights entered into force. The reorganized commission became more active in promoting human rights in the region, especially in its influential 1980 report on human rights in Argentina.[55] In the early 1990s the OAS took some significant steps to alter traditional understandings of sovereignty and nonintervention. At the OAS General Assembly in Santiago in 1991 all thirty-four member states declared "their firm political commitment to the promotion and protection of human rights and representative democracy" and instructed the secretary general to convoke a meeting of the permanent council "in the case of any event giving rise to the sudden or irregular interruption of a democratic government." This "Declaration of Santiago" provided the legal and procedural basis for the rapid regional response to military coups in Haiti and in Peru, and put the OAS in the forefront of international organization efforts to promote democracy.

Foundations and Funders

A handful of private and public foundations have provided funding for human rights organizations. Foundations may be the most autonomous of all the actors in the network. Intergovernmental actors depend on the consensus of their governmental members, and most NGOs

---

[55] Organization of American States, Inter-American Commission on Human Rights, *Report on the Situation of Human Rights in Argentina* (Washington, D.C.: OAS General Secretariat, 1980).

are financially dependent upon membership and foundations. Foundations, however, have independent incomes, and are formally accountable only to self-perpetuating boards of trustees. Peter Bell has argued that the Ford Foundation acted as an "entrepreneur of ideas."[56] Nonetheless, foundations cannot implement their own ideas, but must seek and support other organizations that can.

The most important United States foundation for human rights issues in Latin America has been the Ford Foundation,[57] but a number of European funders have also played key roles, especially European church foundations. In addition, official development assistance agencies and semipublic foundations in Canada, Scandinavia, the Netherlands, and the United States have also funded human rights NGOs.

Before 1975 the big U.S. foundations hardly ever funded international human rights work.[58] From 1977 to 1987, however, such grantmaking grew dramatically, both in numbers of grants and in their total dollar amount. (See Figure 2) In 1968 the Ford Foundation was by far the largest foundation in the United States. One-fifth to one-quarter of the Ford budget has been spent on international activities.[59] In the 1960s and 1970s it had focused on strengthening state administrative capacities in developing countries. Funding human rights activities initially ran against the grain of previous grantmaking priorities, since human rights work was often viewed as attacking the state rather than strengthening it. The impetus for the human rights funding within Ford came from the field offices in Latin America, influenced by political events and ideas in the region.[60]

For years, Ford had supported individual academics conducting social science research. When repressive governments in Latin America fired many of these individuals from their jobs in government or in universities, Ford helped to relocate them abroad or to set up independent research centers in their own countries, thus getting to human rights concerns by way of academic freedom. But even this policy was contentious both within the foundation and between the foundation and the U.S. government.

William Carmichael, Harry Wilhelm, and Peter Bell were key actors in the decision to engage Ford more directly with human rights. Carmichael and Bell worked in Brazil in the 1960s and 1970s and witnessed the im-

---

[56] Peter Bell, "The Ford Foundation as an International Actor," *International Organization* 25 (Summer 1971): 472.

[57] Ibid., pp. 465–78; Jeffrey M. Puryear, "Higher Education, Development Assistance, and Repressive Regimes," *Studies in Comparative International Development* 17 (Summer 1982): 3–35.

[58] The subject of human rights didn't appear in the index of major foundation grants in the U.S. until 1975. The Foundation Center, *The Foundation Grants Index* (New York, 1970–1980).

[59] Bell, "The Ford Foundation," p. 467.

[60] Interview with William Carmichael, New York City, 11 May 1992.

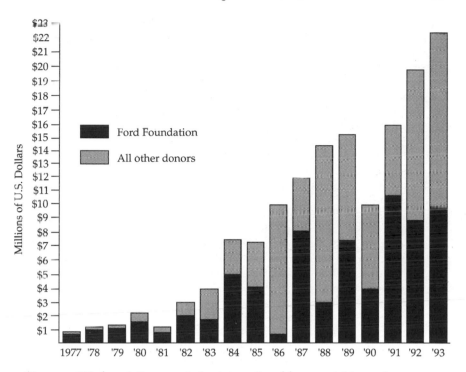

Figure 2. U.S. foundation grants for international human rights work, 1977–91. *Source*: The Foundation Center, *The Foundation Grants Index* (New York: The Foundation Center, all editions, 1977–80), and *Dialog*, electronic data base (New York: The Foundation Center, all years, 1981–91). The figures were compiled from all grants listed under the heading of "human rights" and represent the total contributions of U.S.-based foundations for each year indicated.

pact of repression there. Carmichael "cared passionately about human rights" and "fanned the HR flame" in the foundation.[61] Peter Bell arrived in Brazil shortly after the military coup in 1964. At that time Ford was helping to develop graduate education and research, and Bell broadened the focus beyond the natural sciences and economics to support the other social sciences. He explained how he became involved in individual cases of social scientists who were objects of repression.

> At the time of my arrival in Brazil, there were virtually no Brazilians with graduate training in political science. Indeed, the discipline hardly existed in the country. The Foundation made a grant to a promising group at the Federal University of Minas Gerais to form Brazil's first department of

[61] Interview with Jeffrey Puryear, New York City, 12 May 1992. Puryear discusses the role of the Ford Foundation in Chile in *Thinking Politics: Intellectuals and Democracy in Chile, 1973–1988* (Baltimore: Johns Hopkins University Press, 1994).

political science. I was attending a conference of leading social scientists from around the world which the new department had organized. One of the young professors, Bolivar Lamounier, a Brazilian graduate student who had been doing research for his master's thesis at UCLA, approached me. He said that he had planned to return to UCLA a few days earlier but that he had arrived at the airport to find that his visa to the United States had been canceled. He had been told to go back to the U.S. consul to correct the situation, and he asked me to accompany him and to vouch for his status at UCLA—which I did.

At the consulate itself, the consul insisted on seeing us separately rather than together. When Bolivar emerged from the meeting, he was crestfallen. I then went in to be told that Bolivar had been denied a visa. When I asked why, I was told that he was "the real thing." I asked what that meant, and the consul said that Bolivar was "deep red." I met Bolivar in the anteroom, and we went down the elevator without saying a word to one another. As we emerged, members of the Brazilian secret police grabbed him and took him prisoner. I tried to accompany Bolivar, but was pushed out of the way. I went back up to the consulate, and was told to mind my own business. By the next day, a well-placed Brazilian at the conference was able to locate where Bolivar was being held. Many of the conferees and I boarded a bus for the fort and asked very politely to see the prisoner. Two months later he was released without any charges having been made and (thanks to the support from the UCLA faculty and others) allowed immediately to resume his studies in the U.S.

The role that I had played in this affair seemed very minor to me. All I had done is what any decent person would do. I was surprised therefore that the person then in charge of the Foundation's office in Brazil recommended to our regional director in New York that I be reprimanded or worse. He felt that I had stuck my neck out in an 'un-Foundation-like' way. Fortunately, his memo to New York was answered by a cable from the director, congratulating me on my conduct. As word of the incident spread around Brazil, it seemed to do the Foundation no damage. In fact, it opened new doors to us and appeared to deepen trust in our work.[62]

Later in 1969 the Brazilian government clamped down on some distinguished social scientists and removed them from their jobs in state and federal universities. The blacklisted intellectuals, led by sociologist Fernando Henrique Cardoso, who was to author the seminal text on dependency theory, decided to form a think tank, the Brazilian Center for Analysis and Planning (CEBRAP), which would allow social scientists who had lost their jobs to stay in Brazil at an independent research center. Carmichael and Bell recommended that Ford fund the new center. At this

[62] Peter Bell, "Speech to the Incoming Students," Woodrow Wilson School, Princeton University, 10 September 1983, p. 4–6.

time Bell got a call from the head of the U.S. Agency for International Development (AID) mission in Brazil.

> He expressed a deep concern about the grant we had recommended, and said he was concerned about what such a grant would do to me professionally in the future. I told him that if he had any specific charges against the individuals involved, I would be happy to hear them. He arranged for me to meet with a CIA officer who brought a few files. It was just junk. It showed that a couple of people involved with CEBRAP had had associations with people who were members of the Communist party.[63]

The Ford Foundation headquarters in New York initially rejected the grant, and then, as a result of an internal debate, approved it.[64] Carmichael and his boss Harry Wilhelm argued within Ford not only that the foundation should support intellectual freedom, but also made the argument that having invested in building human capital, the foundation needed to preserve what it had helped create by protecting intellectuals in research institutions.[65] This was one of the first institutional grants to independent research centers of social scientists critical of authoritarianism.

This model was replicated after the military coups in Chile and Uruguay in 1973, and in Argentina in 1976. These early grants fell under the rubric of social science and institution building, but can also be seen as the start of Ford's human rights program. Later, some of these social scientists put Ford field staff in contact with activist human rights organizations like the Vicaría de Solidaridad in Chile and the Academy for Human Rights in Mexico, which began to solicit funding. The Chilean situation finally generated a major policy debate within Ford on what the foundation's policy should be vis-à-vis repressive regimes. In 1977 Ford made an explicit policy choice to include human rights as one of its program priorities; in 1981 human rights and governance became one of the foundation's five main program areas.[66]

Ford was not the only important foundation player. By the late 1970s and early 1980s European and Canadian foundations were also taking up human rights work, and in some cases were involving grantees in foundation decision making to a degree without parallel among U.S. foundations. The large semipublic Dutch foundation Netherland Organization for International Development Cooperation (NOVIB), for example, regularly meets with the organizations it funds, many of which are human

---

[63] Interview with Peter Bell, New York City, 20 March 1992.

[64] CEBRAP went on to play a very influential intellectual and political role in Brazil. With redemocratization, Fernando Henrique Cardoso turned his attention to politics, and was elected president of Brazil in 1994.

[65] Interview with William Carmichael, New York City, 11 May 1992.

[66] Interview with William Carmichael.

rights and women's organizations, to work on a common NOVIB funding strategy for the future. NOVIB also actively encourages contact among the groups it funds (its "partners") in different parts of the world.

NETWORKS AND GOVERNMENTS

Most governments' human rights policies have emerged as a response to pressure from organizations in the human rights network, and have depended fundamentally on network information. For this reason it is hard to separate the independent influences of government policy and network pressures. Networks often have their greatest impact by working through governments and other powerful actors. In the United States the earliest governmental group to work actively on human rights was the House Subcommittee on International Organizations under the chairmanship of Donald Fraser (D-Minn.).[67] Beginning in 1973 this subcommittee held a series of hearings on human rights abuses around the world.[68] The main witnesses providing human rights information in these hearings were representatives of human rights NGOs. Although human rights policy began to form in the U.S. Congress three years before Jimmy Carter was elected president,[69] Carter administration officials gave it a higher profile, and, by lending the weight of the United States to that of progressive European countries in the UN, spurred action in international forums. Under Carter the U.S. State Department's Bureau of Human Rights and Humanitarian Affairs sought contacts with and information from NGOs, which continued to influence executive policy making even during the Reagan and Bush adminstrations.

Network influence within European states centered on foreign affairs and development cooperation ministries. Several European governments set up human rights advisory committees that included NGOs such as Amnesty International, as well as ministries, parliamentarians, and scholars.[70] In some countries the overlap between individuals in government and NGOs is significant. For example, in 1995 both the queen and the foreign minister of the Netherlands were members of AI. Indeed, Dutch policy makers claim difficulty in remembering which hat they are wearing at a particular meeting—academic, member of a leading human

---

[67] Later renamed the Subcommittee on Human Rights and International Organizations.
[68] Interview with John Salzberg, Washington, D.C., April 1991.
[69] See Schoultz, *Human Rights*, pp. 74–88; Forsythe, *Human Rights and World Politics*, pp. 127–59.
[70] Jan Egeland, *Impotent Superpower—Potent Small State: Potentials and Limitations of Human Rights Objectives in the Foreign Policies of the United States and Norway* (Oslo: Norwegian University Press, 1988), pp. 193ff.

rights NGO, member of the NGO governmental advisory board, or government delegate to an intergovernmental organization.

Often, network interactions with government bureaucracies have been mutually reinforcing but not congenial. The U.S. annual human rights reports provide a clear example. Because State Department officials did not want to offend foreign officials or undermine other policy goals, early reports were often weak. The State Department reports, however, did serve as a focal point for human rights groups, which created annual public events by issuing responses to the reports.[71] The reports and counterreports attracted press coverage, and the critiques held the State Department to higher standards in future reporting. In turn, domestic human rights organizations in repressive countries learned that they could indirectly pressure their governments to change practices by providing information on abuses to human rights officers in U.S. embassies for inclusion in the U.S. annual country reports.

The link to government is simultaneously the most powerful and the least dependable aspect of the work of the network, as it often depends on the individuals occupying key posts. Many human rights activists considered Patricia Derian, assistant secretary of state for human rights during the Carter administration, part of the human rights network in the sense that she shared many of their values, and she and her staff were in frequent communication with them. When Reagan took office and Elliot Abrams replaced Derian, the human rights office in the State Department dropped out of the network. Without linkages to governments institutionalized through NGO advisory committees, such changes in personnel can dismantle productive relationships.

The section above discusses the growth and change of each of the parts of the human rights network in the 1970s and 1980s. Each new human rights organization reinforces a reconceptualized view of state sovereignty in which international scrutiny of domestic human rights practices is not only legitimate but necessary. To demonstrate the impact of the network in practice, we need to look at the effectiveness of these pressures in specific cases.

Argentina

Even before the military coup of March 1976, international human rights pressures had influenced the Argentine military's decision to cause political opponents to "disappear," rather than imprisoning them or exe-

---

[71] See, e.g., Human Rights Watch and the Lawyers Committee for Human Rights, *Critique: Review of the Department of State's Country Reports on Human Rights Practices for 1987* (New York: 1988).

cuting them publicly.[72] (The technique led to the widespread use of the verb "to disappear" in a transitive sense.) The Argentine military believed they had "learned" from the international reaction to the human rights abuses after the Chilean coup. When the Chilean military executed and imprisoned large numbers of people, the ensuing uproar led to the international isolation of the regime of Augusto Pinochet. Hoping to maintain a moderate international image, the Argentine military decided to secretly kidnap, detain, and execute its victims, while denying any knowledge of their whereabouts.[73]

Although this method did initially mute the international response to the coup, Amnesty International and groups staffed by Argentine political exiles eventually were able to document and condemn the new forms of repressive practices. To counteract the rising tide of criticism, the Argentina junta invited AI for an on-site visit in 1976. In March 1977, on the first anniversary of the military coup, AI published the report on its visit, a well-documented denunciation of the abuses of the regime with emphasis on the problem of the disappeared. Amnesty estimated that the regime had taken six thousand political prisoners, most without specifying charges, and had abducted between two and ten thousand people. The report helped demonstrate that the disappearances were part of a deliberate government policy by which the military and the police kidnapped perceived opponents, took them to secret detention centers where they tortured, interrogated, and killed them, then secretly disposed of their bodies.[74] Amnesty International's denunciations of the Argentine regime were legitimized when it won the Nobel Peace Prize later that year.

Such information led the Carter administration and the French, Italian, and Swedish governments to denounce rights violations by the junta. France, Italy, and Sweden each had citizens who had been victims of Argentine repression, but their concerns extended beyond their own citizens. Although the Argentine government claimed that such attacks

[72] This section draws upon some material from an earlier co-authored work: Lisa L. Martin and Kathryn Sikkink, "U.S. Policy and Human Rights in Argentina and Guatemala, 1973–1980," in *Double-Edged Diplomacy: International Bargaining and Domestic Politics,* ed., Peter B. Evans, Harold K. Jacobson, and Robert D. Putnam (Berkeley: University of California Press, 1993), pp. 330–62.

[73] See Emilio Mignone, *Derechos humanos y sociedad: el caso argentino* (Buenos Aires: Ediciones del Pensamiento Nacional and Centro de Estudios Legales y Sociales, 1991), p. 66; Claudio Uriarte, *Almirante Cero: Biografía No Autorizada de Emilio Eduardo Massera* (Buenos Aires: Planeta, 1992), p. 97; and Carlos H. Acuña and Catalina Smulovitz, "Adjusting the Armed Forces to Democracy: Successes, Failures, and Ambiguities in the Southern Cone," in *Constructing Democracy: Human Rights, Citizenship, and Society in Latin America,* ed. Elizabeth Jelin and Eric Hershberg (Boulder, Colo.: Westview, 1993), p. 15.

[74] Amnesty International, *Report of an Amnesty International Mission to Argentina* (London: Amnesty International, 1977).

conotituted unacceptable intervention in their internal affairs and violated Argentine sovereignty, U.S. and European officials persisted. In 1977 the U.S. government reduced the planned level of military aid for Argentina because of human rights abuses. Congress later passed a bill eliminating all military assistance to Argentina, which went into effect on 30 September 1978.[75] A number of high-level U.S. delegations met with junta members during this period to discuss human rights.

Early U.S. action on Argentina was based primarily on the human rights documentation provided by AI and other NGOs, not on information received through official channels at the embassy or the State Department.[76] For example, during a 1977 visit, Secretary of State Cyrus Vance carried a list of disappeared people prepared by human rights NGOs to present to members of the junta.[77] When Patricia Derian met with junta member Admiral Emilio Massera during a visit in 1977, she brought up the navy's use of torture. In response to Massera's denial, Derian said she had seen a rudimentary map of a secret detention center in the Navy Mechanical School, where their meeting was being held, and asked whether perhaps under their feet someone was being tortured. Among Derian's key sources of information were NGOs and especially the families of the disappeared, with whom she met frequently during her visits to Buenos Aires.[78]

Within a year of the coup, Argentine domestic human rights organizations began to develop significant external contacts. Their members traveled frequently to the United States and Europe, where they met with human rights organizations, talked to the press, and met with parliamentarians and government officials. These groups sought foreign contacts to publicize the human rights situation, to fund their activities, and to help protect themselves from further repression by their government, and

[75] Congressional Research Service, Foreign Affairs and National Defense Division, *Human Rights and U.S. Foreign Assistance: Experiences and Issues in Policy Implementation (1977–1978)*, report prepared for U.S. Senate Committee on Foreign Relations, November 1979, p. 106.
[76] After the 1976 coup, Argentine political exiles set up branches of the Argentine Human Rights Commission (CADHU) in Paris, Mexico, Rome, Geneva, and Washington, D.C. In October two of its members testified on human rights abuses before the U.S. House Subcommittee on Human Rights and International Organization. Iain Guest, *Behind the Disappearances: Argentina's Dirty War against Human Rights and the United Nations* (Philadelphia: University of Pennsylvania Press, 1990), pp. 66–67.
[77] Interview with Robert Pastor, Wianno, Massachusetts, 28 June 1990.
[78] Testimony given by Patricia Derian to the National Criminal Appeals Court in Buenos Aires during the trials of junta members. "Massera sonrió y me dijo: Sabe qué pasó con Poncio Pilatos . . .?" *Diario del Juicio*, 18 June 1985, p. 3; Guest, *Behind the Disappearances*, pp. 161–63. Later it was confirmed that the Navy Mechanical School was one of the most notorious secret torture and detention centers. *Nunca Más: The Report of the Argentine National Commission for the Disappeared* (New York: Farrar Straus & Giroux, 1986), pp. 79–84.

they provided evidence to U.S. and European policymakers. Much of their funding came from European and U.S.-based foundations.[79]

Two key events that served to keep the case of Argentine human rights in the minds of U.S. and European policymakers reflect the impact of transnational linkages on policy. In 1979 the Argentine authorities released Jacobo Timerman, whose memoir describing his disappearance and torture by the Argentine military helped human rights organizations, members of the U.S. Jewish community, and U.S. journalists to make his case a cause célèbre in U.S. policy circles.[80] Then in 1980 the Nobel Peace Prize was awarded to an Argentine human rights activist, Adolfo Pérez Esquivel. Peace and human rights groups in the United States and Europe helped sponsor Pérez Esquivel's speaking tour to the United States exactly at the time that the OAS was considering the IACHR report on Argentina and Congress was debating the end of the arms embargo to Argentina.

The Argentine military government wanted to avoid international human rights censure. Scholars have long recognized that even authoritarian regimes depend on a combination of coercion and consent to stay in power. Without the legitimacy conferred by elections, they rely heavily on claims about their political efficancy and on nationalism.[81] Although the Argentine military mobilized nationalist rhetoric against foreign criticism, a sticking point was that Argentines, especially the groups that most supported the military regime, thought of themselves as the most European of Latin American countries. The military junta claimed to be carrying out the repression in the name of "our Western and Christian civilization."[82] But the military's intent to integrate Argentina more fully into the liberal global economic order was being jeopardized by deteriorating relations with countries most identified with that economic order, and with "Western and Christian civilization."

The junta adopted a sequence of responses to international pressures. From 1976 to 1978 the military pursued an initial strategy of denying the legitimacy of international concern over human rights in Argentina. At the same time it took actions that appear to have contradicted this strategy, such as permitting the visit of the Amnesty International mission to Argentina in 1976. The "failure" of the Amnesty visit, from the military

---

[79] The Mothers of the Plaza de Mayo received grants from Dutch churches and the Norwegian Parliament, and the Ford Foundation provided funds for the Center for Legal and Social Studies (CELS) and the Grandmothers of the Plaza de Mayo.

[80] Jacobo Timerman, *Prisoner without a Name, Cell without a Number* (New York: Random House, 1981).

[81] See Guillermo O'Donnell, "Tensions in the Bureaucratic Authoritarian State and the Question of Democracy," in *The New Authoritarianism in Latin America*, ed. David Collier (Princeton: Princeton University Press, 1979), pp. 288, 292–94.

[82] Daniel Frontalini and Maria Cristina Caiati, *El Mito de la Guerra Sucia* (Buenos Aires: Centro de Estudios Legales y Sociales, 1984), p. 24.

point of view, appeared to reaffirm the junta's resistance to human rights pressures. This strategy was most obvious at the UN, where the Argentine government worked to silence international condemnation in the UN Commission on Human Rights. Ironically, the rabidly anticommunist Argentine regime found a diplomatic ally in the Soviet Union, an importer of Argentine wheat, and the two countries collaborated to block UN consideration of the Argentine human rights situation.[83] Concerned states circumvented this blockage by creating the UN Working Group on Disappearances in 1980. Human rights NGOs provided information, lobbied government delegations, and pursued joint strategies with sympathetic UN delegations.

By 1978 the Argentine government recognized that something had to be done to improve its international image in the United States and Europe, and to restore the flow of military and economic aid.[84] To these ends the junta invited the Inter-American Commission on Human Rights for an on-site visit, in exchange for a U.S. commitment to release Export-Import Bank funds and otherwise improve U.S.-Argentine relations.[85] During 1978 the human rights situation in Argentina improved significantly. Figure 3 shows that the practice of disappearance as a tool of state policy was curtailed only after 1978, when the government began to take the "international variable" seriously.[86]

The value of the network perspective in the Argentine case is in highlighting the fact that international pressures did not work independently, but rather in coordination with national actors. Rapid change occurred because strong domestic human rights organizations documented abuses and protested against repression, and international pressures helped protect domestic monitors and open spaces for their protest. International groups amplified both information and symbolic politics of domestic groups and projected them onto an international stage, from which they echoed back into Argentina. This classic boomerang process was executed nowhere more skillfully than in Argentina, in large part due to the courage and ability of domestic human rights organizations.

Some argue that repression stopped because the military had finally killed all the people that they thought they needed to kill. This argument disregards disagreements within the regime about the size and nature of the "enemy." International pressures affected particular factions within

[83] Guest, *Behind the Disappearances*, pp. 118–19, 182–83.

[84] *Carta Política*, a news magazine considered to reflect the junta's views concluded in 1978 that "the principal problem facing the Argentine State has now become the international siege (cerco internacional)." "Cuadro de Situación," *Carta Política* 57 (August 1978): 8.

[85] Interviews with Walter Mondale, Minneapolis, Minnesota, 20 June 1989, and Ricardo Yofre, Buenos Aires, 1 August 1990.

[86] See Asamblea Permanente por los Derechos Humanos, *Las Cifras de la Guerra Sucia* (Buenos Aires, 1988), pp. 26–32.

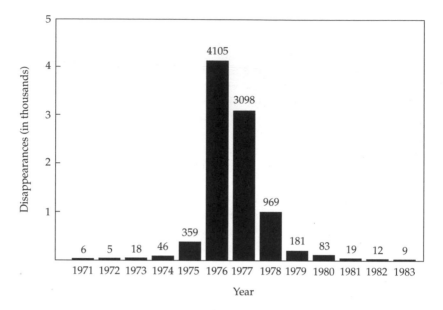

Figure 3. Disappearances in Argentina, 1971–1983. *Source*: Annex to the report of Nunca Mas (Never Again), published by the National Commission on Disappeared People, 1984.

the military regime that had differing ideas about how much repression was "necessary." Although by the military's admission 90 percent of the *armed* opposition had been eliminated by April 1977, this did not lead to an immediate change in human rights practices.[87] By 1978 there were splits within the military about what it should do in the future. One faction was led by Admiral Massera, a right-wing populist, another by Generals Carlos Suarez Mason and Luciano Menéndez, who supported indefinite military dictatorship and unrelenting war against the left, and a third by Generals Jorge Videla and Roberto Viola, who hoped for eventual political liberalization under a military president. Over time, the Videla-Viola faction won out, and by late 1978 Videla had gained increased control over the Ministry of Foreign Affairs, previously under the influence of

---

[87] According to a memorandum signed by General Jorge Videla, the objectives of the military government "go well beyond the simple defeat of subversion." The memorandum called for a continuation and intensification of the "general offensive against subversion," including "intense military action." "Directivo 504," 20 April 1977, in "La orden secreta de Videla," *Diario del Juicio* 28 (3 December 1985): 5–8.

the navy.[88] Videla's ascendancy in the fall of 1978, combined with U.S. pressure, helps explain his ability to deliver on his promise to allow the Inter-American Commission on Human Rights visit in December.

The Argentine military government thus moved from initial refusal to accept international human rights interventions, to cosmetic cooperation with the human rights network, and eventually to concrete improvements in response to increased international pressures. Once it had invited IACHR and discovered that the commission could not be co-opted or confused, the government ended the practice of disappearance, released political prisoners, and restored some semblance of political participation. Full restoration of human rights in Argentina did not come until after the Malvinas War and the transition to democracy in 1983, but after 1980 the worst abuses had been curtailed.

In 1985, after democratization, Argentina tried the top military leaders of the juntas for human rights abuses, and a number of key network members testified: Theo Van Boven and Patricia Derian spoke about international awareness of the Argentine human rights situation, and a member of the IACHR delegation to Argentina discussed the OAS report. Clyde Snow and Eric Stover provided information about the exhumation of cadavers from mass graves. Snow's testimony, corroborated by witnesses, was a key part of the prosecutor's success in establishing that top military officers were guilty of murder.[89] A public opinion poll taken during the trials showed that 92 percent of Argentines were in favor of the trials of the military juntas.[90] The tribunal convicted five of the nine defendants, though only two—ex-president Videla, and Admiral Massera— were given life sentences. The trials were the first of their kind in Latin America, and among the very few in the world ever to try former leaders for human rights abuses during their rule. In 1990 President Carlos Menem pardoned the former officers. By the mid-1990s, however, democratic rule in Argentina was firmly entrenched, civilian authority over the military was well established, and the military had been weakened by internal disputes and severe cuts in funding.[91]

The Argentine case set important precedents for other international and regional human rights action, and shows the intricate interactions of groups and individuals within the network and the repercussions of these interactions. The story of the Grandmothers of the Plaza de Mayo is

---

[88] David Rock, *Argentina, 1516–1987: From Spanish Colonization to Alfonsín* (Berkeley: University of California Press, 1985), pp. 370–71; Timerman, *Prisoner without a Name*, p. 163.

[89] *Diario del Juicio* 1 (27 May 1985), and 9 (23 July 1985).

[90] *Diario del Juicio* 25 (12 November 1985).

[91] Acuña and Smulovitz, "Adjusting the Armed Forces to Democracy," pp. 20–21.

an exemplar of network interaction and unanticipated effects. The persistence of the Grandmothers helped create a new profession—what one might call "human rights forensic science." (The scientific skills existed before, but they had never been put to the service of human rights.) Once the Argentine case had demonstrated that forensic science could illuminate mass murder and lead to convictions, these skills were diffused and legitimized. Eric Stover, Clyde Snow, and the Argentine forensic anthropology team they helped create were the prime agents of international diffusion. The team later carried out exhumations and training in Chile, Bolivia, Brazil, Venezuela, and Guatemala.[92] Forensic science is being used to prosecute mass murderers in El Salvador, Honduras, Rwanda, and Bosnia. By 1996 the UN International Criminal Tribunal for the former Yugoslavia had contracted with two veterans of the Argentine forensic experiment, Stover and Dr. Robert Kirschner, to do forensic investigations for its war crimes tribunal. "'A war crime creates a crime scene,' said Dr. Kirschner, 'That's how we treat it. We recover forensic evidence for prosecution and create a record which cannot be successfully challenged in court.'"[93]

Mexico

The political and human rights situation in Mexico was quite different from that of Argentina. Mexico's elected civilian government had been under the control of the official political party, the Institutionalized Revolutionary party (PRI), since the party was formed in 1929. Massive abuses of the kind that occurred in Argentina after the coup did not occur in Mexico, but abuses were nonetheless common.

The most serious episode occurred in October 1968, when army troops opened fire on a peaceful student demonstration in a central plaza in Mexico City, killing between three and five hundred students and wounding more than two thousand (see Preface). Although single violations of this magnitude did not recur, Mexican human rights organizations reported that approximately five hundred people disappeared in the 1970s, many in the context of a military counterinsurgency campaign against a guerrilla movement.[94] The police routinely used torture to extract confessions from both common and political prisoners; prison con-

---

[92] Cohen Salama, *Tumbas anónimas*, p. 275.

[93] Mike O'Connor, "Harvesting Evidence in Bosnia's Killing Fields," *New York Times*, 7 April 1996, p. E3.

[94] Committee in Defense of Prisoners, the Persecuted, Disappeared Persons, and Political Exiles, "Diez Años de Lucha por la Libertad," 1987, as cited in Americas Watch, *Human Rights in Mexico: A Policy of Impunity* (New York: Human Rights Watch, 1990), p. 35.

ditions were often abysmal; and electoral fraud and press censorship were commonplace.[95] In spite of this record, virtually no international attention was directed to the Mexican human rights situation in the 1970s and early 1980s. The international human rights network which had come into existence by the mid-1970s did not take up the Mexican case, as the more serious violations in Central America and the Southern Cone occupied all its attention. Keeping Mexico off the network's agenda were the existence of an elected civilian government, Mexico's progressive stance on international human rights (it became, for example, a haven for political refugees from Pinochet's Chile, and later a firm critic of human rights violations in El Salvador), and the absence of Mexican human rights organizations.

Mexico had taken a position of firm rhetorical support for the human rights efforts of international organizations, and cultivated its image as a defender of human rights. Mexico argued, however, that the UN's mandate was only to look into massive, systematic rights violations where domestic legal recourse was unavailable.[96] Mexico's verbal support for international norms and the international community's supervision of human rights practices was coupled with a failure to address its own human rights violations.

This situation began to change in the mid- to late 1980s when human rights consciousness began to penetrate Mexican civil society. In 1984 only four human rights NGOs existed in Mexico; seven years later there were sixty, and by 1993 there were more than two hundred.

International attention helped create the political space within which this growth was possible.[97] A key turning point came when Amnesty International activist Mariclaire Acosta and a group of prestigious Mexican intellectuals, activists, and politicians set up the Mexican Academy for Human Rights in 1984. The academy focused attention on human rights issues in Mexico, trained human rights practitioners, and fostered research and education. Its founders explicitly designed the academy as an academic institution rather than an activist group, hoping to provide a forum for the human rights debate in Mexico without confronting the government on specific issues.[98] The academy received strong support from the Ford Foundation, which provided the bulk of its funding during

[95] Ibid., p. 1.

[96] Statement by the Chief of the Mexican Delegation, Mr. Claude Heller, on theme 12 of the agenda in the 44th period of session of the Commission of Human Rights, Geneva, 8 March 1988, p. 1, 3 (mimeo, trans. by author).

[97] Jonathan Fox and Luis Hernández, "Mexico's Difficult Democracy: Grassroots Movements, NGOs, and Local Government," *Alternatives* 17 (1992): 184–85; Human Rights Watch, *Human Rights Watch World Report* (New York: Human Rights Watch, 1993), p. 131.

[98] Interview with Rodolfo Stavenhagen (founding member of the academy), Buenos Aires, 26 October 1992.

its first five years.[99] The 1985 earthquake in Mexico City spurred the growth of independent organizations in Mexico, and fueled concern with human rights. The discovery of the bodies of several prisoners who had apparently been tortured, during the excavation of the headquarters of the office of the Federal District Attorney General, stirred national outrage.[100] Furthermore, when the Mexican government was paralyzed in its response to the earthquake, civil society organized and international NGOs and funders stepped in to clean up. This collaboration broke down old assumptions in Mexico that all political activity must be channeled through the state, and created new confidence in the capacity of the NGO sector.[101]

The next stage began when the international human rights NGOs first addressed the Mexican situation. With the wave of redemocratization in the hemisphere, human rights had improved in many countries that previously had been targets of the network. Network members could now focus attention on the more ambiguous situations involving endemic violations under formally elected governments. The first reports by an international nongovernmental human rights organization came when Americas Watch released a 1984 report on Mexico's treatment of Guatemalan refugees, and Amnesty International issued a 1986 report on rural violence in Mexico.[102] (When the AI researchers first visited Mexico they found no human rights official in the government or human rights NGO to contact.) Although these reports upset the Mexican government because they breached its carefully cultivated image as a defender of human rights,[103] government practices did not change.

Change did begin after 1988, however, when a changed domestic and international political context made human rights a more salient issue. The split of the ruling party, PRI, before the 1988 presidential election, led to a political challenge from the left in the form of the Democratic Revolutionary Party (PRD) led by Cuauhtémoc Cárdenas. Then in 1990 Mexico initiated discussions with the United States and Canada over a free trade agreement. Both of these situations made the Mexican government more sensitive to charges of human rights violations.

[99] This included an initial two-year grant of $150,000, and a follow-up grant of $375,000.
[100] Americas Watch, *Human Rights in Mexico*, pp. 9–10.
[101] Interview with Rodolfo Stavenhagen; telephone interview with Christopher Welna, 8 October 1992. On the importance of the earthquake in contributing to the growth of civil society, see Dan La Botz, *Democracy in Mexico: Peasant Rebellion and Political Reform* (Boston: South End Press, 1995), pp. 65–73.
[102] Americas Watch, "Guatemalan Refugees in Mexico: 1980–1984" (New York: Human Rights Watch, 1984); Amnesty International, *Mexico: Human Rights in Rural Areas* (London: Amnesty International, 1986).
[103] Interview with Sebastian Brett (AI researcher on Mexico), Santiago, Chile, 3 November 1992.

In 1990 Americas Watch issued a seminal report on human rights conditions in Mexico. After noting the Mexican government's careful cultivation of its pro-human rights image, the report documented killings, torture, and mistreatment by the police during criminal investigations; disappearances; election-related violence; violence related to land disputes; abuses against independent unions; and violations of freedom of the press—all abuses that, the report argued, had become institutionalized in Mexican society.[104] The Americas Watch report received coverage in the U.S. and Mexican press and attracted significant attention in Washington, where the initial negotiations for the North American Free Trade Agreement were under way.

Until 1990 the U.S. Congress had never held hearings on human rights in Mexico. Yet a few months after the Americas Watch Report was issued, such hearings took place in the subcommittees on Human Rights and International Organizations and on Western Hemisphere Affairs of the House of Representatives. In addition to testimony from the State Department, the subcommittees heard testimony from AI and Americas Watch.[105]

The Inter-American Commission on Human Rights did not accept any Mexican cases until 1989–90, when it took on three. Brought by members of a major opposition party, the National Action party (PAN), all three alleged that the PRI was responsible for electoral irregularities. The Mexican government adopted a rigid position that if a "State agreed to submit itself to international jurisdiction with respect to the election of its political bodies, a *State would cease to be sovereign*," and that any commission conclusion on elections would constitute an intervention, according to the OAS Charter.[106]

Given that the American Convention on Human Rights guaranteed the right to vote and be elected, the IACHR asserted the admissibility of the complaints and its own competence to decide issues related to elections. Taking into account the Mexican government's ratification of the American convention, its failure to express reservations at that point with regard to the issue of elections, and the shared understandings and practices of other states in the region, the IACHR concluded that the Mexican position was unfounded, and it recommended that the Mexican government reform its internal electoral law to make effective the political

[104] Americas Watch, *Human Rights in Mexico*, p. 1.
[105] "Current Developments in Mexico," hearing before the Subcommittees on Human Rights and International Organizations, and on Western Hemisphere Affairs, of the Committee on Foreign Affairs, House of Representatives, 101st Congress, 2d sess., 12 September 1990 (Washington, D.C.: U.S. Government Printing Office, 1990).
[106] Organization of American States, *Annual Report of the Inter-American Commission on Human Rights 1989–1990* (Washington, D.C.: OAS General Secretariat, 1990), pp. 103–5 (emphasis added).

rights of the convention.[107] In other words, the IACHR underscored a quite different interpretation of sovereignty from that of the Mexican government, which it justified by reference to the shared understandings and practices of other states in the region, and to previous Mexican government actions that created precedents constraining its future options.

Under pressure from the IACHR, domestic political parties, and human rights organizations, and in response to the widespread allegations of fraud in the 1988 elections, the Mexican government entered into negotiations with political parties in 1990, and began to modify electoral laws and procedures.

In June 1990 the Mexican government created the National Commission on Human Rights.[108] The administration of Carlos Salinas de Gortari was concerned that Mexico might be subject to heightened scrutiny from both the U.S. administration and Congress in the context of future free trade negotiations and subsequent ratification debates.[109] Both President Salinas and his successor, Ernesto Zedillo, have been sensitive to Mexico's external image and to the international repercussions of domestic human rights complaints, sometimes taking preemptive measures to project the image of their concern with human rights. Engaging in electoral reform and creating the National Commission on Human Rights defused the issue by making it appear that the Mexican government had its problems under control.

That Mexico's national commission was a response to international pressure is underscored by the timing of its creation, and by the fact that its reports were published simultaneously in Spanish and English and shipped via international express mail to representatives of key human rights organizations in the United States. Three events converged shortly before the commission's creation. Norma Corona Sapien, a leading human rights activist, was murdered on 21 May 1990 after spearheading an investigation that concluded that federal judicial police were responsible for earlier killings. Also in May 1990, the IACHR rendered a decision finding Mexico in violation of the OAS American Convention on Human Rights. Finally, the Americas Watch report came out in June, just days before Salinas and President George Bush were to announce their intention to begin negotiations for a U.S.-Mexican free trade agreement. To pre-

---

[107] *Annual Report of the Inter-American Commission on Human Rights 1989–1990*, pp. 106–23.

[108] Jorge Luis Sierra Guzmán et al., *La Comisión Nacional de Derechos Humanos: Una visión no gubernamental* (Mexico, D.F.: Comisión Mexicana de Defensa y Promoción de los Derechos Humanos, 1992), p. 1.

[109] According to Denise Dresser, "foremost among the priorities of Salinas's foreign policy is the avoidance of diplomatic conflicts that might sabotage Mexico's shared economic interests with the U.S." "Mr. Salinas Goes to Washington: Mexican Lobbying in the United States," conference paper 62, presented at the research conference, "Crossing National Borders: Invasion or Involvement," Columbia University, 6 December 1991, p. 5.

empt negative publicity about Mexican human rights practices, President Salinas established the National Human Rights Commission four days before the meeting with Bush.[110]

Although the commission has been criticized for lacking sufficient independence from the government to serve as a watchdog agency,[111] evidence suggests that in many cases it has been an effective advocate for human rights.[112] Since its formation the Mexican government has approved procedures to prevent the use of evidence from confessions in trials, a practice which had led to routine use of torture during interrogation after arrests.[113] Also, the commission has investigated and denounced conditions in some of the country's worst prisons.[114]

During the peasant uprising in Chiapas in 1994 it became clear that the government could no longer control information as it had in 1968. The guerrillas, the Zapatista National Liberation Army (EZLN), "demonstrated a sophisticated awareness of the international press and other transnational actors."[115] The press and domestic and international NGOs monitored the conflict closely, and electronic mail became one of the main mechanisms through which the EZLN communicated with the world. Faced with a much greater perceived threat to national security than the students had posed in 1968, the Mexican government acted with much greater restraint and opted for a political solution in Chiapas because it was now "accountable to constituencies beyond its borders" which had "raised the political costs of repression." The events in Chiapas in turn "opened up a window of opportunity for domestic and foreign actors in favor of democracy," by forcing the government to engage in more significant electoral reform.[116] Governmental, intergovernmental, and nongovernmental election observers helped guarantee that the 1994 elections were relatively free of fraud (thus paradoxically legitimizing the PRI victory).

In summary, we can divide the Mexican case into three historical stages, each of which provides some evidence for our argument that ad-

[110] Ellen L. Lutz, "Human Rights in Mexico: Cause for Continuing Concern," *Current History* 92 (February 1993): 79.

[111] Emilio Krieger, "Prólogo," in Sierra Guzmán et al., *La Comisión Nacional de Derechos Humanos*, p. ix.

[112] Ellen Lutz discusses the commission's "hard-hitting recommendations in over 300 cases," many of which included cases that have been the focus of NGOs. "Human Rights in Mexico," p. 80.

[113] "Mexico: Human Rights Come to the Fore," *Latin America Update*, Washington Office on Latin America (January–April 1991), pp. 1, 6.

[114] Americas Watch, *Prison Conditions in Mexico* (New York: Human Rights Watch, 1991), p. 46.

[115] Denise Dresser, "Treading Lightly and without a Big Stick: International Actors and the Promotion of Democracy in Mexico," in *Beyond Sovereignty: Collectively Defending Democracy in the Americas*, ed. Tom Farer (Baltimore: Johns Hopkins University Press, 1996), p. 334.

[116] Ibid., pp. 334–35.

vocacy networks helped improve human rights practices. During the first stage, in 1968–69, the massacre of students in Mexico City provoked no sustained international response because the international human rights network did not yet exist. Even high levels of mobilization among students worldwide at that time did not produce any significant show of solidarity with their Mexican counterparts. During the second stage, from 1970 to 1988, lower-level endemic human rights abuses continued. Although the human rights network emerged during this period, it did not work on Mexico, and there was no condemnation of these practices, nor did the situation change. In the third stage, from 1988 to 1994, the international network in collaboration with recently formed domestic human rights groups, provoked a relatively rapid and forceful response from the Mexican government, contributing to a decline in human rights violations and a strengthening of democratic institutions.[117]

CONCLUSIONS

In this chapter we have argued that international human rights pressures can lead to changes in human rights practices, helping to transform understandings about the nature of a state's sovereign authority over its citizens. Although the cases of Argentina and Mexico are not sufficient to confirm this argument, the contrast between them provides substantiation for it and suggests it is worth further study.[118] The international human rights network has not always been effective in changing understandings or practices about human rights. In Latin America, for example, network activities failed to stem massive violations in Guatemala in the 1970s and 1980s, and endemic abuses in Colombia in the 1990s; elsewhere we might point to China and Cambodia. The central question then becomes, under what conditions can the international human rights network be effective? The cases suggest some possible answers.

In both Mexico and Argentina nongovernmental actors documented violations and raised global concern about them. Later, international and regional organizations produced reports building upon early NGO inves-

[117] Some observers give international pressures little credit for promoting democracy in Mexico, failing to take into account the international pressures and domestic changes in the post-1989 period that are the basis of the argument presented here. See, e.g., Lorenzo Meyer, "Mexico: The Exception and the Rule," in Abraham F. Lowenthal, ed., *Exporting Democracy: The United States and Latin America: Case Studies* (Baltimore: Johns Hopkins University Press, 1991), pp. 93–110.

[118] Cases similar to Argentina might include Uruguay and Chile. Mexico is unique, both for the lack of attention it received on human rights issues initially and for the rapidity of its subsequent response. Other cases of semidemocratic governments where international pressures have led to change include the Dominican Republic during the 1978 elections and, more recently, Paraguay.

tigations. NGOs also provided the information that served as the basis for altered governmental policies. Because domestic human rights NGOs are a crucial link in the network, where these groups are absent, as in Mexico initially, international human rights work is severely hampered.

Could foreign government pressure and domestic political pressure have changed human rights practices without the involvement of the advocacy network? In both cases foreign governments placed pressure on human rights violators only *after* nongovernmental actors had identified, documented, and denounced human rights violations, and had pressured foreign governments to become involved. Because repression in Argentina was secret, and the junta diplomatically skilled, the truth about human rights abuses there probably would have remained hidden without the detailed documentation and diffusion of information by the international network. In contrast to Chile, where television crews and embassy officials could attest to the scale of violations, uncovering the Argentine government's responsibility for disappearances required an intensive effort by many parts of the network working collectively, without which foreign governments could not have exerted diplomatic pressure on the Argentine government. The first such pressures followed the release, nearly a year after the coup, of the AI document detailing the Argentine government's responsibility for the practice of disappearances.

In the case of Mexico, foreign governments failed even to notice endemic human rights abuses there for almost two decades. Here we have an especially clear contrast between the situation before and after the network existed, and before and after it took up the Mexican case. When the network did not exist, there was virtually no international response to the massacre of students in 1968. Until the network began to work on Mexico the human rights situation there remained unknown internationally. Only after the nongovernmental organizations within and outside Mexico began to document human rights abuses and alert the press and policymakers (and only within the context of the free trade negotiations), did the Mexican government improve its human rights practices.

A network's existence and its decision to focus on abuses in a particular country is a necessary but not sufficient condition for changing human rights practices. Many argue that human rights pressures would not be effective against strong states that can impose significant costs on the states that pressure them. Network activists admit that they have been less effective against states that superpowers consider important to their national security interests: countries such as Saudi Arabia, Israel, Turkey, China, and Pakistan.[119] The vulnerability of the target state is thus a key factor in network effectiveness.

---

[119] Interview with Michael Posner, New York City, 19 March 1992.

One aspect of target vulnerability is the availability of leverage. The United States and European countries provided Mexico and Argentina substantial amounts of military and economic assistance and trade credits. In the case of Mexico, in addition, the United States and Canada were negotiating a free trade agreement that the Mexican government believed was necessary for further economic development. This gave the network many avenues for leverage, which it used quite skillfully, lobbying its several governments to limit, condition, or cut aid, and arguing against trade credits or agreements until human rights goals were met.

What is often missed in the debate over the apparent "failure" of human rights policy in China is that virtually none of the classic military and economic levers exist. As a result, the human rights network has been forced to advocate a fairly drastic policy of revoking "most favored nation" (MFN) trading status. Even the most forceful efforts to constrain Latin American military regimes never resorted to this mechanism, and there is no consensus in the United States over the use of MFN for human rights purposes. Furthermore, human rights and democracy leaders in China have been divided on the question of limiting trade for human rights purposes because many believe that increasing China's economic openness would ultimately stimulate political openness. The Chinese case is negative substantiation for the argument presented here: a weak, repressed, and divided domestic movement, combined with little possibility for leverage politics, constitutes exactly the conditions under which we would *not* expect successful human rights pressures.

But small or weak countries that are vulnerable targets will not necessarily be more amenable to international network pressures. Haiti and Guatemala, for example, resisted international human rights pressures for a longer time than did larger countries like Mexico and Argentina. In the realm of human rights, it is the combination of moral and material pressure that leads to change. Transforming state practices has come about from linking principled ideas to material goals: military aid, economic aid, and trade benefits. Significant material pressure may be ineffective, however, where leaders are unconcerned with the normative message. Pressures are eventually most effective against states that have internalized the norms of the human rights regime and resist being characterized as pariahs. Although this is difficult to ascertain, certain aspects of national identity or discourse may make some states vulnerable to pressures. In the case of Argentina, a liberal tradition, a national identity focused on European culture, and military justification of repression as a defense of "Western and Christian civilization" made it more difficult for the government to ignore criticism of international actors. Recently some Asian states have successfully resisted international human rights pressures by attempting to create a new national identity linked to traditional beliefs—the so-called Asian values—which rejects the rights discourse by counterposing values that stress communities rather than individuals and duties rather than rights. Most Latin American countries, with a longer liberal tradition, have a harder time articulating a legitimate counter-discourse to the discourse of human rights.

Effective human rights networking does not imply a simple victory of norms over interests. The networks were influential within states because they helped to shape a reformulation of how national interest was understood at times when global events were calling into question traditional understandings of sovereignty and national interest. Especially during a period of profound global flux, foreign policymakers are often uncertain not only about what the national interest is, but also about how best to promote it. Advocacy networks have served effectively as carriers of human rights ideas, inserting them into the policy debate at crucial moments when policymakers were questioning past policy models.

A realist approach to international relations would have trouble attributing significance either to the network's activities or to the adoption and implementation of state human rights policies. Realism offers no convincing explanation for why relatively weak nonstate actors could affect state policy, or why states would concern themselves with the internal human rights practices of other states even when doing so interferes with the pursuit of other goals. For example, the U.S. government's pressure on Argentina on human rights led Argentina to defect from the grain embargo of the Soviet Union. Raising human rights issues with Mexico could have undermined the successful completion of the free trade agreement and cooperation with Mexico on antidrug operations. Human rights pressures have costs, even in strategically less important countries of Latin America.

In liberal versions of international relations theory, states and nonstate actors cooperate to realize joint gains or avoid mutually undesirable outcomes when they face problems they cannot resolve alone. These situations have been characterized as cooperation or coordination games with particular payoff structures.[120] But human rights issues are not easily modeled as such. Usually states can ignore the internal human rights practices of other states without incurring undesirable economic or security costs.

In the issue of human rights it is primarily principled ideas that drive change and cooperation. We cannot understand why countries, organizations, and individuals are concerned about human rights or why countries respond to human rights pressures without taking into account the

---

[120] See, e.g., Arthur A. Stein, "Coordination and Collaboration: Regimes in an Anarchic World," *International Organization* 36:2 (Spring 1982): 299–324.

role of norms and ideas in international life. Jack Donnelly has argued that such moral interests are as real as material interests, and that a sense of moral interdependence has led to the emergence of human rights regimes.[121] For human rights, as for the other issues in this book, the primary movers behind this form of principled international action are international networks.

---

[121] Donnelly, *Universal Human Rights*, pp. 211–12.

CHAPTER 4

Environmental Advocacy Networks

Environmental advocacy networks differ in important respects from the human rights networks discussed in the preceding chapter. For one thing, they are not as clearly "principled." Though environmentalism has a strong ethical dimension, in the traditional anthropocentric sense of "stewardship" or in biocentric claims in the name of an earth ethic, actors in environmental advocacy networks may invoke professional norms or interests as well as values. Environmentalism is less a set of universally agreed upon principles than it is a frame within which the relations among a variety of claims about resource use, property, rights, and power may be reconfigured. A good example, discussed below, is the environmentalist campaign around secure land use rights for traditional forest dwellers. When network actors have different medium- or long-term agendas, networks can become sites for negotiating over which goals, strategies, and ethical understandings are compatible. Because transnational advocacy networks normally involve people and organizations in structurally unequal positions, this negotiation is always politically sensitive.

Since environmentalists are often talking about public goods such as clean water or air rather than recognized "rights," they have a harder time giving their campaigns a human face—and must choose whether to do so. Environmental issues are treated in a wide range of institutional arenas. How activists frame an environmental conflict may determine its institutional location as well as the receptivity of target audiences. Urban pollution issues are often framed in terms of public health; Brazilian rubber tappers recast a land conflict into one over forest conservation. Despite its obvious disadvantages, jurisdictional confusion rewards entrepreneurship; venue shifting is especially common in this issue area.

For the state that is the ultimate target, stakes may be quite high (and multilayered). All advocacy networks challenge boundaries: human rights activity challenges state sovereignty, and international protests around violence against women demand public intervention in private social relations and challenge cultural norms. International environmental campaigns generally raise claims about property (public and private) and sovereignty, involving substantial economic costs and thorny domestic political conflicts.

ORIGINS OF ENVIRONMENTAL NETWORKS

Transnational environmental networking has a long history. Naturalists at the turn of the century corresponded to promote early conventions protecting migratory birds. After the Second World War the International Union for the Conservation of Nature and Natural Resources (IUCN), a hybrid organization that includes in its membership states and government agencies and also nongovernmental organizations, often served as a clearinghouse for international projects.[1] When the UN was formed, environmental problems fell under different agencies, with little coordination. The UN Educational, Scientific, and Cultural Organization (UNESCO), created in 1946, was formed to promote educational and scientific activities as well as collaboration among specialists and NGOs.[2] It was particularly instructed to work with the International Council of Scientific Unions (ICSU), a scientific coordinating body created after the First World War, whose Scientific Committee on Problems of the Environment (SCOPE) was created in 1969.

By the end of the 1960s, environmental experts agreed on the need for stronger institutions of international collaboration. The 1968 Biosphere conference[3] recommended action by governments and the UN system. The biosphere idea provided one model for a shift in the ideational basis of the conservation movement—one that promoted greater international collaboration and sought greater understanding of human activities.[4]

[1] Founded in 1948 with 18 state members and 107 conservation organizations, by 1990 the IUCN included 62 states, 114 government agencies, and 436 NGOs.

[2] J. Eric Smith, "The Role of Special Purpose and Nongovernmental Organizations in the Environmental Crisis," *International Organization* special issue on "International Institutions and the Environmental Crisis," ed. David A. Kay and Eugene B. Skolnikoff, 26:2 (Spring 1972): 308.

[3] Intergovernmental Conference of Experts on a Scientific Basis for a Rational Use and Conservation of the Resources of the Biosphere.

[4] "Biosphere" refers to the domain of life—a region whose prevailing conditions enable incoming solar radiation to produce the geochemical changes needed for life to occur. Since matter and energy change their form during evolution, all living matter is ultimately genetically connected throughout geologic time. See Lynton Keith Caldwell, *International Environmental Policy*, 2d ed. (Durham, N.C.: Duke University Press, 1990), pp. 25–28; and Peter Haas, *Saving the Mediterranean: The Politics of International Environmental Cooperation* (New York: Columbia University Press, 1990), pp. 19–25.

UNESCO's Man and the Biosphere Program, begun in 1971, was intended to stimulate such collaboration.

In 1968 Sweden introduced a resolution calling for a UN-sponsored conference on the human environment, which it offered to host. Sparked by Sweden's concern with transboundary acid rain from European industry, the conference was "to focus attention of governments and public opinion on the importance and urgency of this question, and also to identify those aspects of it that can only or best be solved through international cooperation and agreement." The result was the 1972 UN Conference on the Human Environment in Stockholm. As the conference was highly politicized from the outset, the role of NGOs was enhanced: the UN wanted their input without alienating their governments, and offered facilities for a concurrent environmental forum of NGOs.[5]

This first NGO forum parallel to a UN official conference pioneered a transnational process that would become absolutely central to the formation and strengthening of advocacy networks around the world. As it developed, the NGO forum format led to dialogue, conflict, creativity, and synergy. The face-to-face contact helped activists from different backgrounds and countries recognize commonalities and establish the trust necessary to sustain more distant network contacts after the conference was over.

To the consternation of those seeking more international collaboration, the Stockholm conference highlighted divisions between more and less developed countries on the relationship between environment and development. In the wake of decolonization, the new southern majority in the UN General Assembly had promoted an assertive pro-development agenda with the formation of the Group of 77 as a developing country bloc and with proposals for a "New International Economic Order".[6] After the gloomy projections of such world modeling experiments as the Club of Rome's 1972 report, *The Limits to Growth*, however, environmentalists seemed inalterably opposed to improvement in third world standards of living.[7] Concurrent attempts to theorize about ecologically responsible development models got little attention in developed countries. When preparations for Stockholm revealed the extent of north–south polarization, conference secretary-general Maurice Strong convoked a commission of experts to produce a report on the relationship between

[5] Anne Thompson Feraru, "Transnational Political Interests and the Global Environment," *International Organization* 28:1 (Winter 1974): 31–60.
[6] See Stephen D. Krasner, *Structural Conflict* (Berkeley: University of California Press, 1985).
[7] Donella H. Meadows, Dennis L. Meadows, Jorgen Randers, and William W. Behrens III, *The Limits to Growth* (New York: New American Library, 1972). See discussion in John McCormick, *Reclaiming Paradise: The Global Environmental Movement* (Bloomington: Indiana University Press, 1989), pp. 75–78.

environment and development; the resulting Founex report prefigured by almost a decade much of the 1980s discussion of sustainable development.[8]

But even for 1972, the "north–south" characterization of the divide was too simplistic. The internationalist Swedish position contrasted with a U.S. position that actively resisted linkages between environment and development. The Swedes argued that redistribution of global resources was not just a moral imperative but a realistic response to the obvious limits to growth. They pledged $5 million over five years toward the $100 million target for an Environment fund, and asked nations to make contributions in addition to other development assistance. During the preparations for Stockholm, the U.S. voted against a resolution that environmental protection not be allowed to pose a threat to third world development, the State Department arguing that the resolution "introduced developmental issues extraneous to the main purpose of the conference, which was to focus world attention on the global problems of the human environment."[9] Under attack for what Swedish prime minister Olaf Palme called "ecocide" in Vietnam and Southeast Asia, the U.S. sought as far as possible to bar "political" issues from the Stockholm agenda.

In contrast to these divisions among developed countries, third world states seemed unified on substance. Vying for leadership roles at the conference, delegations from India, Brazil, and newly admitted China stressed poverty as the great polluter and development as the solution. "How can we speak to those who live in villages or slums about keeping the oceans, the rivers and the air clean" asked Indira Gandhi, "when their own lives are contaminated at the source?"[10] Stressing sovereignty over resources and development, delegates from China and Brazil accused the industrialized north of using environmental arguments to try to keep developing countries subordinate.[11] This apparent unity of developing countries masked a more complex reality: Brazil's military government, for example, which so eloquently pleaded the cause of poor nations in the international arena, was simultaneously presiding over one of the most significant income redistributions from poor to rich in the country's history.

[8] UN General Assembly, "Development and Environment: Report by the Secretary-General," A/CONF.48/10 (22 December 1971), reprinted as a special issue of *International Conciliation* 586 (January 1972).

[9] U.S. Department of State, *U.S. Participation in the U.N., 1971* (Washington, D.C.: U.S. Government Printing Office, 1972), Publication 8675, p. 117, cited in Deborah L. Guber, "The U.S. at Stockholm: Putting Politics above Progress," unpublished paper, Yale University, 1992.

[10] Marcus F. Franda, "Mrs. Gandhi Goes to Stockholm," *South Asia Series* 16:10 (1972): 2, cited in Wendy Weiser, "The Position of India at Stockholm," unpublished paper, Yale University, 1992.

[11] João Augusto de Araujo Castro, "Environment and Development: The Case of the Developing Countries," *International Organization* 26:2 (Spring 1972): 401–16.

Defining the conflict over environment and development in north–south terms portrays nation-states (and economic agents associated with them) as unitary actors in the international arena. This is a strategic image that states, and sometimes nonstate actors as well, deploy in particular kinds of international arenas. However, although structural inequality plays a constitutive role in the identities of developing and developed country actors, it is only one of the factors that shape those identities. Values, principles, and shared experiences help relationships to develop that cut across the north–south antimony for both state and non-state actors.

The Stockholm conference sparked the creation of institutions around which transnational environmental networks would mobilize. It was also a landmark in the evolution of ideas about the relationship between environment and development, marking an ideational shift that brought new actors and issues into environmental debates. Attended by representatives of 114 governments, the conference signaled that the environment was a legitimate concern for the international community. Besides producing declarations and recommendations, the conference led to the establishment of the UN Environmental Program (UNEP).

During the 1970s and early 1980s few environmental organizations developed independent strategies around global issues. The International Union for the Conservation of Nature continued to promote collaboration among conservationists and coordinate information exchange through publications and regular conferences, working in tandem with the World Wildlife Fund (WWF). The IUCN's hybrid character gave it special access to international policy-making; recalling its role at Stockholm, the organization's director general estimated that 95% of national delegations included an active IUCN member.[12] The organizations of scientists and conservationists formed an "epistemic community" around a variety of environmental issues,[13] providing many of the links that brought scientists together in conferences, in joint research, and, increasingly, in policy advocacy.

Conservationists spent the decade after Stockholm developing a response to the environment vs. development debate. In March 1980, the IUCN, World Wildlife Fund, and United Nations Environment Program launched a joint World Conservation Strategy at simultaneous ceremonies in thirty countries. Recognizing that "the separation of conservation from development . . . [is] at the root of current living problems,"

---

[12] Lee Talbot, "From the D.G.'s Desk," *IUCN Bulletin* 13:4–6 (April–June 1982): 31.

[13] Peter Haas defines epistemic community as "transnational networks of knowledge-based communities that are both politically empowered through their claims to exercise authoritative knowledge and motivated by shared causal and principled beliefs." See "Do Regimes Matter: Epistemic Communities and Mediterranean Pollution Control," *International Organization* 43 (Summer 1989): 377–403.

IUCN's Robert Allan told journalists at the launching ceremonies that "too often we assume that people are destroying the environment because they are ignorant, when in fact they have no other choice."[14] The groups' strategy included suggestions for national legislative reforms and conservation goals. It introduced the idea of "sustainable development," later in the decade popularized in the report of the World Commission on Environment and Development as "development that meets the needs of the present without compromising the ability of future generations to meet their own needs."[15]

Changes in ideas about the relationship between development and environmental protection encouraged more participation by actors in developing countries—state actors, local scientists and conservationists, and other agents promoting social change. The resulting multiplicity of voices, views of development, and understandings of the relationship between human beings and nature increased through the action of a new set of players in the international environmental field—transnational advocacy networks—that emerged in the early 1980s and addressed themselves both to national and international institutions and broader international publics. Their advocacy went well beyond the traditional conservation agenda; increasingly, defenders of nature had to come to terms with the need to defend also the rights of peoples.

THE INSTITUTIONAL CONTEXT

International treatment of environmental issues is more recent and less bounded than treatment of human rights issues. Increasing numbers of diverse intergovernmental organizations are involved with the environment, with frequently overlapping mandates. The UN Environmental Program, established in 1972, is the main environmental intergovernmental organization, but has less money, staff, and institutional history than other UN agencies that consider themselves better equipped to deal with environmental issues, such as the UN Development Program (UNDP), and the Food and Agriculture Organization (FAO).[16] Although UNEP was the lead UN agency in most of the major environmental conventions of the 1970s and 1980s, other agencies produced codes of conduct and other

---

[14] Joanne Omang, "Conservation Strategy Mapped by 30 Nations," *Washington Post*, 6 March 1980, p. A13 (from Nexis).

[15] World Commission on Environment and Development, *Our Common Future* (Oxford: Oxford University Press, 1987), p. 43.

[16] See McCormick, *Reclaiming Paradise*, pp. 106–24; Gareth Porter and Janet Welsh Brown, *Global Environmental Politics* (Boulder, Colo: Westview Press, 1991), pp. 46–53; and Lynton Keith Caldwell, *International Environmental Policy*, 2d ed. (Durham, N.C.: Duke University Press, 1990), pp. 71–83.

normative instruments; for example, the 1986 International Code of Conduct on the Distribution and Use of Pesticides was drafted by the FAO. UNEP has played a subsidiary role on the tropical forest issue, with major initiatives taken by other UN agencies and the World Bank.

Specialized intergovernmental treaty organizations such as the International Whaling Commission (IWC), the Antarctic Treaty Consultative Parties, and the International Tropical Timber Organization (ITTO) structure relations between governments and NGOs around particular issues. The IWC, for example, was created in 1946 by the International Convention for the Regulation of Whaling, at the initiative of the United States. Like its predecessor agreements, the convention was a nonbinding instrument; any member state could escape from an IWC provision by giving notice within ninety days. The commission was made up of one representative from each state that was party to the convention, and was not limited to whaling states, a factor that in the 1980s facilitated a normative transition in the organization. Whaling became a major rallying point for environmental NGOs in the late 1970s and 1980s, involving Friends of the Earth, Greenpeace, and many other organizations in campaigns that generated wide media attention; these groups recognized the strategic opportunity provided by the convention's structure, and lobbied nonwhaling states to join the treaty organization.[17] The success of the whaling campaign encouraged environmental NGOs to develop strategies around other treaty organizations.

Multilateral development banks, especially the World Bank, have become important actors on environmental questions. Since the early 1970s the World Bank has considered itself a leader among multilateral agencies in this area.[18] It created an environmental unit in 1971, and in 1974 its executive directors adopted a principle of environmental lending. In 1980 the World Bank and UNEP promoted adoption by the major development banks and multilateral agencies of a "Declaration of Environmental Policies and Procedures Relating to Economic Development."[19] Beginning with Robert McNamara, World Bank presidents have stated repeatedly their commitment to sustainable development. Although in practice environmental considerations have rarely played a significant role in lending policy, the bank's normative commitment offered an opportunity that environmental advocacy groups were later to seize.

---

[17] Peter J. Stoett, *Atoms, Whales, and Rivers: Global Environmental Security and International Organization* (Commack, N.Y.: Nova Science Publishers, 1995), chapter 5.

[18] Philippe Le Prestre, *The World Bank and the Environmental Challenge* (Selinsgrove, Pa.: Susquehanna University Press, 1989).

[19] The following organizations joined in the declaration: African Development Bank, Arab Bank for Economic Development of Africa, Asian Development Bank, Caribbean Development Bank, Inter-American Development Bank, World Bank, the Commission of the European Communities, the Organization of American States, the UNDP, and UNEP.

THE RISE OF ADVOCACY ORGANIZATIONS

In the middle and late 1980s the mass media began to pay increased attention to international environmental issues. The Bhopal and Chernobyl disasters, the discovery in the mid-1980s of a hole in the ozone layer over the Antarctic, and developing scientific consensus over the risk of global climate change associated with augmented concentrations of "greenhouse" gases like CO_2 and methane, all contributed to a widened public interest in the global environment.

In the second half of the 1980s membership in the major U.S. environmental organizations grew rapidly. During this period in which computers became widely used, all major environmental organizations began to employ direct mail techniques for fundraising and managing membership lists.[20] Though the data does not support a causal linkage here, some of the most rapid growth occurred in organizations most associated with global campaigns.[21] Between 1985 and 1990 membership in the Environmental Defense Fund (EDF) doubled, then doubled again between 1990 and 1991. The Natural Resources Defense Council (NRDC) grew 2.7 times between 1985 and 1990, as did the Nature Conservancy. The World Wildlife Fund–US grew 5.6 times, and Greenpeace more than doubled (from 400,000 to 850,000.). Total membership of ten organizations for which continuous data are available grew from 4,198,000 in 1976 to 5,816,000 in 1986 and 8,270,000 in 1990.[22]

Some of these organizations brought new, more confrontational approaches into the environmentalist repertoire, ranging from the litigation and regulatory negotiation approaches of the NRDC and EDF to the Quaker-inspired witness and direct action approach of Greenpeace. Greenpeace and Friends of the Earth (FOE) employed creative combinations of

[20] Robert Cameron Mitchell, Angela G. Mertig, and Riley E. Dunlap, "Twenty Years of Environmental Mobilization: Trends among National Environmental Organizations," in *American Environmentalism: The U.S. Environmental Movement, 1970–1990*, ed. Angela G. Mertig and Riley E. Dunlap (Philadelphia: Taylor and Francis, 1992), pp. 11–25.

[21] No causal linkage can be inferred because these same organizations were among the most active domestically; indeed, international activities take up a fraction of their staff time. Without a careful analysis of returns to particular direct mail appeals, it is impossible to say which new members responded to domestically oriented or internationally oriented mailings. It is worth noting that for most U.S. environmental NGOs, "membership" denotes contributors, but does not imply participation in decision-making.

[22] The ten organizations are: The Environmental Defense Fund, Friends of the Earth, The Izaak Walton League of America, The National Audubon Society, The National Parks and Conservation Association, The National Wildlife Federation, Natural Resources Defense Council, The Nature Conservancy, The Wilderness Society, and The World Wildlife Fund–US. Data from National Wildlife Federation, *The Conservation Directory* (Washington, D.C.: National Wildlife Federation, 1976, 1982, 1986, 1990). Data for 1976 on the National Audubon Society come from Thaddeus C. Trzyna and Eugene V. Coan, eds., *World Directory of Environmental Organizations* (Claremont, Calif.: Public Affairs Clearinghouse, 1976).

confrontation, lobbying, and other institutional strategies in the whale campaigns of the late 1970s and early 1980s. These and other advocacy and direct action groups were increasingly impatient with the longstanding IUCN persuasion strategy of linking scientists and policymakers.

Greenpeace and FOE were both conceived from the outset as international organizations, albeit decentralized ones. Both grew from the social activism of the late 1960s and early 1970s, with its critique of materialism and its appreciation of nature.[23] Greenpeace, founded in Vancouver in 1971, focused its protests during the 1970s on nuclear test sites and whaling, sending small boats into U.S. or French nuclear test areas or into direct confrontations with Japanese or Soviet whaling ships. By 1985, when the French intelligence service blew up Greenpeace's ship the *Rainbow Warrior* in Auckland harbor in New Zealand, the organization had offices in seventeen countries and a total membership of around 1.2 million; its 1992-93 annual report claimed 1,330 people working in 43 offices in 30 countries, with over 5 million supporters in 158 countries. Friends of the Earth, formed in 1969 in the United States, was intended from the beginning as an international organization. By the early 1980s FOE had organizations in 25 countries; in 1996 that number was up to 54.[24]

Besides the international NGOs, many national organizations have small but active international programs. Members of the international divisions of the National Wildlife Federation, the Natural Resources Defense Council, the Environmental Policy Institute, and Environmental Defense Fund were core initiators in 1983-84 of the NGO campaign to make multilateral banks more environmentally responsible, with early support from other organizations. Their contacts in developing countries were often with multi-issue development NGOs rather than with environmental organizations—linkages that highlighted relationships among environmental, human rights, and development issues.[25]

In developing countries as well, social movements and NGOs concerned with the environment multiplied rapidly during the 1980s, influenced by the spread of environmentalist ideas and by nationally specific historical circumstances. In Latin America, the wave of democratic transitions in the 1980s provided fertile ground for new organizations of all

[23] Robert Paelke, *Environmentalism and the Future of Progressive Politics* (New Haven: Yale University Press, 1989).

[24] Robin Morgan and Brian Whitaker, *Rainbow Warrior* (London: Arrow Books, 1986), pp. 120–21, cited in McCormick, *Reclaiming Paradise*, p. 145; Tom Burke, "Friends of the Earth and the Conservation of Resources," in *Pressure Groups in the Global System*, ed. Peter Willetts (New York: St. Martin's Press, 1982), pp. 104–24. Current figures for Greenpeace and FOE were obtained from the Worldwide Web home pages of Greenpeace International and FOE–US, December 1996.

[25] See Barbara J. Bramble and Gareth Porter, "NGO Influence on United States Environmental Politics Abroad," in *The International Politics of the Environment*, ed. Andrew Hurrell and Benedict Kingsbury (Oxford: Oxford University Press, 1992).

kinds. Older conservation organizations were joined by new urban and rural movements with different approaches to the relationships between development goals and their social and environmental consequences. The period of democratization also saw the birth or expansion of many professionalized grassroots support organizations, eventually referred to as NGOs.[26] The spread of NGOs accompanied the worldwide crisis of and disaffection with the left, as socially concerned activists sought other vehicles by which to "make a difference."

Advocacy NGOs in South and Southeast Asia followed upon a long tradition of communitiy organizations and NGOs formed to work among the poor. In the mid-1970s, disenchanted with conventional approaches to development, advocacy groups began to work to support communities' efforts to empower themselves, claim rights, and espouse alternative conceptions of development. Many believed that an environmentally sound use of resources was integral to this process. In some countries these efforts seemed increasingly to depend on democratization of political institutions.[27] In 1983, a directory published by the environmental organization Sahabat Alam Malaysia of environmental NGOs in the Asia-Pacific region listed 162 organizations.

Until the early 1980s few environmental NGOs had the time or money for international networking. To share resources, NGO lobbying and information bureaus were established to monitor the activities of UN agencies and the European Economic Community.[28] IUCN membership also provided access to information, and many NGOs sought and won consultative status before relevant UN agencies. Parallel NGO meetings have taken place at all major UN environmental events since Stockholm, as activists tried to persuade governments to address problems they viewed as pressing. But by the middle of the 1980s many NGOs were frustrated with the limitations of these arenas.[29] A growing number of or-

[26] On NGOs in Latin America, see Thomas Carroll, *Intermediary NGOs: The Supporting Link in Grassroots Development* (West Hartford, Conn.: Kumarian Press, 1992); Rubem César Fernandes, *Privado Porém Público: O Terceiro Setor na América Latina*, 2ª edição (Rio de Janeiro: Civicus/Relume Dumará, 1994); Leilah Landim, "A Invenção das ONGs, do Serviço Invisível à Profissão sem Nome," Ph.D. diss., PPGAS, Museu Nacional, Universidade Federal de Rio de Janeiro, 1993.

[27] David C. Korten, "The Role of Nongovernmental Organizations in Development: Changing Patterns and Perspectives," in *Nongovernmental Organizations and the World Bank: Cooperation for Development*, ed. Samuel Paul and Arturo Israel (Washington, D.C.: The World Bank, 1991), p. 29.

[28] Burke, "Friends of the Earth," pp. 117–19. On the European Environmental Bureau, see Hubert David, "Europe's Watch Dog," *IUCN Bulletin* 15:1–3 (January–March, 1984), p. 21.

[29] At the 16th IUCN General Assembly in Madrid, in 1984, a report by Tom Stoel (NRDC) and Delmar Blasco (Environmental Liaison Centre) expressed NGO dissatisfaction with the organization's recognition of and support for their work. "NGOs and IUCN," *IUCN Bulletin* 15: 10–12 (October–December, 1984), p. 108. It is interesting to note that the Madrid Assembly also marked the admission of Greenpeace to the IUCN, over the opposition of some of its more traditional members.

ganizations in both developed and developing countries began to use cheaper and faster means of communication, and cheap air travel facilitated face-to-face encounters that would have been unthinkable even a decade before.

As environmentalists began to seek more proactive forms of transnational activity, other advocacy networks had already developed this new kind of practice. Seeking a more focused way of targeting abuses by transnational corporations in developing countries, in the mid-1970s the International Baby Food Action Network had launched an almost unprecedented global campaign against the promotion of infant formula in the developing world. This network pioneered new forms of international cooperation as it coordinated a boycott of the Nestlé Corporation and lobbied in favor of a corporate code of conduct for marketing of breast milk substitutes (a code that the World Health Organization and UNICEF adopted in 1981). One of the most active nodes of the baby food network was the International Organization of Consumer Unions, headed for the first time by someone from a developing country, and working out of Penang, Malaysia. Unlike the northern consumer movement, the Malaysians raised concerns not only with product safety, but also working conditions, corporate responsibility, social justice, and ecological awareness.[30]

Sometimes new environmental organizations grew out of older NGOs. Sahabat Alam Malaysia (SAM), Malaysia's Friends of the Earth affiliate founded in 1977, is one of a whole family of organizations and networks spun off from the Consumer Association of Penang. SAM, in turn, hosted the founding meeting for the Asian–Pacific Peoples' Environmental Network in Penang in 1983, and SAM and the Consumer Organization of Penang spawned the Third World Network in late 1984 and the World Rainforest Movement (initially World Rainforest Network) in 1986. Their campaigns gained visibility in the north in part through close links with the British journal *The Ecologist,* whose brand of political ecology contained a stronger critique of existing development models than did most U.S. environmental advocates. Some networks borrowed tactics from the baby food network. The Pesticides Action Network, for example, came to international attention in June 1985 when it launched a campaign to have banned a "dirty dozen" most dangerous chemicals. Formed around issues

[30] On the infant formula campaign, see Kathryn Sikkink, "Codes of Conduct for Transnational Corporations: The Case of the WHO/UNICEF Code," *International Organization* 40:4 (Autumn 1986): 815–40. For a more recent journalistic account see Naomi Bromberg Bar-Yam, "The Nestlé Boycott," *Mothering,* 22 December 1995, pp. 56ff. (from Nexis). On the consumer movement and transnational networking, see Leon Lindsay, "Drive Led by World Consumer Group: Fighting Pesticide 'Dumping' in Third World," *Christian Science Monitor,* 21 December 1982, p. 13; and Leon Lindsay, "Computers Aid Third-World Consumers to Claim Rights," *Christian Science Monitor,* 9 December 1982, B28.

with strong environmental dimensions that affected identifiable communities in the third world, these networks laid the groundwork for much subsequent organizing.

Thus, fueling the emergence of advocacy networks in the mid-1980s were new ideas about the relationship between environment and development; more organizations and new communications technologies; and opportunities to influence new international institutions concerned with the environment or transform the missions of older ones. To this we should add a dramatic increase in private (foundation) and public funding available for environmental activities. Finally, as neoliberal antistatism (or in some cases frustration with bureaucratic inefficiencies) swept through development circles in the advanced industrial countries, NGOs became a favored alternative for funneling development aid. None of these circumstances was sufficient by itself. Ideas, opportunities, and even resources frequently go unnoticed. Characteristic of advocacy networks is the political entrepreneurship of a (usually) small number of individuals who recognize new political opportunities, and join with others to address them strategically.[31]

There are now literally hundreds of environmental networks, making up a loose web of interconnection out of which particular subsets work together on specific campaigns. (At the same time, other subsets, sometimes involving the same organizations in quite different alliances, are involved in separate campaigns or activities.) These organizations produce and process enormous amounts of information. A rapid perusal of environmental conferences (newsgroups) on the computer networks comprising the Association for Progressive Communications reveals a daunting quantity of publicly available information. In addition, organizations and individuals involved in a campaign maintain regular contact by E-mail, fax, telephone, and radio.

Throughout this book we have concentrated on networks that link activists in more developed with those in less developed countries, working on situations where identifiable victims are being physically harmed, which allows advocates to portray issues in terms of right and wrong. The claim about harm is a distinctive feature of advocacy networks. The environmental issues that most easily lend themselves to such portrayals involve displacement of traditional peoples or destruction of their livelihoods. These make for powerful appeals, and not surprisingly some of the best-known transnational networks have arisen to oppose deforestation and/or large dams.

[31] Doug McAdam, John D. McCarthy, and Mayer N. Zald, "Introduction," in *Comparative Perspectives on Social Movements*, ed. McAdam, McCarthy, and Zald (Cambridge: Cambridge University Press, 1996), pp. 1–22; and Sidney Tarrow, *Power in Movement: Social Movements, Collective Action and Politics* (Cambridge: Cambridge University Press, 1994).

However similar the issues involved, the kinds of networks and strategies that develop around them may differ. Differences may arise over how a problem is understood, how it is framed, and what kinds of solutions seem appropriate. Linkages between environment and development issues are inherently political; they involve property relations, profitability of investments, rents, markets, and distribution of income and wealth, as well as access to and power over institutions. Differences over how to approach these issues have an ideological dimension that makes environment and development struggles easier to characterize in left–right terms than are many of the other issue areas we discuss here— however much the actors involved may resist such a characterization.

Two of the best-known cases of transnational environmental networking involve deforestation in the Brazilian Amazon and the Malaysian state of Sarawak. We chose these cases because we expected them to illustrate differential impact, one case involving a central point of leverage (the World Bank in the Amazon case) and the other involving none. Instead we came to appreciate how different strategic contexts and political opportunities, different kinds of domestic organizations and resources, and different ideas and worldviews influenced quite different strategic framings of the deforestation problem.

TROPICAL DEFORESTATION

In the 1980s awareness of global issues stimulated by ozone and climate change negotiations gave a new urgency to older concerns like tropical deforestation. By the end of the decade many northerners saw deforestation as the epitome of third world environmental problems. In the United States, rainforest campaigners focused on the Brazilian Amazon; deforestation in Southeast Asia, proceeding at equal or greater speed, mobilized publics in Europe and Japan more than it did in the United States.[32]

The term "tropical deforestation" only became part of the environmentalist's daily vocabulary in the early 1970s. Before that, concern with tropical forest loss fell under the rubric of habitat protection. The 1968 Latin American Conference on Conservation of Renewable Natural Resources had no session on forests,[33] and there is no entry for forests, deforestation, or tropical forest in the index for volume 2 of the *IUCN Bulletin*, which covers from 1967–71. The problem had yet to be named.

[32] See Norman Myers, "The Anatomy of Environmental Action: The Case of Tropical Deforestation," in *The International Politics of the Environment*, pp. 430–54.

[33] Conference co-sponsored by the IUCN, UNESCO, and FAO. E. J. H. Berwick, "The Bariloche Conference," *IUCN Bulletin* 2:7 (April–June, 1968), p. 50.

The IUCN took up the tropical forest issue for the first time in 1972, in response to the Brazilian government's decision to accelerate colonization and development projects in the Amazon. UNESCO picked up on the problem as the first project of its Program on Man and the Biosphere. A letter to Brazil's president Emílio Garrastazú Médici, jointly signed by IUCN president Harold J. Coolidge and WWF president Prince Bernhard of the Netherlands, pointed out "the need for careful consideration of the environmental problems involved in Amazonian development."[34] Not surprisingly, the Brazilian government was not pleased.

Concern grew rapidly. At the urging of NGOs, in 1973 a number of UN agencies and the Organization of American States cosponsored international meetings of scientists, government representatives and representatives of international agencies to discuss guidelines for economic development of Latin American and Southeast Asian tropical forest areas.[35] By 1974, the IUCN and the WWF considered tropical rainforests "the most important nature conservation programme of the decade."

Scientists and conservationists also pushed the rainforest issue in the United States, and President Carter called tropical forest loss a crucial global issue. In 1977, an Environment and Natural Resources sector was added to the U.S. Foreign Assistance Act, and the Agency for International Development (U.S.–AID) began to sponsor projects aimed at natural resource management. Congress held hearings on tropical deforestation in 1980,[36] and the United States put pressure on the UN General Assembly and UNEP to take action.[37] Those initiatives quickly foundered under President Reagan, and several of the most important tropical forest countries (including Brazil, Zaire, Colombia, Venezuela, and Burma) refused to participate in UNEP meetings on the subject.

The network of scientists and conservationists that initially worked on the tropical forest issue fits very nicely into Haas's definition of an epistemic community. Either by becoming part of the policy process or by working through NGOs or international organizations, its members hoped to persuade people of goodwill to adopt rational guidelines for tropical forest use. Tropical forest experts held meetings, shared information, and discussed strategies and action plans. But the epistemic community was relatively small; a handful of people carried the issue alone.

[34] "The Opening Up of Brazil," *IUCN Bulletin* 3:5 (May 1972): 18.
[35] *IUCN Bulletin*, 4:7 (June 1973); 4:12 (November 1973). The Latin American meeting was held in Caracas, Venezuela, in February; a similar meeting was held in May in Bandung, Indonesia.
[36] House, Subcommittee on International Organizations of the Committee on Foreign Affairs, 96th Cong., 2nd sess. 7 May, 19 June, and 18 September 1980.
[37] UNEP, with the FAO, UNESCO, and UNCTAD, held a meeting of about fifty experts from six developed and fourteen developing countries from 25 February to 1 March 1980 on conservation as part of sustainable use of tropical forests. See *IUCN Bulletin* 11:5 (May 1980).

Frustrated with the meager results of their efforts, several organizations initiated studies and negotiations in the early 1980s to seek new ways of intensifying and broadening their influence. As conservationists' focus shifted from preservation to sustainable development, they needed a better understanding of how human populations—including indigenous peoples—interacted with forests. Around the same time, the newly formed World Resources Institute worked with the UNDP, FAO, and the World Bank on a proposed tropical forestry action plan, FAO designated 1985 as the International Year of the Forest, and WWF launched a highly successful fund-raising campaign around tropical forests.

In sum, the first decade of activity around tropical forests created networks of scientists and policymakers who produced and exchanged a great deal of information, placed the issue on the agendas of a variety of international organizations, and expanded the issue from one concerned primarily with trees and soils to one that at least recognized the problems of indigenous peoples. The 1980 IUCN/WWF/UNEP World Conservation Strategy recognized the need to integrate discussions of development and environment, and IUCN's network of scientists and policymakers tried to stimulate governments to engage in rational resource planning. There was not yet an attempt to gain leverage over recalcitrant actors in the system.

THE MULTILATERAL DEVELOPMENT BANK CAMPAIGN

As conservation organizations diversified their approaches, a new group of actors appeared on the scene, determined to extend to the international arena the kinds of advocacy tactics that had served them well in environmental campaigns in the United States. In 1983 a small group of individuals in Washington, D.C., began to form a network of activists and organizations to target multilateral bank lending in developing countries.[38]

The NGO campaign around multilateral bank lending differed from traditional environmentalist campaigns by focusing not on a particular substantive issue, but rather on a set of political relationships within which activists believed they could obtain leverage. They chose the multilateral banks for their potential impact on the incorporation of environmental concerns into development policy in the third world.

This campaign was clearly a case where strategy moved from the domestic to the international arena. The stress on leverage followed two

---

[38] Although this new grouping introduced a shift in strategic focus, there was some overlap with earlier initiatives; NRDC had already served as lead organization in the IUCN on tropical forests. See *IUCN Bulletin* 11:5 (May 1980); Ronald Brownstein, "Success Story: Environmentalists amid the Ruins," *Amicus Journal*, Fall 1983, pp. 32–35.

decades of environmental litigation in the United States, where lawyers from environmental NGOs successfully used the National Environmental Policy Act (NEPA) and other measures to extend the range of environmental protection in a variety of areas, including the international activities of U.S. agencies.[39] By the late 1970s these lawyers had begun to concentrate more on influencing administrative and regulatory processes. Several key multilateral bank campaign activists were lawyers—Bruce Rich of the Natural Resources Defense Council (NRDC) and later the Environmental Defense Fund (EDF), Barbara Bramble of the National Wildlife Federation, and David Wirth of the NRDC.[40] Stephan Schwartzman, an anthropologist who joined the group in 1984 after returning from his dissertation fieldwork in the Brazilian Amazon, contributed a strong concern with traditional peoples.

While the activists in Washington, D.C., were developing their strategies, *The Ecologist* in Britain weighed in with a January 1985 special double issue on the World Bank. Introduced by an "Open Letter to Mr. Clausen, President of the World Bank," the issue included a contribution from Bruce Rich on multilateral development banks, as well as case studies that included Brazil's Polonoroeste project. Subsequently *The Ecologist* would be at the forefront of a radical critique of the bank's policies and was particularly active in promoting campaigns around World Bank projects in Asia. Although our focus here is on the institutional strategies of the Washington-based campaign, *The Ecologist* played an important networking role, beyond its importance for disseminating information about bank projects and campaigns.[41]

The multilateral bank campaign was not intentionally organized around tropical deforestation. Activists involved in it would eventually try to influence bank policies in a variety of areas (energy, water, resettlement) and in specific projects. The activist critique of the environmental impact of bank projects focused at least as much on their human impact as on their effect on wildlife or natural resources. In the 1986 campaign pamphlet *Bankrolling Disasters*, Schwartzman described the Polonoroeste project in Brazil, the Indonesian Transmigration project, (involving resettlement from Java to less populated parts of the archipelego), the Narmada Dam project in India, and a cattle ranching project in Botswana—all of which involved migration or resettlement issues along with environmen-

[39] See Tom Turner, "The Legal Eagles," *Amicus Journal*, Winter 1988, pp. 25–37.

[40] EDF and NRDC were both formed to pursue NEPA suits. See Lettie McSpadden Wenner, "The Courts and Environmental Policy," and Helen M. Ingram and Dean E. Mann, "Interest Groups and Environmental Policy," *Environmental Politics and Policy: Theories and Evidence*, ed. James P. Lester (Durham, N.C.: Duke University Press, 1989), pp. 238–60, 135–57.

[41] Edwin Goldsmith, "Editorial, Open Letter to Mr. Clausen, President of the World Bank," *The Ecologist* 15:1/2 (1985): 4–8.

tal destruction.[42] This evolution lends weight to the argument that cases involving physical harm or loss of livelihood are particularly susceptible to transnational advocacy campaigning; it is not obvious that for a campaign designed to promote environmental preservation this should be so.

Donor influence helped consolidate the multilateral development bank campaign. In 1987 the Charles Stewart Mott Foundation asked the Sierra Club, the Environmental Defense Fund, the Environmental Policy Institute (later Friends of the Earth), the National Wildlife Federation, and the Natural Resources Defense Council to design a five-year plan for the campaign, on the basis of which the Foundation awarded $1.8 million between 1988 and 1992 to advocacy NGOs. Other foundations joined the effort, but the Mott Foundation's initiative was a strong incentive to strategic activity.[43]

The campaign's goal was to change the behavior of multilateral banks (especially the World Bank), making their projects at least less destructive to the environment and at best positively beneficial. This aim would require effecting changes in the banks' project cycles, personnel, internal organization, and permeability—that is, access to information, and breadth of consultation with those affected by the banks' activities. To bring home the need for such changes, the campaigners began with a substantive critique of particular projects.

Deforestation in the Brazilian Amazon

One of the first cases for the campaigners was the World Bank's loan to Brazil's Polonoroeste program, an effort to rationalize seemingly out-of-control colonization in the Brazilian northwest. The timing—the project began in 1981—placed it just on the cusp of Brazil's democratization process; the first free gubernatorial elections took place in 1982, and Brazil's first civilian president since the 1964 military coup took office in 1985. Democratization stimulated political and social organization and greater circulation of information. Although Rondônia, the area where the Polonoroeste project was mainly to be implemented, lagged behind the rest of Brazil on all of these counts, the overall loosening of political controls affected this region as well.[44] By 1985 many Amazonian areas previously classified as national security zones came under civilian control. Unfortunately the mil-

---

[42] Stephan Schwartzman, *Bankrolling Disasters* (San Francisco: Sierra Club, 1986). *The Ecologist* 16:2/3 (1986) devoted an entire special issue to the transmigration project.

[43] David A. Wirth, "Environment and the International Financial Institutions: The Next Steps," Report from the Sierra Club Center for Environmental Innovation to the Charles Stewart Mott Foundation, 16 December 1992.

[44] Although the project included neighboring Mato Grosso, most campaign activities centered on Rondônia.

itary's withdrawal from its customary role as guardian of order in the Amazon allowed levels of violence, particularly in land conflicts, to rise.

Colonization in the northwestern territory (as of 1981, a state) of Rondô-nia took off during the 1970s, pulled by the completion of a road and promises of free land, and pushed by the concentration of landholdings in the south and northeast. Rondônia's population increased from 111,064 in 1970 to 904,298 in 1985. The World Bank agreed to finance part of the Polonoroeste development program, but with misgivings. The loan was in-tended to pave the main highway through the state and implant social infra-structure in colonization areas; the bank insisted as well on components insuring protection of ecological and indigenous areas. Although bank offi-cials knew that such programs might intensify settlement and further aggra-vate deforestation, they reasoned that if the Brazilian government carried out its plans without bank participation the prospects would be worse.[45]

The most vocal early critics of the loan were anthropologists who saw the destabilizing impact deforestation was having on Amerindian popu-lations and did not expect the Brazilian government to respect the bank's demand for demarcation of indigenous areas. Indigenous rights organi-zations like Cultural Survival, Survival International, and the Anthropo-logical Resource Center in Cambridge, Massachusetts, were among the first to sound the alarm. Anthropologist David Price, hired by the World Bank to report on the situation of the Nambiquara Indians in the project area, went public with criticism of the project after feeling that his dire predictions were being ignored by bank staff.[46]

The Polonoroeste Network and the Bank

Social networks of foreign and Brazilian anthropologists were crucial for the early stages of the external critique of Polonoroeste. When Steve Schwartzman returned to the United States from fieldwork among the Krenakore Indians in Xingu National Park, he quickly began to participate in campaign activities in the name of Survival International. Information on Polonoroeste came from the Ecumenical Center for Documentation and Information (CEDI) in Brazil, where anthropologist Carlos Alberto Ri-cardo headed up an indigenous rights project, from several anthropolo-gists who had been consultants on the project, from the filmmaker Adrian Cowell, and from a few other journalists and academics.[47] It did not, at this stage, come from organizations on the ground in Rondônia.

[45] World Bank, Operations Evaluation Department, "World Bank Approaches to the En-vironment in Brazil: A Review of Selected Projects, volume 5: The POLONOROESTE Program," 30 April 1992.
[46] David Price, *Before the Bulldozer: The Nambiquara Indians & The World Bank* (Cabin John, Md.: Seven Locks Press, 1989).
[47] Interview with Stephan Schwartzman, Environmental Defense Fund, Washington, D.C., 10 November 1989.

In the United States, campaigners lobbied key congressional appropriations committees and the Treasury Department in an attempt to influence positions taken by U.S. executive directors of the multilateral banks. This strategy proved unexpectedly successful. In May 1983, campaign organizers testifed before congressional committees on the lack of environmental impact assessments for multilateral development bank projects, and in June produced dramatic testimony from David Price accusing the bank of watering down his negative assessment of Polonoroeste's indigenous component.[48] By 1984, the Polonoroeste case had become a focus of congressional inquiry.

Between 1983 and 1986 the U.S. Congress held seventeen hearings related to MDBs and the environment. Wisconsin senator Robert Kasten, chair of the Foreign Operations Subcommittee of the Senate Appropriations Committee, became a very important ally; his desire to increase U.S. influence at the World Bank fit very nicely with the environmentalists' agenda.[49] Congressional committee chairs had direct leverage over the bank through their power of appropriation; in addition, they got the Treasury Department involved in its capacity as the liaison with the U.S. executive director for the bank.

The World Bank is vulnerable to U.S. pressure because of its system of weighted voting, by which the United States, the United Kingdom, Germany, Japan, and France have 40 percent of the voting shares; these countries also provide the lion's share of money for the International Development Agency (IDA), the bank's soft loan facility. Beginning in the late 1970s, negotiations over IDA replenishment became increasingly complicated, and the bank did not want to see yet another roadblock established in this process.

In December 1984, and again in 1986, the U.S. Congress adopted a set of recommendations suggested by NGOs to strengthen the bank's environmental performance.[50] In 1985, largely as a result of the MDB campaign, the World Bank temporarily suspended disbursements for Polonoroeste on the grounds that the Brazilian government was violating loan conditions on protecting natural and indigenous areas; this was the first loan

[48] Bruce M. Rich, attorney, NRDC, representing WWF, Sierra Club, FOE, and Izaak Walton League, and Brent Blackwelder, director, Water Resources Project, Environmental Policy Institute, testimony before House Appropriations Committee, Subcommittee on Foreign Operations, May 1983, on Foreign Assistance and Related Programs Appropriations for 1984, part 3. Y4.Ap6/1:F76/3/984/pt. 3; and House Subcommittee on International Development Institutions and Finance of the Committee on Banking, Finance, and Urban Affairs, 98th Cong., 1st sess., 29 June 1983.

[49] Bruce Rich, Mortgaging the Earth: The World Bank, Environmental Impoverishment, and the Crisis of Development (Boston: Beacon Press, 1994), pp. 117–25.

[50] House Subcommittee on International Development Institutions and Finance of the Committee on Banking, Finance, and Urban Affairs, 96th Cong., 2d Sess., December 1984. On the role of Congress, see LePrestre, The World Bank, pp. 191–93; and Rich, Mortgaging the Earth, pp. 113–31.

suspension on such grounds. In 1985, the Senate Appropriations committee attached a strongly worded environmental report to the foreign aid appropriation bill asking U.S. executive directors of multilateral development banks to promote a series of reforms in project design and implementation.[51] The World Bank's decision to create a top-level environmental department in 1987 was designed to stem the rising tide of criticism. In his speech at the World Resources Institute announcing the changes, bank president Barber Conable referred to Polonoroeste as something the new department was designed to prevent from happening.

The Impact of Local Organizing

At this stage of the campaign Brazilian NGOs and individuals served mainly as informants. This changed in the second half of the 1980s, for two reasons: first, the connection some Washington activists forged with rubber tapper organizers from Acre, Brazil had a deep influence on their subsequent activity; and second, other instances of transnational environmental networking, in which third world (especially Asian) activists played a more central role, highlighted the importance of local protagonists. Information on multilateral bank activities became more widely available, also, and opportunities for organizations to share their experiences and discuss strategy increased. The most visible opportunity was the annual NGO meeting held parallel to the annual meeting of the World Bank and the International Monetary Fund (IMF) beginning in 1986.

For the initial group of multilateral bank campaigners, contact established in 1985 with the Acre rubber tappers was a watershed event. Francisco "Chico" Mendes was the leader of a group of rubber tappers (gatherers of natural latex from rubber trees) who had been fighting since 1975 to guarantee land use rights and improve the living standards of forest peoples. They were central to rural union organizing in the state of Acre, and had close relationships with other social movements in the area during Brazil's transition to democracy. Anthropologists working in Brazilian NGOs met with Steve Schwartzman in Washington in 1985, and recognized a potential synergy between the multilateral bank campaign and the rubber tappers' struggle; subsequently Schwartzman attended the founding meeting of the National Council of Rubber Tappers in Brasília.[52]

[51] House Subcommittee on Foreign Operations and Related Agencies of the Committee on Appropriations, hearings on Foreign Assistance and Related Programs Appropriations for 1986, pt. 6, 99th Cong., 1st sess., 1985, pp. 750–815, especially 766–67.
[52] For a detailed discussion of the development of rubber tapper organizing in Acre and its relation to multilateral bank campaign activists, see Margaret E. Keck, "Social Equity and Environmental Politics in Brazil: Lessons from the Rubber Tappers of Acre," *Comparative Politics* 27 (July 1995): 409–24.

The relationship that developed between the bank campaigners and the rubber tappers was mutually beneficial. It took the teeth out of accusations that rainforest destruction was simply a concern of privileged northerners. Over time, it helped activists from distant political and social universes to understand better their different perspectives on the same problems, and to build elements of a common understanding. For the rubber tappers, who had struggled for a decade against the encroachment of cattle ranchers on forest they had traditionally used, contact with the bank campaigners gave them access to international opinion- and decision-making arenas that they could not have gained on their own. When they joined forces to influence a proposed road project in Acre for which Brazil sought Inter-American Development Bank funding, a struggle for land rights waged by rural unions became simultaneously a struggle to preserve the standing forest.

In December 1988 Chico Mendes was murdered by hired guns of irate landowners. But he had made his point abroad. Invited by the bank campaigners to Washington and Miami to meet with members of the U.S. Congress and with multilateral bank officials, he had helped make the rubber tappers' proposal to create "extractive reserves" in the Amazon one of the few concrete illustrations of the "sustainable development" idea. By linking environmental destruction to a concrete picture of how local populations lived in the forest, environmentalists were able to make the tropical forest issue real to an international public.

The murder of Chico Mendes had enormous symbolic impact—so much so that it made page one of the *New York Times*. It embodied at the same time an issue—deforestation in the Amazon—and a set of complex social relationships in which the roles of rubber tapper, cattle rancher, the justice system, Brazilian government programs, multilateral development banks, and North American and European taxpayers all became transparent. The rubber tapper case thus reinforced an approach to tropical deforestation that focused on social relations. This approach is very different from one that sees forest loss as a set of technical or scientific issues to be resolved by experts, or from one that looks at it primarily in terms of trees and wildlife.

The relationship with the Acre rubber tappers had important ramifications for transnational networking on the environment. It showed that testimony from those most directly affected by bank projects was often a more powerful organizing tool than information produced by outside experts. Calls for participation in the early stages of project design by those likely to be affected by a bank-funded project became a constant of activist critiques. Notably, the third world social movements whose participation the campaigners advocated focused overwhelmingly on the human dimension of environmental change.

The negotiation of different goals in the context of network activity is one of the most interesting dimensions of this story; this is a process by which the principled basis of the networks comes to include the recognition of differences as well as claims on behalf of a universal good. By the late 1980s the preferred language of the campaign had become a language of "partnership" in which genuine links between organizations of those suffering harm and those speaking for them were crucial to a campaign's legitimacy. Building partnerships, however, is fraught with difficulties.[53]

Distinct visions of the tropical forest problem produce very different proposals for its solution. The development of a committment to the communities affected by bank projects often placed advocates at loggerheads with borrowing country governments, as well as the bank. If on the one hand this put environmentalists in a position long familiar to human rights and indigenous advocates, it also potentially politicized their commitment beyond what many in their organizations were prepared to support. Advocates who traveled between Washington and the Amazon especially had to negotiate a fine line between the lobbying and pressure strategies they employed at home and the requirements of grassroots support in the areas affected by bank projects.

From Polonoroeste to Planafloro

In 1986 technical personnel in the Rondônia state government began to work with World Bank staff on a successor project to Polonoroeste. Based on a zoning plan, this new project, called the Planafloro, was intended to prevent further ecological damage by helping to intensify agricultural activity in settled areas, and institutionalize varying degrees of environmental protection for the remainder of the state.[54] In 1990, in the midst of the approval process, the Environmental Defense Fund led the bank campaign network in a series of objections that relevant local groups had not been consulted on the project.[55]

---

[53] David A. Wirth, "Legitimacy, Accountability, and Partnership: A Model for Advocacy on Third World Environmental Issues," *Yale Law Journal* 100:8 (June 1991): 2051–52.

[54] The acronym Planafloro comes from the project's Portuguese name, Plano Agropecuário e Florestal de Rondônia (Agriculture, Livestock, and Forest Plan of Rondônia). The World Bank called it the Rondônia Natural Resources Management Project. The potential for conflict is already clear in the different names given it.

[55] See Bruce Rich et al. to Mr. E. Patrick Coady, Executive Director, World Bank, 9 January 1990; Osmarino Amancio Rodrigues and Ailton Krenak to Shahid Husain, Vice President for Latin America of the World Bank, 11 December 1989; Bruce Rich et al. to Luis Coirolo [sic], Latin America and the Caribbean Regional Office, Brazil Division, World Bank, 19 December 1988; Francisco Mendes Filho to Barber Conable, President, World Bank, 13 October 1988; Bruce Rich and Stephan Schwartzman to Mr. S. Shahid Husain, 22 February 1980; S. Shahid Husain to Frank E. Loy, Chairman of the Board, Environmental Defense Fund, 5 March 1990; Bruce Rich and Steve Schwartzman to Shahid Husain, 14 May 1990; José Lutzenberger, National Environmental Secretary, to Barber Conable, 22 March 1990. This correspondence with its attachments is collected in packets that are available from EDF.

In response to the bank's claim that such consultations had taken place, Washington environmentalists requested information from their contacts in Rondônia. Brazilian groups reported that rubber tappers, rural workers, and indigenous organizations knew little or nothing about the project, but had requested information and expressed interest in discussing it. Brazilian and foreign NGO representatives simultaneously raised the issue with the newly appointed environmental secretary, José Lutzenberger, who asked the bank to suspend consideration of the project until consultations could take place. This forced the bank's hand, and the project was taken off the agenda of the executive directors. There were other objections to the loan too; the Ministry of the Economy installed in 1990 wanted to cut foreign borrowing, and doubted the Rondônia state government's ability to repay.

In 1990–91 rubber tappers, indigenous peoples, and rural unionists held a series of meetings, partially funded by the National Wildlife Federation, to discuss the Planafloro project. The meetings helped stimulate the self-organization of the first two groups; rubber tapper and indigenous organizations were weak in Rondônia, and advisory NGOs and competing national indigenous organizations were contending among themselves to organize them.

Incentives for local groups to become organized were high. With foreign attention focused on the Amazon and the approach of the 1992 "Earth Summit" in Rio de Janeiro, money and media attention were available as never before. Conflicts among NGOs in the region were smoothed over, and in 1991 the Rondônia NGO Forum was created. This forum became the formal NGO interlocutor from Rondônia for the Planafloro project and another large environmental project, the Amazon Project sponsored by the Group of Seven (G-7). With NGO agreement, the Planafloro returned to the World Bank's docket in 1991. The bank pressed the Rondônia state government to accept as part of the project's governance structure, a deliberative council that gave NGOs voting parity with state secretariats to decide on the project's operating plans, and seats in the planning commissions.[56]

Although this was one of the biggest procedural victories of the campaign, it did not immediately produce results. The organizations in the forum did not have enough local clout to make their positions effective, and the state government did not intend for them to gain such clout. Nonetheless, local groups gained access to information and greater capacity to monitor government actions. They could then assess government claims in the light of direct experience and demand that the bank be held accountable.

---

[56] See Margaret E. Keck, "Brazil's Planafloro: The Limits of Leverage," in *The Struggle for Accountability: The World Bank, NGOs, and Grassroots Movements*, ed. Jonathan Fox and L. David Brown (Cambridge, Mass.: MIT Press, 1998 forthcoming).

Although the Rondônia activists did try to use hearings in the Brazilian Congress and lawsuits in Brazilian courts to stop violations of the zoning plan, ultimately their best strategy remained one that put the onus of restraining the Brazilian government onto the World Bank. This is a case where a boomerang strategy resulted from the political weakness of actors rather than from complete blockage of access, as in the human rights cases; transnational networking helped to amplify local demands by resituating them in different arenas with more potential allies.

In June 1994, only a year after the loan's disbursements had begun, the NGO forum resigned from the deliberative council, reporting multiple violations of the loan agreement. A bank mission brokered a short-lived agreement between the NGOs and the state government, but in November 1994 the forum decided to collaborate with Friends of the Earth (and eventually Oxfam as well) in bringing a formal claim that the Planafloro was violating the bank's own policies before the newly established World Bank Inspection Panel. Friends of the Earth, with funding from the Dutch agency NOVIB to finance research, presented the claim to the bank on 14 June 1995.

Although it was ultimately rejected, simply filing the claim produced a flurry of activity. The Rondônia state government and the Brazilian federal government signed a long-delayed agreement committing the Federal Land Institute to respect the state's zoning plan, and reserves whose demarcation had been unaccountably delayed were suddenly demarcated. Bank personnel finally took a serious look at the project's shortcomings, and proposed revisions that they hoped might overcome previous gridlock.

The Organization of the Network

In defining the network, we need to distinguish between that part of it that follows any particular project closely and the multilateral bank campaign network generally. Within the latter there is a division of labor, and different individuals and groups act as leads on particular areas of expertise. It is possible to list actual network participants at any point in the campaign. For example, a reasonable measure of the members of the United States–Canada bank campaign network could be gleaned from the list of participants at a 1991 strategy meeting, called in conjunction with the Mott Foundation, to discuss the bank campaign's next steps.[57]

The Planafloro network reactivated connections forged in the campaigns around Polonoroeste and the Acre rubber tappers. EDF's Steve

[57] See list provided in Wirth, "Environment and the International Financial Institutions," appendix A.

Schwartzman played a leading role in coordinating the Washington side of the multilateral bank campaign's activities on Brazil, and activists from Friends of the Earth and the World Wildlife Fund (WWF) were important on the European side. With the approach of the 1992 "Earth Summit" in Rio de Janeiro, several other European and international NGOs became more active: Italy's FOE affiliate began to develop an Amazon program by working with Brazilian NGOs on the G-7 Amazon project, and Greenpeace, newly installed in Brazil, began a series of occupations of illegal timbering operations. The WWF also established a Brazilian branch after UNCED. Both Greenpeace and WWF developed close relationships with indigenous rights NGOs. Establishment of Brazilian branches of international NGOs diversified local NGOs' access to information and allies. Oxfam–UK, which had been active in the Amazon region in the early to mid-1980s, became so again.

Personal connections were crucial. Schwartzman had gotten to know individuals in Rondônia who worked with rubber tappers, via the National Council of Rubber Tappers. In a conversation with a social worker and rubber tapper organizer from Rondônia at a meeting of the national council, he discovered that the bank's claims about having consulted local NGOs on the Planafloro were suspect. Berkeley graduate student Brent Millikan, who had previously spent several years doing masters research in Rondônia during the Polonoroeste period, was back doing doctoral research beginning in the late 1980s; a member of the San Francisco-based Rainforest Action Network, Millikan knew the bank campaigners, had considerable experience in the state, and had close relations with scholars of the region. Wim Groenvelt, the Dutch expatriate head of the Institute for Pre-History, Anthropology, and Ecology (IPHAE), had close links with European and Brazilian forestry groups. Several organizations that became involved in the Rondônia NGO forum were themselves parts of other networks: The Indigenous Missionary Council (CIMI) was a pastoral activity of the Brazilian Catholic church; the state rural union confederation was affiliated with the national labor confederation CUT.

The quality of the local nodes of the advocacy network was more important in the Planafloro campaign than with Polonoroeste. "Local participation" became an important part of such campaigns in the 1990s, made so by the publicity given to the Acre rubber tappers and several other campaigns where vigorous grassroots protest was a crucial element, such as the Narmada dam campaign in India. On the Polonoroeste project foreign NGOs had spoken freely in place of the Brazilians on whose behalf they claimed to act, but with the Planafloro project accountability issues were raised more often.

In the early 1990s EDF and Oxfam, recognizing the need for a more solid Brazilian domestic base for the multilateral development bank campaign, sponsored a meeting in Brasília in March 1993 for Brazilian environmental and indigenous NGOs, to form a Brazilian campaign network. In principle, this national network was to make multilateral bank-related activities more sensitive to national political dynamics. Although slow to get off the ground, by mid-1996 the Brazilian network had a strong national coordination and regular information exchange.

Network Strategies

The Planafloro experience fits the boomerang pattern described in previous chapters. Unable effectively to influence the activities of the state government and of federal agencies acting in Rondônia at the state level, local groups applied pressure either at the national or international levels.[58] In the United States, activists lobbied Congress and the Treasury Department. In addition, inclusion of NGOs in the Planafloro's governance structure legitimized their intervention to an unprecedented degree. However, Brazilian NGO strategies were complicated by the pervasive crisis of governance and economy that Brazil was experiencing for most of the period. The Planafloro was only one, and far from the most egregious, of the abuses of public authority that competed for attention.

Such abuses were all the more striking given the Brazilian administration's adroit use of "green" public relations. Soon after Fernando Collor's election to the presidency in 1989, he stunned environmentalists by appointing internationally known ecologist José Lutzenberger secretary of the environment. Asked by a *New York Times* reporter for his impression, Steve Schwartzman called the appointment "stupefyingly positive."[59] Hopes that the advocacy network had penetrated to the heart of the environmental decision-making apparatus proved elusive, however. Collor's environmentalism was more show than substance, and Lutzenberger was a colorful but ineffective minister. Nonetheless, governmental machinery did become more accessible. The Brazilian Environment and Renewable Resources Institute (IBAMA) through its traditional peoples program, began to support rubber tapper and indigenous organizing.

The Planafloro strategy was primarily an accountability strategy, attempting to leverage environmental, land, and indigenous rights policy by asking the World Bank to hold Brazilian government institutions to the commitments they had made. Although initially reluctant to exert major pressure on Brazil, bank personnel became increasingly resentful

---

[58] This strategy was employed by the early civil rights movement in the U.S. See Doug McAdam, *Political Process and the Development of Black Insurgency, 1930–1970* (Chicago: University of Chicago Press, 1982).

[59] James Brooke, "Defender of Rainforest Is Named Secretary of Environment in Brazil," *New York Times*, 6 March 1990, p. C5.

at taking the heat themselves for failures on the Brazilian side, and began to monitor the project more closely. Eventually, weakly organized local movements and NGOs in Rondônia gained experience.

The multilateral bank campaign has clearly had an impact on World Bank procedures; as with most institutional change, external pressures reinforced internal reformers. The 1987 World Bank reorganization created a central environmental department and environmental units within each of the bank's four regional offices. By 1990 some sixty new positions had been created.[60] Over the next few years the World Bank's role in environmental issues grew. After 1990 it helped elaborate the G-7's Amazon project, and later assumed management of the Global Environmental Facility, a funding mechanism for national projects in the areas of climate change, ozone depletion, and biodiversity. The bank's 1992 reorganization added a central vice presidency for environmentally sustainable development (within which is also located the Social Policy and Resettlement Division).[61] Further reform followed upon network agitation over the Sardar Sarovar Dam project on the Narmada River in India. In that case the World Bank convoked an independent commission to report on the project's status. After the Commission's June 1992 report and an NGO campaign around the tenth replenishment of IDA monies in 1993, the Bank created a semi-independent inspection panel and instituted a new information policy, both in response to NGO demands. The inspection panel was "empowered to investigate complaints from people directly affected by Bank projects regarding violations of World Bank policy, procedures, and loan agreements."[62] The information policy essentially declassified a wide range of World Bank documents, making them available for public scrutiny.[63]

OPENING THE FLOW OF INFORMATION

The ability to generate and use information strategically is the main asset of transnational advocacy networks. What kinds of information are

[60] See Jeremy J. Warford and Zeinab Partow, *World Bank Support for the Environment: A Progress Report* (Washington, D.C.: World Bank Development Committee, 1989), no. 22; and Bruce Rich, "The Emperor's New Clothes: The World Bank and Environmental Reform," *World Policy Journal* 7 (Spring 1990): 305–29.

[61] Nüket Kardam, in "Development Approaches and the Role of Policy Advocacy: The Case of the World Bank," *World Development* 21:11 (1993): 1773–86, explains policy change by looking at variation in organizational independence, the fit between new issues and older conceptions of mission, and the roles of internal and external advocates. She focuses on strategic efforts by internal advocates within the bank to build towards new approaches to social issues.

[62] Lori Udall, "The World Bank and Public Accountability: Has Anything Changed?," November 1995 draft chapter for Fox and Brown, *The Struggle for Accountability*.

[63] See Lori Udall, *A Citizens' Guide to the World Bank's Information Policy* (Washington, D.C.: Bank Information Center, 1994).

strategically necessary? Who gains access to it and how? How, and how well, does information circulate in the network?

Success in engaging such an institution as the World Bank over a project or policy requires, besides certain kinds of expertise, physical access to documents. Without regular access to bank personnel, one may not even know that documents exist. Thus a special responsibility fell upon NGOs in Washington where the World Bank is located.

Two innovations greatly increased opportunities for information sharing in 1986: the beginning of yearly NGO meetings held parallel to the meetings of the Bretton Woods institutions, and the establishment of the Bank Information Center. Chad Dobson, who arrived to organize the first and stayed to set up the second, brought a background in the peace movement, and considerable organizing experience to the bank campaign in Washington. "In 1986," Dobson recounts, "Marian Edey, who was head of the League of Conservation Voters, called me and asked if I would do a rally and conference at the bank here, because she knew that in '82 I had done one in Central Park, in the peace movement, that had been enormously successful." [Dobson was coordinator of the June 12th Rally Committee, which brought an estimated 800,000 people to a nuclear freeze march in New York City.] I reminded Marian that there was a difference between peace and environment and between Washington and New York, but she said she didn't care."[64]

Chad Dobson was a born organizer—a talent he credits to his Mormon upbringing. Between 1982 and 1986 he worked for the Field Foundation, organizing voter registration projects for them and for other foundations, starting the Arms Control Computer Network, and tackling the MX missile in Utah. After the call from Edey, Dobson pulled together an umbrella organization of Washington NGOs, to organize the conference and demonstration.[65] At the meeting, activists from Europe and developing countries called for the creation of an organization specifically designed to share information.[66] Encouraged by Randy Hayes of the Rainforest Action Network, Dobson agreed to start the Bank Information Center (BIC)—in effect, a network service institution.

Dobson's foundation experience helped him raise start-up grants, after which BIC picked up funding from the Mott Foundation, from NOVIB to provide information to its southern partners, and from WWF to provide information to its partners. Dobson began to cultivate relationships with

---

[64] All material in quotes in this section is from an interview with Chad Dobson, Washington, D.C., 20 May 1996.

[65] The group included FOE, National Wildlife Federation, WWF, Rainforest Action Network, EDF, Greenpeace, and others.

[66] Dobson remembers *The Ecologist* and Oxfam particularly in relation to the call for an information-sharing institution.

bank personnel and with U.S. government officials who could help gain access to information. He also set out to create an advisory board of potential information users outside of Washington, especially non-Americans.

Dobson's activities and BIC helped to open up the multilateral development bank campaign beyond the small network of activists that had gotten it off the ground. Besides providing documentation, that meant opening up discussions of strategy. One venue for doing that was the institution of the parallel conference, and increased contact among activists from different parts of the world who met there. Broadening the network also changed it.

> The earliest connections were clearly environmental. And of course that bias was from the Washington environmental groups. When we started bringing southerners here, they didn't talk about species . . . The real connection was [made] when they started coming and saying "you can't protect the environment when the people are suffering the way they are." I think it really was [after] getting southerners here . . . that you had people changing and saying, well, we're talking about sustainable development . . . But it absolutely started out as a rainforest thing.

BIC also tried to broaden strategy discussions in Washington beyond the core group. This effort eventually spawned the "Tuesday group," begun in 1989 in response to the Pelosi amendment[67] and U.S.–AID's mandate to scrutinize environmentally problematic multilateral development bank projects. The Tuesday group was initially composed of organizations with sister organizations in Europe (such as Friends of the Earth, Greenpeace, and the WWF). Recognizing that many of their southern partners could not work with their own governments, NGOs would work with the U.S. government to come up with a position. Government representatives normally included the Environmental Protection Agency, the State Department, U.S.–AID, and the Treasury Department. The idea was to use international networks to get European governments on board. Eventually, the meetings were open to any NGO that wanted to attend. Here was a case where government officials committed to improving environmental performance actively sought NGO collaboration.

With the creation of a more open information policy at the World Bank, Dobson hoped that more southern and other non-Washington groups would begin to ask for the documents to which they were entitled. As or-

---

[67] Presented by Congresswoman Nancy Pelosi and authored largely by the Sierra Club, the 1989 amendment affected Title XIII of the International Financial Institutions Act. It requires the Secretary of the Treasury to instruct the U.S. Executive Directors of multilateral banks to vote against any environmentally significant project unless an environmental assessment or a comprehensive environmental summary has been made available to the board members at least 120 days before it meets on a project.

ganizations gain access to information for themselves, they lose some of
their dependence on intermediaries, and the networks shed some part of
their structural inequality. They begin, then, more nearly to approximate
the horizontal relationships to which they aspire.

The Campaign against Deforestation in Sarawak

Another case of deforestation that began to receive considerable attention in the late 1980s was the extremely rapid logging of tropical timber
in the Malaysian state of Sarawak, on the island of Borneo. Logging had
already decimated the forests of neighboring Sabah, but received little
public attention. Sarawak was different, for three reasons: (1) a change in
the international institutional context for discussion of tropical forestry
issues, with establishment of the International Tropical Timber Organization, provided a new campaign focus, following upon a relatively
successful effort to target a similar organization on the whaling issue;[68]
(2) strong connections between deforestation and native land rights issues brought environmental and indigenous rights campaigners together, especially in Europe, and the actions of Bruno Manser, an amateur
anthropologist who had lived with a nomadic people in Sarawak called
the Penan, dramatized their plight; and (3) the case was taken up vigor-
ously by a Malaysian organization, Sahabat Alam Malaysia, that was already a member of Friends of the Earth International as well as several
other mainly southern, transnational networks.

Background

Sarawak and Sabah are the two Malaysian states located on the northern coast of Borneo. They enjoy significant autonomy under the country's
federal system, with the ability to control customs, civil service, and immigration (Sarawak requires a passport for visitors from peninsular
Malaysia). Sarawak also controls the revenues from timber concessions,
the result of an agreement at the time of joining the federation that gave
peninsular Malaysia, in return, control over oil revenues. As a result of
this deal, the federal government in Kuala Lumpur has been able to deny
responsibility for logging practices in Sarawak.

With the exception of a severe recession in 1986, Malaysia's GNP has
grown at 6–8 percent per annum since the early 1970s. A series of five-
year plans have worked toward the goal, articulated in Prime Minister

---

[68] Kunda Dixit, "Japan: Groups Mobilize to Save Tropical Rainforests," *Inter Press Service,*
12 March 1987 (from Nexis).

Mahathır Mohamad's "Vision 2020" program, of being a fully industrialized economy by the year 2020. Industry currently represents around 70
percent of the nation's exports. Timber is second to oil as a revenue producer in the primary sector.

The country is a multi-ethnic state.[69] The shadow of ethnic conflict has
hung heavily over Malaysia since an explosion of violence in 1969. Although preferential treatment is given to Malays, the benefits of development are very widely distributed. Given the image of rapid modernization
which is currently a central component of Malaysia's political identity, the
idea that Dayak (indigenous) land rights should be secured in part to preserve traditional lifeways commonly portrayed as backward does not fit
with the image of a country racing toward the twenty-first century.
Malaysia has been ruled by a large multi-party coalition headed by the
UMNO-Baru (United Malays National Organization), a Muslim–Malay
party, since independence in 1957, and overtly ethnic politics is seen by
dominant groups as potentially destabilizing.

Logging in peninsular Malaysia declined significantly between 1975
and 1985 as a conservationist National Forestry Policy (which does not
affect Sarawak and Sabah) came into effect. At the same time, log output
in Sarawak increased from 4.4 million cubic meters in 1976 to 12.2 million
in 1985.[70] Although in theory logging in Sarawak was tightly controlled
from the outset, enforcement has been practically nonexistent; both the
geographical constraints of hill logging and the economic incentives for
cutting beyond the targets are very strong. Briefly, timber concessions under the control of state politicians are granted (sold) for short-term logging licences to timber companies, whose motivation to log selectively
and with care in areas designated for protection is virtually nil.[71]

Logging decimated traditional forms of livelihood, meanwhile accelerat-
ing the integration of Dayak communities into the state's cash economy.
Although logging brought short-term jobs to native communities, it eroded
soils, polluted rivers and reduced fish stocks, eliminated wildlife formerly
hunted for food, and increased flooding. Employment benefits ended
when the logging companies moved on to the next area. Attempts by
Dayak communities to gain the rights to log in their own areas have been
unsuccessful, as have most attempts to have areas declared communal

[69] Sarawak's population is about 40 percent Dayaks (the collective name for native
groups, largely Christian and animist), 30 percent Chinese, 20 percent Malay, and the rest
small tribal groups. For the country as a whole, Malays constitute about half of the population, Chinese 35 percent, Indians 9 percent, and non-Muslim natives 6.6 percent.

[70] Evelyne Hong, *Natives of Sarawak: Survival in Borneo's Vanishing Forests* (Penang: Insti-
tut Masyarakat, 1987), p. 125.

[71] See Marcus Colchester, *Pirates, Squatters and Poachers: The Political Ecology of Disposses-
sion of the Native Peoples of Sarawak* (London: Survival International/INSAN, 1989), pp.
29–33.

forests and thus protected from the loggers.[72] Making land rights effective has been a losing struggle in the state. Logging hit especially hard for the still partially nomadic Penan people of the Baram region, for whom the forest provided food and home.

Dayak resistance came to international attention beginning in March 1987, when the Penan set up barricades on logging roads in the Upper Baram. Use of this tactic quickly spread throughout the region to other Dayak groups (the Kenyah, Kayan, Lambawang, and Kelabit). Activities in at least sixteen logging camps were halted. Although this is not the first time that barricades were used against loggers, it is the first time they were part of a sustained campaign, and the first time the resistance received so much attention.[73]

What elements projected the Sarawak conflicts onto a broader stage in 1987? First, interrelated political crises at the national and state levels amplified their importance. Malaysia had undergone a severe recession in 1986, with per capita income declining by 15.7 percent. Criticism of the government became pervasive both in the governing coalition and the opposition, mainly concerning access to decision-making.[74] Within Sarawak, rising Dayak nationalism since 1983 had spawned the first explicitly ethnic political party in the state (Parti Bansa Dayak Sarawak—PBDS).[75] Prime Minister Mahathir began to fear for his coalition. In addition, by early March 1987 Sarawak was in the midst of its own political crisis, significant for the present story because of revelations about official corruption in granting timber concessions. This multifaceted crisis formed the backdrop for the logging blockades.[76]

Second, tropical forests had become increasingly visible on the international agenda by the mid-1980s. In March 1983 sixty four countries had agreed to establish an International Tropical Timber Organization (ITTO).[77] Composed of producers and consumers of tropical timber, the

[72] Ibid., pp. 37–44. A fascinating account of attempts by one longhouse (community) to make sense of this process is found in William Bevis, *Borneo Log: The Struggle for Sarawak's Forests* (Seattle: University of Washington Press, 1995), chapter 10.

[73] According to Reuters, the Ibans frequently blocked logging roads to protest against inadequate (or nonexistent) compensation for damage to their land. Reuters North European Service, "Malaysia's Disappearing Tropical Forests," 12 June 1985, (from Nexis). For chronology and account of the blockades, including a collection of news clippings, see World Rainforest Movement/Sahabat Alam Malaysia, *The Battle for Sarawak's Forests* (Penang, Malaysia: World Rainforest Movement/Sahabat Alam Malaysia, 1989).

[74] Gordon P. Means, *Malaysian Politics: The Second Generation* (New York: Oxford University Press, 1991), pp. 193–94.

[75] The party wanted to raise the status of the Iban language, address the problems of defining traditional land rights in a modern setting, and deal with the impact of logging on native populations. "Mahathir lets Sarawak Rivals Fight It Out," *Financial Times*, 14 March 1987 (from Nexis).

[76] For the concessions system, see Colchester, *Pirates, Squatters, and Poachers*, pp. 29–33.

[77] After six years of negotiations in the UN Conference on Tropical Timber held under the auspices of UNCTAD in Geneva.

new group was given a mandate to consider global resource management issues. Then in 1985, declared the International Year of the Forest, the UN Food and Agriculture Organization, the World Bank, and the UN Development Program, working with the World Resources Institute, produced the Tropical Forestry Action Plan and published "Tropical Forests: A Call for Action." The resulting International Tropical Forest Timber Agreement and Action Plan, passed in June 1986 in Geneva, was to be implemented by the International Tropical Timber Organization, headquartered in Yokohama, Japan.[78] The ITTO council met for the first time in March 1987, at the same time that the blockades of logging roads began to spread throughout the Baram region of Sarawak.[79]

Logging in Sarawak was already high on the agenda of others who met in Yokohama as the ITTO council convened in March 1987, specifically the Japan Tropical Forest Action Network (JATAN) and Friends of the Earth International, which convened a parallel conference in the same city to discuss Japan's tropical timber imports from Southeast Asia. JATAN, with some meticulous research of its own, uncovered a joint venture between James Wong, head of the Sarawak timber firm Limbang Trading Company and the Japanese company C.Itoh which stood to profit from the construction of a road, funded by the Japan International Cooperation Agency (JICA), to the logging concession the two companies were working in Long Napir. (Wong was also secretary of the Environment and Tourism for Sarawak). JATAN brought the case to the Japanese Diet (as JICA funding is supposed to be restricted to projects that benefit local people), and although no action resulted from the hearings, C.Itoh quietly paid back the loan and broke off its relations with the Limbang Trading Company.[80]

The third factor that brought Sarawak logging wide attention was that local protests were linked to international publics through two different network nodes. One was the charismatic (and enigmatic) Bruno Manser, a Swiss national who had lived with the Penan for a number of years and who apparently helped to organize the blockade; and the other was Sahabat

---

[78] Critiques of the action plan followed soon after it was published. See for example, Vandana Shiva, "Forestry Myths and the World Bank: A Critical Review of Tropical Forests: A Call for Action," *The Ecologist* 17:4/5 (1987): 142–49. A more extensive critique is Marcus Colchester and Larry Lohmann, *The Tropical Forestry Action Plan: What Progress?* 2d ed. (Penang: World Rainforest Movement, 1990). Indeed, it was precisely because the plan was unable to stem the tide of deforestation that the FAO proposed in 1990 that negotiations begin for an international forest convention.

[79] For an assessment of the ITTO by a forest campaigner, see Marcus Colchester, "The International Tropical Timber Organization. Kill or Cure for the Rainforests?," in *The Earthscan Reader in Tropical Forestry*, ed. Simon Rierberger (London: Earthscan Publications, 1991), pp. 185–207.

[80] "Japan: Groups Mobilize to Save Tropical Rainforests," *Inter Press Service*, 12 March 1987 (from Nexis); Bevis, *Borneo Log*, pp. 140–44.

Alam Malaysia, one of a set of interrelated organizations based in Penang. Involved in a variety of environmental campaigns in peninsular Malaysia, SAM had an office in Marudi, Sarawak, run by Harrison Ngau, a Kayan from the Baram region. SAM was also the Malaysian member of Friends of the Earth International. SAM provided logistical support for the blockades, and arranged for twelve native representatives to go to Kuala Lumpur, where they met with the acting prime minister and a variety of high government officials.[81] Although Dayak customary rights to land were recognized in law, the state government continued to violate them.

Before the blockades in 1987, forest campaigners had already begun to mount an international campaign involving deforestation in the region. At a meeting of FOE International in Penang in September 1986, everyone was looking for a way to influence the tropical timber trade, especially with regard to Japan. FOE–U.K. promoted the view that a campaign needed an institutional lever such as International Tropical Timber Organization. Experience with the International Whaling Commission in the antiwhaling campaign was undoubtedly a factor in that assessment. Others preferred to work for export bans and timber boycotts. Although organizations in the network concentrated on different aspects of the campaign, these were not seen as mutually exclusive.[82]

Both SAM and Bruno Manser quickly sought international attention for the blockades.[83] Marcus Colchester of Survival International went to Sarawak in April 1987 to gather information in preparation for an international campaign. The need for such a campaign began to look even more pressing in October, when the federal government responded to rising tensions by arresting 106 people under the Internal Security Act, among whom, in addition to opposition party activists, were environmental and social welfare activists and lawyers. Harrison Ngau was one of those arrested, as was a SAM attorney. Subsequently, the Sarawak government began mass arrests at the blockades, and succeeded in dismantling them.[84] In January 1988 a team from Survival International, FOE International, and IUCN spent two weeks meeting with native peoples, NGOs, lawyers, and government officials.[85]

---

[81] See *The Battle for Sarawak's Forests*, pp. 23–32.

[82] See Fred Pearce, *Green Warriors* (London: Bodley Head, 1991), pp. 182–90.

[83] SAM had previously gotten support from its international contacts (especially Survival International) on campaigns to halt plans for the Bakun Dam in Sarawak in 1985–86, and the Tembeling Dam project in Taman Negara park in 1982. On the latter, see Sahabat Alam Malaysia, *The State of the Malaysian Environment 1983–84: Towards Greater Environmental Awareness* (Penang: Sahabat Alam Malaysia, 1983), pp. 63–66.

[84] Marcus Colchester remembers this period as "the first time the 'internet' (as it is now called) really hummed with campaign information from national and local levels 'up' to the international supporters." Personal communication, 6 December 1996.

[85] *The Battle for Sarawak's Forests*, p. 48.

Despite passages of a forest amendment bill in late 1987 that made interfering with logging operations a criminal act punishable with a heavy
fine and imprisonment, the blockades were repeated. From 1988 into the
1990s, they offered a powerful symbol of resistance and a continuing
stimulus to network activities though they were of little value in producing concessions from state officials. Although the Penan Association and
longhouse organizations continued to try to gain land titles or communal
forest designations, the logging went on.

Framing the Sarawak Conflict

The Sarawak campaign has different meanings for different groups of
proponents. For people influenced by the experiences of Bruno Manser,
who emerged from his hiding place in the forest and somehow returned
to Europe in 1990, the nomadic Penan tribesmen were the symbolic center of the story. Organizing with the Penan at the center has created powerful images of an exotic and lost people fighting a heroic battle for the
forest in the interest, it is implied, of all of us. Not surprisingly, this vision
of the conflict has generated the most powerful media images. Filmmak-
ers, journalists, and photographers have in the main placed the Penan at
the center of their accounts. Although the Penan are indeed an important
part of the Sarawak story, several other frames have produced different
kinds of strategies and engaged different constellations of actors.

Some organizations, including the World Rainforest Movement's Forest Peoples' Program, SAM, Survival International, and *The Ecologist*,
have placed primary emphasis on indigenous land rights, which is also a
central issue in Evelyne Hong's influential book *Natives of Sarawak*. Without secure land title, they argue, the structural inequalities that prevent
Dayak populations from resisting timber interests can never be addressed. This cogent vision of the problem is less resonant internationally
than the Penan story, and one with which transnational networks have
more difficulty organizing.[86] The causal chain is fairly long, and the
remedies difficult to devise.

The other main transnational strategy that emerged from the Sarawak
case was its embedding in a broader campaign around tropical or rainforest timber (and in some cases temperate and boreal timber as well). This
decentralized strategy has allowed space for considerable variation in organizational activities. Its main components have been consumer boycotts,
targeting corporations and particular kinds of businesses (Mitsubishi,

---

[86] For a comparative treatment illustrating this argument, see Marcus Colchester and
Larry Lohmann, eds., *The Struggle for Land and the Fate of the Forests* (Penang: World Rainforest Movement, 1993).

Do-it-Yourself stores, for example), persuading local or state governments to refrain from using tropical timber in construction projects, pressuring national governments and the European Union for tropical timber bans, pressuring ITTO members to develop sustainability requirements, and, increasingly, "eco-labeling." A large number of organizations have adopted these strategies, shared information, and collaborated on certain activities, though sometimes disagreeing over where to direct energies at particular stages.

This campaign involves a number of loosely connected subcampaigns with different organizational sponsors.[87] A central role, though not always a coordinating one, has belonged to the constellation of organizations headquartered in Penang–SAM, the Asian-Pacific People's Environmental Network, the Third World Network, and the World Rainforest Movement. By the early 1990s the campaign was focused on logging in Papua New Guinea, Guyana, and Brazil (in all of which Sarawak logging companies have expanded their operations).

Particular donors have been extremely important to this network. NOVIB, because it makes a special effort to build relationships among the organizations it funds, provides important linkages among network nodes. As a major funder of SAM, NOVIB was especially well placed. As with the other networks we have studied, meetings held parallel to official ones such as those of the ITTO Council and the World Bank/IMF meetings are also important networking opportunities.

Campaign Strategies around Sarawak's Forests

The Sarawak campaign's efforts to set in motion a boomerang strategy had some effect, but fell far short of success. From taking Dayak representatives to meet with officials in Kuala Lumpur and foreign capitals to contesting the information Malaysian representatives presented in international forums, the network mobilized vast quantities of information and testimony. Repeated barricades of logging roads were powerful symbols of resistance. Demanding that the Malaysian federal government intervene to control or block log exports from Sarawak, the network hoped

[87] Along with those already mentioned, a partial list would include Friends of the Earth in the U.K., Sweden, and the U.S., Greenpeace International's Rainforest Campaign in the Netherlands, the Rainforest Action Network and the Bank Information Center in the U.S., the Rainforest Information Center and Rainforest Action Group in Australia, the Center for Science and Environment in India, the Japan Tropical Forest Action Network and its spinoff the Sarawak Campaign Committee, WWF in Switzerland and its international affiliates, Urgewald in Germany, Robin Wood in Germany and France, Probe International, and various First Nations groups in Canada. In addition to the Consumer Association of Penang and its spinoffs in Malaysia, there is also the Malaysian Environmental Protection Society (EPSM), and the Malaysian Nature Society. Partial list composed from documents and news reports, with help from Chad Dobson of the Bank Information Center, Washington, D.C.

to exert moral leverage. No effective material leverage was available—no World Bank loans in relevant areas, for example, or strategically placed aid programs. However, because Malaysia aspired to leadership in the Southeast Asian region, the idea that it would respond to moral leverage seemed a credible one. Moral leverage proved insufficient, however, to overcome Prime Minister Mahathir's dependence on the votes of Sarawak's political elites to maintain his broad coalition government. Moreover, there is some evidence that Mahathir's willingness to stand up to U.S. and European critics on this issue may even have enhanced his regional prestige.

Beyond the matter of leverage, however, the tropical timber campaign implicitly proposed a different kind of relationship between north and south than existed in the Brazilian case. From the perspective of most of the Sarawak campaigners, the blame for overexploitation of timber in the region belonged even more to importers than it did to the exporter. Without demand, went the argument, there would be no supply.[88] Thus the campaign was framed and focused quite differently from those waged around World Bank projects; instead of focusing the energies of activists in developed countries on a developing country target, it asked them to target their efforts at home.

The reasons for the difference were both ideological and logistical. First, there was no single source of leverage that provided the same purchase over the Sarawak situation that the World Bank seemed to offer in Rondônia. The central government's insistence that it had no authority over timber extraction in Sarawak was not a fiction; the tradeoff between centralizing oil revenues and leaving timber revenues to the states of East Malaysia had been a crucial compromise at the time of federation. For Sarawak's politicians, growing rich from timber concessions, there was simply no incentive—positive or negative—to stop logging. Because of Mahathir's dependence on a very broad coalition, the political costs of attempting to intervene might have been very high. Furthermore, the Malaysian NGOs that provided the bridge between the Dayak populations in Sarawak and the transnational network were not anti-development—though they wanted to see development's fruits distributed more justly—and believed that first world governments and NGOs should not use the environmental issue as a weapon to prevent third world countries from developing autonomously. This argument was especially salient in international debates during the preparatory process for the 1992 UN Conference on

---

[88] See S. M. Mohamed Idris, "Speech of Acceptance of the Right Livelihood Award at Swedish Parliament," 9 December 1988, in *The Battle for Sarawak's Forests*, pp. 186–90. Idris was president of SAM.

Environment and Development in Rio de Janeiro.[89] The tropical timber campaign therefore focused attention on the industrialized world, that rabidly consumed Sarawak's tropical hardwoods.

The Tropical Timber Campaign and Its Effects

Campaigning around tropical timber had the advantage of decentralization, which allowed for a variety of activities and styles—from Rainforest Action Network activists climbing Mitsubishi office buildings to hang boycott banners and parading with huge Godzilla figures to protest Japanese tropical hardwood imports to WWF's more sober negotiations over sustainability guidelines with corporations.

Organizations in Germany, the United Kingdom, and the Netherlands launched boycotts in 1988. On a motion from a Dutch Green party delegate, the European Parliament voted in 1988 to recommend Malaysian timber bans to European Union (EU) members until its logging became sustainable. The EU Commission subsequently overturned that recommendation, but as a symbol of protest it garnered much publicity. In May 1989 Australia's Rainforest Action Group, which had already called for a boycott, deployed swimmers and kayaks to Malaysian timber-bearing ships. The Rainforest Action Network in the United States declared a boycott of Mitsubishi, and Friends of the Earth did the same in Europe.

In addition to corporate boycotts, environmental organizations organized hundreds of local government boycotts of the use of tropical timber in municipal construction. This strategy was very successful in Europe; by November 1990 local boycotts had so incensed Malaysians and Indonesians that they threatened trade retaliations. In 1993 and 1994 Japanese activists stepped a similar local campaign.[90]

These protests had little effect on logging. In 1990, timber operators in Sarawak cut a record eighteen million cubic meters of tropical hardwood logs. In early 1990, angry at foreign pressure, the Malaysian government had asked the ITTO to assess the question of sustainability. The ITTO team reported in May 1990 that Sarawak was logging at eight to ten times a sustainable level.[91] The report recommended a reduction in log output by 1.5 million cubic meters a year. In 1992 the Sarawak government

[89] See Martin Khor, "The State of Cooperation in the Present World Situation: A Critique," in *Development, International Cooperation and the NGOs: I International Meeting of NGOs and the United Nations System Agencies,* (English version) ed. Instituto Brasileiro de Análises Sociais e Econômicos/UN Development Programme (Rio de Janeiro, 1992), pp. 45–62.

[90] Sarawak Campaign Committee, "Japan Rainforest Campaign Update," 25 February 1996, from Econet conference wrm. rainforest, topic 211.

[91] Diane Jukofsky, "Problems and Progress in Tropical Forests," *American Forests* 97: 7–8 (July 1991) (from Nexis).

claimed it would comply with the recommendation, but regulations continued to be weakly enforced, and illegal logging is common.[92]

But the trade issue had clearly become a serious one. In October 1991 Prime Minister Mahathir gave the keynote address at the meeting of the Association of Southeast Asian Nations (ASEAN) economy ministers, saying that ASEAN countries must speak with one voice against campaigns linking trade and environmental issues, and that the threats these posed to development had reached serious proportions.

In 1992 the campaign in Europe intensified. Friends of the Earth for the first time endorsed green labeling, after an extensive consumer survey in the United Kingdom showed that over 90 percent worried about the rainforest (though 60 percent did not know which hardwoods were tropical timber). The following year, Dutch NGOs signed a covenant with the Dutch government and timber importers, establishing a 1995 deadline for restricting tropical timber imports to those from sustainable sources; by the end of the summer the covenant had been signed by 240 timber companies accounting for 95 percent of the Dutch market. Malaysian representatives to a 1993 ITTO meeting attacked the covenant as discriminatory, as it restricted developing country imports but did not apply the restrictions to other timber producers.[93] Austria also provoked Malaysian ire: in 1992, the Austrian government passed a tropical timber ban, only to retract it the following year when Malaysia threatened to retaliate against Austrian goods. In response to a threatened Swiss ban, Malaysia offered to target Nestlé.

Measuring the impact of the tropical timber campaign requires that we define clearly the goals the campaign intended to reach. For those who wanted to preserve the nomadic lifeways of the Penan and the forest in which they lived, the campaign failed. Only a few hundred Penan remain in the forest. The rest live in longhouses, many work in timber camps and others suffer from the chronic unemployment that has beset communities throughout the region as the loggers move on. For those who wanted to fuel a struggle for land rights, the campaign continues. SAM has helped to organize several hundred community associations, for which security of tenure remains the precondition for any kind of community development activity. Although the transnational network does not exert direct leverage over this question, the campaign nonetheless provides some degree of protection to local efforts. For those who wanted to stop tropical

[92] Michael Vatikiotis, "Clearcut Mandate," *Far Eastern Economic Review* 156:43 (28 October 1993) (from Nexis). See also Michael Ross, "The Political Economy of Logging in Southeast Asia: Clientelism, Misregulation, and Reform," paper presented at American Political Science Association, Chicago, Ill., 31 August–3 September 1995. (Cited with permission.)

[93] "Netherlands Timber Suppliers Say Campaign to Reduce Tropical Timber Imports Undermines Agreement," *Reuter Textline: Financieele Dagblad*, 12 January 1994 (from Nexis).

timber logging in Sarawak, the campaign also failed. Sarawak will be logged out in five years, and Sarawakian timber companies are now repeating the process in Guyana and Papua New Guinea. The substantive goals of the Sarawak campaign, in other words, were not met.

In some respects, though, the efforts of the NGO networks and activists were remarkably successful. The Malaysian newspaper *Business Times* reported in October 1995, "Malaysia's timber exports to Europe have fallen by half since 1992 due to pressures from environmental groups on local and municipal governments in Europe to boycott or ban tropical timber products."[94] Tropical timber imports into the Netherlands fell by 50 percent between 1990 and 1995, "mainly as a result of an NGO boycott campaign."[95] Everyone seems to agree that the campaign succeeded in reducing consumption of tropical timber in some of the major importing countries.

If we see the tropical timber campaign as pursuing procedural rather than substantive goals, that is, a change in the international timber trading regime, then it has had some limited success. Campaign activities raised the salience of the issue and eventually placed it on the trade agenda. Unlike subsequent environmentalist attempts to use the trade agenda, as in the dispute over the effects of tuna fishing on dolphins, a forum was in place in which the issues could be ajudicated—the ITTO. Within the ITTO, beyond pressuring the institution to send investigative missions to logging areas and hold states accountable to their commitments, activists in the network have forced debates on the social dimensions of logging and on customary and common property arrangements. However, the new international tropical timber agreement negotiated in 1994 was far weaker than expected. Although it sets the year 2000 as a target for reaching sustainable forest management, the targets are weakly presented in the agreement, and contribution to a fund to help producers meet the goals remains voluntary. Consumer countries agreed to a nonbinding commitment to apply similar guidelines for managing their own forests, but they refused the demand of tropical forest countries that the agreement include timber from temperate and boreal forests. This was a retreat from the commitment made at Rio in 1992 for a global approach to forest issues.

CONCLUSIONS

More than the other network campaigns examined in this book, rainforest campaigns are built on the tensions between recognizing structural

[94] Joycelyn Lee, "Malaysia: Timber Exports to Europe Halved Since 1992," *Reuter Textline: Business Times* (Malaysia), 17 October 1995, (from Nexis).
[95] "Netherlands—Tropical Timber Ban," *National Trade Data Bank Market Reports*, 8 December 1995 (from Nexis).

causes and designing strategies that seek remedies by placing blame on, and influencing the behavior of, particular actors. Furthermore, the struggles they entail over meaning, power, and access to resources highlight the north-south dimension found in many network campaigns. The campaigns include participants whose understandings have been changed by their ongoing conversation with what anthropologist Anna Tsing calls people in out-of-the-way-places.[96] And, since these are stories about the real world, the campaigns include participants whose understandings have not been changed at all.

Environmental advocacy networks have not so much gotten the tropical forest issue onto the agenda—it was already there—as they have changed the tone of the debate. To the frequent consternation of the epistemic community of scientists and policymakers who had succeeded in placing it on the agenda initially, the advocacy networks deliberately politicized the issues. While the epistemic community had sought to design sound policies and tried on the basis of their authoritative knowledge to persuade governments to adopt them, advocacy networks looked for leverage over actors and institutions capable of making the desired changes. Advocacy networks also insisted on different criteria of expertise. Although they did not deny the expertise of the scientists, they demanded equal time for direct testimony about experience. And within the networks they also cultivated the strategic expertise of good organizers. The issue, especially for the multilateral bank campaigners, was not ultimately forests, or dams, or any other particular environmental issue, but leverage over institutions that make a difference.

The advocacy networks helped to broaden the definition of which information and whose knowledge should shape the agenda on tropical forest issues. In the process, they won seats at the bargaining table for new actors. Their campaigns created a new script for sustainable forest management projects, with roles for "local people," "NGOs," and so forth. We must be careful not to exaggerate the power of the individuals and groups that play these roles, relative to that of states, economic actors like corporations, or multilateral organizations (the Planafloro deliberative council is a good example). Nonetheless, once these roles have been legitimized, organizations like the World Bank must address them.

How much change have transnational advocacy networks produced in the tropical forest issue? Because the networks are not the only reform-minded actors engaged, exact attributions of influence are difficult. The multilateral development bank campaign would certainly not have had much success without the collaboration of network members inside the

[96] Anna Lowenhaupt Tsing, *In the Realm of the Diamond Queen* (Princeton: Princeton University Press, 1993).

bank. At the levels of both discursive and procedural change the network has been remarkably successful. Multilateral development banks increasingly claim to be addressing environmental objectives in loans, and there is some evidence that they have begun to eliminate high-risk projects much earlier in the project evaluation cycle. Besides having adopted the discourse of sustainable development, the bank has also implemented important procedural changes, including the information policy. Under increased pressure from the United States after the 1989 Pelosi amendment, all of the multilateral banks are taking the environmental assessment process more seriously.

Similarly, though less dramatically, the tropical timber campaign has had considerable success in promoting discursive change and some success with procedural change as well. Malaysia, as well as other tropical forest states, has begun at least to use the discourse of sustainable forestry, whether or not much has changed in practice. Malaysia has also adopted action plans phasing out unsustainable logging, and has begun to encourage local wood processing. The ITTO has adopted somewhat more stringent standards for movement toward demonstrably sustainable forestry practices. Green labeling, about which forest campaign advocates are quite divided, has not yet proved itself; should it change behavior in the ways that its proponents hope, this may stimulate further steps from the ITTO.

Among the people whose testimony generated the sharpest images of the impact of deforestation on lives, signs of success are harder to find. In Sarawak the transnational advocacy campaign has had very little impact. Logging goes on with its ecological and human impacts. In Rondônia, rubber tappers in the areas protected by the Planafloro will, at least for now, maintain use rights over a demarcated territory. Amerindian reserves will be demarcated as well, but they remain vulnerable to encroachment by goldminers, loggers, and even settlements, as long as the state continues omissive in enforcement. Furthermore, what they have won will not be easily extended to other rubber tappers, to other indigenous peoples, to others with insecure tenure.

The different outcomes in the two cases reflect in part the different kinds of campaigns, but even more they suggest that environmental issues fit differently into different configurations of domestic political struggle. Both Sarawak and Rondônia are on the geographic and demographic frontiers of their respective national life. Sarawak, nonetheless, has considerably more leverage over its central government than does Rondônia, for reasons of both political economy and governing coalitions. Domestic political structures, political cultures, and coalition behavior are important factors here. Timing also matters. The kind of nationalist discourse of modernization offered by the Mahathir government In Malaysia has long fallen on cynical ears in northern Brazil; this is not to say that nationalism no longer resonates there, but that Brazilians are less likely than Malaysians to imagine that the benefits of modernization will be shared.

Both states and NGOs are learning new languages with which to address old problems. Although the problem may not become more tractable in translation, the linkages that networks create make possible the search for common ground—what in the next chapter is called a "common advocacy position."

CHAPTER 5

Transnational Networks on Violence against Women

Susana Chiarotti, one of the founding coordinators of Indeso-Mujer in Rosario, Argentina, has given a dramatic description of the moment when the issue of violence against women began to crystallize:

We began to make the connection between violence and human rights when a "compañera" from Buenos Aires brought us the article by Charlotte Bunch on "Women's rights as human rights," which she got at a meeting in California on Leading the Way Out. I was the only one in my group that read English and when I read it, I said to myself, "Hmmm . . . a new approach to human rights. This we have not seen before. And a new approach to violence as well." So I told the other women in my group, "It seems to me that this would be the key to end our isolation." Women's groups are not isolated from each other, but society's reception of us is "there are the women again with their stuff." "This new approach," I said, "would be very interesting, because we could recruit a lot of people who are not going to be able to say no." So I translated the article for them during our meetings. See how powerful theory is? I am an activist, but this theoretical piece made a great difference in our work. Later, we learned about the petition campaign calling for UN recognition of women's rights as human rights. We thought the petition was a useful tool because it was so well crafted. Its language is irrefutable; you would have to cover yourself with shame if you didn't accept it. This began a new conceptualization of the violence theme, and we started to bother people from human rights organizations to broaden their vision. . . . I think that for us it is a strategic lesson, in the sense that it tells us, "Let's look for more allies. And to find them, let's look for languages that cannot be rejected."[1]

Violence against women is an issue that has arrived late and dramatically for the international women's movement, differing radically from the classic issues of suffrage, equality, and discrimination around which women have long mobilized.[2] In the 1970s it was on the agenda of neither the women's movement nor international human rights groups. The main normative legal code on women's rights, the Convention for the Elimination of All Forms of Discrimination against Women (drafted in the 1970s and adopted in 1979), does not mention violence against women. The thirty articles of this otherwise comprehensive document establish detailed norms on matters of equality and opportunity. But they contain not a single word about rape, domestic or sexual abuse, female genital mutilation, or any other instance of violence against women.[3] This chapter examines the transnational campaign on violence against women, exploring how international women's networks first converged around the issue and inserted it into global discourse.

Violence against women did not become a topic for transnational social movement or network actions until the early 1980s, and did not become an object of UN activity until 1985. Once on these agendas, however, the issue moved to the fore rapidly. By the mid-1990s it had become the most important international women's issue, and the most dynamic new international human rights concern. At the UN Conference on Women in Beijing in 1995, violence against women was a "centerpiece of the platform," one of four issues given special prominence.[4] By mid-1995 violence against women had become a "common advocacy position" of the women's movement and the human rights movement.

How can we explain both its absence from international debate before the 1980s, and the rapid attention it attracted once it emerged? The story of the emergence of violence against women as an international issue shows how two previously separate transnational networks around human rights and women's rights began to converge and mutually transform each other. The network built around violence against women thus

[1] Center for Women's Global Leadership, *International Campaign for Women's Human Rights, 1992–1993 Report* (New Brunswick, N.J.: Rutgers University, 1993), p. 24.
[2] Arvonne Fraser, "International Organizing on Violence against Women," public lecture, University of Minnesota, 12 November 1994.
[3] The only mention is in one article that calls on governments to suppress traffic in women and exploitation of prostitution. Article 6, Convention on the Elimination of All Forms of Discrimination Against Women, adopted and opened for signature, ratification, and accession by the UN General Assembly resolution 34/180 of 18 December 1979. Entry into force, 3 September 1981.
[4] Steven Mufson, "UN Women's Meeting Settles Key Disputes," *Washington Post*, 14 September 1995, p. A15.

could draw upon preexisting communication networks that were receptive to the "new ideas of the incipient movement."[5] Not all new ideas "resonate" with the submerged networks they seem made for; this one, however, resonated across significant cultural and experiential barriers. Other "women's issues" that seemed to be candidates for international campaign activity failed to do so. In the mid-1970s "women and development" began to be discussed in UN circles and by some governments and NGOs, and although it received significant institutional support, no major advocacy campaign was ever organized around the issue. Likewise, some activists urged international action against the practices of veiling and purdah in many Muslim societies, even going so far as to refer to it as "female apartheid." Yet veiling has not provoked an international campaign, but only isolated protests by women in these particular societies. Finally, one competitor to the women's rights movement at both the UN Population Conference in Cairo and the Women's Conference in Beijing was an international profamily and antiabortion network. Yet despite the extensive power the Catholic church hierarchy wielded in alliance with this movement, it failed to dominate the platforms of the two conferences, nor did it form as extensive or influential an international network as the one around women's human rights. How can we explain these differences in network formation and network success?

THE EMERGENCE OF THE INTERNATIONAL WOMEN'S NETWORK

The women's movement in the United States first popularized the modern usage of the word "network" to refer to interconnected groups of people when they coined the term "old boys' network" to criticize the informal contacts men used to further professional goals, often through exclusive men-only clubs. From that initial critique, women went on to imitate and innovate with the network model.[6] More than any other groups, women's organizations use the terms "network" and "networking" to describe their interactions. Indeed, many international women's groups are named "networks" (The International Feminist Network, Latin American and Caribbean Feminist Network against Domestic and Sexual Violence, Asian Women's Research and Action Network).[7]

---

[5] Jo Freeman, "The Origins of the Women's Liberation Movement," *American Journal of Sociology* 78:4 (January 1973): 32.

[6] Fraser, "International Organizing."

[7] See, for example, *International Feminism: Networking against Female Sexual Slavery*, Report of the Global Feminist Workshop to Organize against Traffic in Women, Rotterdam, the Netherlands, 6–16 April 1983, ed. Kathleen Barry, Charlotte Bunch, and Shirley Castley (New York: International Women's Tribune Centre, 1984); and Jessie Bernard, *The Female World from a Global Perspective* (Bloomington: Indiana University Press, 1987), p. 157.

Today's women's networks have their roots in the abolitionist movement of the 1800s and the subsequent international campaign for woman suffrage, discussed in Chapter two. Feminist theorists refer to the suffrage campaign as the "first wave" of feminism, and the movement beginning in the 1960s as the "second wave."[8] Like the suffrage movement, second-wave networks were fostered by international conferences; the emergence of modern international organizations provided more arenas for women's issues.

The Inter-American Commission on Women, started in the 1920s, was one of the groups instrumental in getting the provision on equal rights for women into the UN Charter, and recommending the formation of the UN Commission on the Status of Women. The UN Economic and Social Council (ECOSOC) established this commission in the late 1940s, along with the Commission on Human Rights (which received more institutional support).[9]

The second wave of international organizing on women began in the 1960s and early 1970s, as ideas originating with feminists in the United States and Europe sparked global debate.[10] The Commission on the Status of Women drafted the Declaration on the Elimination of Discrimination against Women, adopted in 1967, and then began work on a convention. Adopted in 1979, the Convention on the Elimination of All Forms of Discrimination Against Women entered into force in 1981.

This convention dealt mainly with discrimination, defined as "any exclusion or restriction of women on the basis of sex in the political, economic, social, cultural, civil or any other field." The 1967 declaration and the resulting convention mention discrimination and equality in practically every article, but never refer to violence against women.[11] Discrimination and equality were the master frames of the women's movement in the United States and in Europe, and the UN system. The discrimination frame did not always include the concerns of third world women's organizations, however, as revealed in many of the debates at the International Women's Year Conference in Mexico City in 1975.

The emergence of international women's networks was more intertwined with the UN system than the other networks discussed in this book. Chronologies of the international women's movement are largely a litany of UN meetings: Mexico, Copenhagen, Nairobi, Vienna, Cairo, Bei-

[8] Hester Eisenstein, *Contemporary Feminist Thought* (London: Unwin, 1984), p. 6.
[9] Sandra Coliver, "United Nations Machineries on Women's Rights: How Might They Better Help Women Whose Rights Are Being Violated," in Ellen Lutz et al., eds., *New Directions in Human Rights* (Philadelphia: University of Pennsylvania Press, 1989), pp. 28–32.
[10] Bernard, *The Female World*, pp. 109–22.
[11] The convention mentions "discrimination" twenty-nine times, "equal" or "equality" thirty-four times, "human rights" five times, but makes no mention of violence, rape, abuse, or battery.

jing. The current wave of organizing internationally on women's issues gained momentum during International Women's Year (IWY) and the UN Decade for Women (1976–85),[12] which in turn catalyzed networks around women's rights. The three conferences—in Mexico City (1975), Copenhagen (1980), and Nairobi (1985)—that spanned the UN Decade for Women served as locations to build and connect the emerging international network. Preparations for the population conference in Cairo in 1994 and the women's conference in Beijing in 1995 further extended and solidified the network. In each of the cities, increasingly large parallel conferences of NGOs took place at the same time as the official conferences; more than 14,000 women from 150 countries attended the NGO forum in Nairobi, and 20,000 attended the one in Beijing in 1995.

International conferences did not create women's networks, but they legitimized the issues and brought together unprecedented numbers of women from around the world. Such face-to-face encounters generate the trust, information sharing, and discovery of common concerns that gives impetus to network formation. The NGO meeting in Mexico City encouraged a group of women to found the International Women's Tribune Centre, which used the mailing list generated at Mexico City to keep in touch with individuals and groups around the globe, and expanded it to include new groups. Lucille Mair of Jamaica, secretary general of the Copenhagen conference, said of the Mexico City conference: "Mexico City focused on some of the fundamental issues . . . but it also did something that, while less tangible, may be in some ways more important than anything else: It established a network."[13] Today the Tribune Centre is a communication link for 16,000 individuals and groups working on behalf of women in 160 countries.[14] The NGO meeting at the Nairobi conference spawned many new regional networks, including three on women, law, and development that would be especially involved in the issue of violence against women: the Latin American Committee for the Defense of Women's Rights, the Asia-Pacific Forum on Women, Law, and Development, and Women in Law and Development in Africa.[15] World conferences also sped up ratification of the Convention on the Elimination of All Forms of Discrimination Against Women, and prodded states to change practices.[16]

---

[12] On the origins of the IWY see Hilkka Pietila and Jeanne Vickers, *Making Women Matter: The Role of the United Nations* (London: Zed Books, 1990), p. 73.

[13] Arvonne Fraser, *U.N. Decade for Women: Documents and Dialogue* (Boulder, Colo.: Westview, 1987), p. 71.

[14] *The Tribune: A Women and Development Quarterly*, newsletter 45 (July 1990).

[15] Elisabeth Friedman, "Women's Human Rights: The Emergence of a Movement," in *Women and Human Rights: An Agenda for Change*, ed. Julie Peters and Andrea Wolper (New York: Routledge, 1994), p. 24.

[16] Pietila and Vickers, *Making Women Matter*, p. 6.

Women's groups in Latin America took the lead in the use of network styles of communication, becoming models for other women's organizations around the world. Chilean women host one of two offices for ISIS International, a major women's information and communication service that links 150 countries. Latin American women often set up documentation centers connected to advocacy and grassroots groups.[17]

But at the same time that the Mexico conference encouraged network formation, it also revealed a major division among women's organizations. The conference disintegrated into a heated debate among feminists from Western countries who stressed discrimination, and women from the developing world who stressed what they considered the more pressing issues of development and social justice that affected both men and women. Often portrayed as a north-south split, these divisions also existed within northern and southern groups.[18] They continued beyond Mexico City, and indeed were exacerbated by debates over Zionism and racism at the next conference in Copenhagen.

The north-south tensions within the women's movement began to recede at the UN women's conference in Nairobi in 1985, the first one that made substantial recommendations on the issue of violence against women. These two facts are not unrelated; convergence around the issue of violence against women was the result of creating a category for discussion and action that linked concerns of women around the world.

One of the first efforts to bridge the gap between north and south was the debate over women and development,[19] stimulated by the overlap of the second UN Development Decade with the Decade for Women. Ester Boserup's pathbreaking 1970 book, *Women's Role in Economic Development*, had highlighted the issue, especially the key role of women as agricultural producers, and the U.S. Agency for International Development had created a Women and Development Bureau in 1973. The action plans issuing from the three women's decade conferences strongly reflected development language and concerns. Yet the issue of women and development never spawned a major global network or campaign. Its demands are important but prosaic: more credit opportunities for rural women, change in laws about property rights and inheritance, more equitable sharing of work between men and women, training programs, improved agricultural extension, water connections,

[17] Catherine Reeve, "Latinas Lead the World in Networking," *Chicago Tribune*, 10 July 1994, Womanews section, p. 1.

[18] See the discussion of divisions within the Latin American women's movement in Nancy Saporta Sternback et al., "Feminisms in Latin America: From Bogotá to San Bernardo," *Signs* 17:2 (Winter 1992): 393–434.

[19] We are indebted to Petrice Flowers and Helen Kinsella for helping us think about the evolution of the women and development movement, and how it related to the issue of violence against women.

roads, etc.[20] Even the most ardent advocates of the women and development approach began to be disillusioned by the mid-1980s with the disappointing results of early programs to increase women's economic participation. Many activists believed that women's economic position could not improve without addressing the root problems of women's subordinate status, and of global economic inequalities, but these concerns were so systemic that they defied individual or group efforts to effect change.

The issue of violence, on the other hand, appeared to offer clearer avenues for activism. Charlotte Bunch, head of the Center for Women's Global Leadership at Rutgers University, says, "sometimes deceptively, sometimes usefully, you feel like you can do something about it. There are everyday things you can do about it, from wherever you are."[21] Violence and development could also be linked, since in many cases violence against women limited the role they could play in development. Some of the most innovative groups to take on the women and development issue, like the Women, Law, and Development groups, later became leaders in the campaign for women's human rights.[22]

NAMING THE PROBLEM: DEFINITIONS OF VIOLENCE AGAINST WOMEN

From its first use, the term "violence against women" encompassed a range of practices in diverse locations, from household brutality to the violence of state security forces. But to start with definitions is to jump over the process through which the network helped "create" the issue, in part through naming, renaming, and working out definitions, whereby the concept "violence against women" eventually unified many practices that in the early 1970s were not understood to be connected.

What existed first was not the general category "violence against women" but separate activist campaigns on specific practices—against rape and domestic battery in the United States and Europe, female genital mutilation in Africa, female sexual slavery in Europe and Asia, dowry death in India, and torture and rape of political prisoners in Latin America. It was neither obvious nor natural that one should think of female genital mutilation and domestic abuse as part of the same category. The category "violence against women" had to be constructed and popularized before

[20] See the section on "Women, Poverty, Food Security, and Economic Empowerment," in "NGO Proposed Amendments to the African Platform for Action," 5th African Regional Conference on Women, NGO Forum, 12–15 November 1994, Dakar, Senegal, pp. 26–27.

[21] Interview with Charlotte Bunch, New York City, 21 February 1996.

[22] Margaret Schuler, "Violence against Women: An International Perspective," in *Freedom from Violence: Women's Strategies from around the World*, ed. Margaret Schuler (New York: UNIFEM, 1992), pp. 3, 6.

people could think of these practices as the "same" in some basic way. Yet activists cannot make just any category stick. This one caught on because in some way it "made sense" and it captured the imagination. As one Latin American activist pointed out, "the violence theme is very evocative. No woman can help but feel it as her own. I don't think any one of us can say that she has never felt violence against her. It crosses all our lives."[23] At the same time, the category served some key strategic purposes for activists trying to build a transnational campaign because it allowed them to attract allies and bridge cultural differences. This strategic focus forced transnational activists to search for a basic common denominator—the belief in the importance of the protection of the bodily integrity of women and girls—which was central to liberalism, and at the same time at the core of understandings of human dignity in many other cultures.

The earliest "official" definition of the term "violence against women" was developed not in the UN but in the Organization of American States (OAS), which adopted the Inter-American Convention on the Prevention, Punishment, and Eradication of Violence against Women in 1994. It defined violence against women as "any act or conduct, based on gender, which causes death or physical, sexual, or psychological harm or suffering to women, whether in the public or private sphere."[24] This definition was considerably narrower than one proposed in 1991 which also included indirect acts that intimidated or humiliated women, maintained them in sex-stereotyped roles, or denied them human dignity, whether or not these acts caused physical or mental injury or suffering.[25]

A new focus on violence in the private sphere was the major conceptual innovation that the issue of violence against women contributed to international human rights discourse. Traditional human rights work had focused on trying to get governments to stop doing something (for instance, torturing or imprisoning people). Certainly some violence against women is carried out by the state, as when rape is used as an instrument of ethnic cleansing in Bosnia, or prison guards are particularly abusive in their treatment of women prisoners; but most violence against women is carried out by private individuals, within the household or community. In cases like female genital mutilation or dowry death, the

---

[23] Susana Chiarotti, quoted in *International Campaign for Women's Human Rights 1992–1993 Report*, Center for Women's Global Leadership, p. 25.

[24] The convention was adopted by acclamation at the 24th regular session of the General Assembly of the OAS on 9 June 1994, in Belém de Pará, Brazil. As of 2 June 1997, twenty-six member states had ratified it.

[25] Inter-American Commission on Women, OAS, "Suggested Preliminary Draft for the Preparation of an Inter-American Convention on the Prevention, Punishment, and Eradication of Violence against Women," in the "Report on the Results of the Meeting of Experts to Consider the Viability of an Inter-American Convention on Women and Violence," 5–9 August 1991, Caracas, Venezuela, p. 17.

key perpetrators may even be other women, including mothers or mothers-in-law. The new international attention to violence against women implied rethinking the boundaries between public and private (as had the antislavery and anti-footbinding movements).[26]

Like the inter-American convention, the nonbinding UN Declaration on Violence against Women stresses violence that results in physical, sexual or psychological harm occurring in public or private life.[27] The OAS convention includes a list of types of violence against women, such as rape, battery, sexual abuse, torture, trafficking in persons, forced prostitution, kidnapping, sexual harassment, and violence perpetrated or condoned by the state. The UN declaration adds dowry-related violence, female genital mutilation and other traditional practices harmful to women, nonspousal violence, and violence related to exploitation.

Scope of the Problem

Scholars using demographic data estimate that between sixty and one hundred million women are "missing" in the world as a result of the most extreme forms of violence against female infants, girls, and women.[28] In China, which accounts for the majority of the missing women, births of some female children may not be reported to authorities, as a way of evading the strict one-child policy. But for the most part, "missing" means that these women and girls are prematurely dead from sex-selective abortion, female infanticide, differential access to food and medical care for girls, and other forms of gender violence. The figure of sixty million is larger than the combined combat death tolls from the First and Second World Wars yet the problem is virtually unknown to scholars and to the general population. Charlotte Bunch has argued that these women and girls should be considered just as much "disappeared" as are victims of state repression.[29]

This phenomenon is only the tip of the iceberg, in that it accounts for only gender-based violence that leads to death. In millions of other cases gender-based violence does not kill its victims, but may scar them physically

[26] Karen Brown Thompson argues that the increasing global concern with women's rights and children's rights represents a shift in the international public-private boundaries that has far-reaching implications for state-citizen relations. "Global Norms concerning Women's and Children's Rights and Their Implications for State-Citizen Relations," Ph.D. dissertation, University of Minnesota, 27 April 1997.

[27] Article 1, "Declaration on Violence Against Women," UN Commission on the Status of Women, 1992 (adopted by the UN General Assembly, Fall 1993).

[28] Amartya Sen, "Millions of Women are Missing," *New York Review of Books*, 20 December 1990; Ansley J. Coale, "Excess Female Mortality and the Balance of the Sexes in the Population: An Estimate of the Number of 'Missing' Females," *Population and Development Review* 17:3 (September 1991): 521.

[29] Interview with Charlotte Bunch.

or emotionally. The World Bank estimates that between 80 and 114 million girls and women in the world have undergone genital mutilation, which can cause long-lasting physical pain and ongoing health problems.[30] The global health burden of such violence against women, as measured by healthy years of life lost, is "comparable to that posed by other risk factors and diseases already high on the world agenda, including AIDs, tuberculosis, cancer, and cardiovascular disease."[31]

But however serious the problem appears on the basis of this data, it did not in and of itself generate a response on the part of governments or international agencies. Only after a major social movement and network campaign emerged around the issue in the late 1980s and early 1990s did it begin to be incorporated into regional and international discourses. Having called attention to these issues, the network has begun to develop an information base and a normative consensus on change. As with all the networks we consider in this book, certain issues lend themselves more easily to transnational organizing, but change never occurs before actual groups organize and press for it.

This argument is consistent with one Mary Katzenstein makes in her work on getting gender violence onto the public agenda in India. Katzenstein argues that when body politics (rape, dowry death, wife beating, and burning of widows) reach the public agenda, "the prerequisite appears to be the activities of autonomous women's organizations as the initiators of public debate." While state-initiated actions put issues involving women's economic welfare on the agenda, it was women's groups outside of govenment that got body politics on the agenda.[32]

Origins and Development of the Campaign

Feminists put issues of rape and domestic violence or battering on the agenda of the women's movement in the United States and Western Europe in the mid-1970s, but violence tended to concern the local rather than the mainstream national women's organizations.[33] The issue emerged

[30] World Bank, *World Development Report 1993: Investing in Health* (Washington, D.C.: International Bank for Reconstruction and Development, 1993), p. 50.

[31] Lori L. Heise, with Jacqueline Pitanguy and Adrienne Germain, *Violence against Women: The Hidden Health Burden*, World Bank Discussion Paper, #255 (Washington, D.C.: The International Bank for Reconstruction and Development, 1994), p. 17.

[32] Mary Katzenstein, "Getting Women's Issues onto the Public Agenda: Body Politics in India," *Samya Shakti* 6 (1991–1992): 3–4.

[33] Leslie R. Wolfe and Jennifer Tucker, "Feminism Lives: Building a Multicultural Women's Movement in the United States," pp. 435–62, and Jane Jenson, "Extending the Boundaries of Citizenship: Women's Movements of Western Europe," pp. 405–34, in *The Challenge of Local Feminisms: Women's Movements in Global Perspective*, ed. Amrita Basu (Boulder, Colo.: Westview Press, 1995), survey the development of women's movements in the United States and Western Europe, and mention the issues of domestic abuse and violence against women only in passing. We are indebted to Mary Katzenstein and Sally Kenney for bringing to our attention the centrality of issues of violence to local feminist groups in the U.S. and Europe, and for feminist writers of the 1970s.

locally as women organized in their communities to offer services to victims of rape and domestic abuse.[34] Violence was also a central theme of consciousness-raising groups, and of more radical feminist theorists who galvanized the women's movement in the 1970s.[35]

Activists opened the first shelters for battered women in London in 1971 and in the United States in 1974. In 1975 Fran Hosken founded *Women's International Network (WIN) News*, a quarterly journal of information on women's issues excerpted from correspondence and other publications, which began with discussion of domestic violence as a crucial international issue. Hosken is best known for her outspoken and controversial leadership in the campaign over female genital mutilation, but *WIN News* was also a consistent source of information on many forms of violence against women. These fledgling efforts, however, were still too weak for the issue of violence against women to become a focus at the international women's year conference in Mexico City in 1975.

But at the March 1976 First International Tribune on Crimes against Women, held in Brussels, two thousand women from forty countries spoke out on family violence, wife beating, rape, prostitution, female genital mutilation, murder of women, and persecution of lesbians (the proceedings were carried on radio in some parts of the world). The International Feminist Network (IFN), coordinated by ISIS International, grew out of the Brussels meeting.[36] The IFN was intended to serve as an action network similar to Amnesty International; in practice, however, it was more sporadic than its organizers had hoped.

The movement to combat violence against women also has roots in local action in the developing world. Locally based projects and coalitions such as GABRIELA in the Philippines, Mujeres por la Vida in Chile, and various women's groups in India and Bangladesh working on dowry-death had begun work on issues of violence in the mid- to late 1970s.[37] The two main strands of action came from women's groups in Latin America and from Asian groups working on the issue of so-called "comfort women" in army brothels used by Japanese soldiers during the Second World War. It is estimated that 200,000 women, 80–90 percent of whom were forcibly detained in Korea, were registered as sex slaves for

---

[34] See Claire Reinelt, "Moving onto the Terrain of the State: The Battered Women's Movement and the Politics of Engagement," pp. 84–104 in *Feminist Organizations*, ed. Myra Marx Ferree and Patricia Yancey Martin (Philadelphia: Temple University Press, 1995).

[35] For example, Susan Brownmiller, *Against Our Will: Men, Women, and Rape* (New York: Simon and Schuster, 1975); and Mary Daly, *Gyn/Ecology: The Metaethics of Radical Feminism* (Boston: Beacon Press, 1978).

[36] *ISIS International Bulletin* 8 (Summer 1978).

[37] Jane Roberts Chapman, "Violence against Women as a Violation of Human Rights," *Social Justice* 17:2 (Summer 1990):61; and Radha Kumar, "From Chipko to Sati: The Contemporary Indian Women's Movement," pp. 65–66, and Roushan Jahan, "Men in Seclusion, Women in Public: Rokeya's Dream and Women's Struggles in Bangladesh," p. 102, in *The Challenge of Local Feminisms*; Katzenstein, "Women's Issues," p. 6.

the Japanese army during the war.[38] The issue first attracted attention in 1976 when Korean activist Kim Il Myon published a pathbreaking book *The Emperor's Forces and Korean Comfort Women* based on government sources and war memoirs, though not on the testimony of the comfort women themselves.[39]

Later, women's groups in Korea and elsewhere drew attention to the experience of the comfort women as it applied to current violence against women. For many years the main concern of Korean women's groups had been the prevalence of sex tourism, mainly from Japan, and of prostitution around U.S. bases. In the 1980s some of these groups began to see that the history of the comfort women, "simultaneously shocking from the standpoints of morality, feminism, and patriotism," could be used to arouse feelings against sex tours.[40] The campaign was hampered, however, by the lack of firsthand accounts by comfort women themselves. Despite the trauma they had suffered, women were afraid to come forward, use their real names, or offer public testimony because of the shame such an admission would bring to their families. One of the first women to testify publicly about her experiences as a comfort woman and initiate legal action against the Japanese government did so only because all her immediate family were dead.

The case of the comfort women underscores the importance of personal testimony for networks in diverse cultural settings, even where such testimony is perceived as profoundly shameful. "All the research, rhetoric and war memoirs were as nothing until the women were prepared to come forward and speak out against their exploitation. . . . It was not until the comfort women rose to cry out, that research and activists could turn the subject into an issue."[41]

The comfort woman issue, like the issue of female genital mutilation, involves language distinctions that may be important for network campaigns. While many thought that the term "comfort women" masked the brutality of the practice, most NGOs working on the issue used that expression nonetheless. More recently, however, the Korean Council for the Matter of Comfort Women has started to use a different title: Council for the Women Drafted into Sexual Slavery by Japan.

Diverse groups throughout Latin America began to work on issues of violence in the late 1970s and early 1980s. Many were initially concerned with state violence against women. Activists pointed to the unique vul-

[38] Charlotte Bunch and Niamh Reilly, *Demanding Accountability: The Global Campaign and Vienna Tribunal for Women's Human Rights* (New York: Center for Women's Global Leadership and UNIFEM, 1994), p. 34.
[39] George Hicks, *The Comfort Women: Japan's Brutal Regime of Enforced Prostitution in the Second World War* (New York: W. W. Norton, 1994), pp. 22, 278.
[40] Ibid., pp. 175–76.
[41] Ibid., p. 22.

nerability of women prisoners for whom rape, torture, and sexual en-
slavement were often a routine part of imprisonment. When scholars began to recognize such acts not only as aberrant behaviors but part of
broader "societal archetypes and stereotypes" that were manipulated by
torturers,[42] they focused attention on deeper patterns of subordination
and violence against women, in the private as well as the public sphere.
Although women's organizations still encountered arguments that gender equality was less important than class and political oppression, they
expanded their work on gender violence during this period, often with
strong support from working-class women.[43]

The seeds of an international network on violence against women were
planted in a series of meetings at the UN Women's Conference in Copenhagen in 1980. Charlotte Bunch, who had organized a set of panels on international feminist networking at the nongovernmental forum held
parallel to the official conference, recalls:

> We observed in that two weeks of the forum that the workshops on issues
> related to violence against women were the most successful . . . they were
> the workshops where women did not divide along north-south lines, that
> women felt a sense of commonality and energy in the room, that there
> was a sense that we could do something to help each other. . . . It was so
> visible to me that this issue had the potential to bring women together in
> a different way, and that it had the potential to do that without erasing
> difference. Because the specifics of what forms violence took really were
> different. There were some things like domestic battery that really were
> everywhere, but what people chose to put as their first issue was differ-
> ent. So you get a chance to deal with difference, and see culture, and race,
> and class, but in a framework where there was a sense that women were
> subordinated and subjected to this violence everywhere, and that nobody
> has the answers. So northern women couldn't dominate and say we know
> how to do this, because the northern women were saying: "our country is
> a mess; we have a very violent society." So it created a completely differ-
> ent ground for conversation. . . . It wasn't that we built the network in that
> moment. It was just the sense of that possibility.[44]

One of the earliest attempts to realize that possibility came in 1981 at
the first feminist Encounter for Latin America and the Caribbean in 1981.
Participants proposed to call November 25 the "Day against Violence
against Women," in honor of three sisters from the Dominican Republic

---

[42] Ximena Bunster-Burotto, "Surviving beyond Fear: Women and Torture in Latin America," in *Women and Change in Latin America,* ed June Nash and Helen Safa (South Hadley,
Mass.: Bergin and Garvey, 1985), p. 299.

[43] Sonia Alvarez, *Engendering Democracy in Brazil: Women's Movements in Transition Politics*
(Princeton: Princeton University Press, 1990), pp. 134–36

[44] Interview with Charlotte Bunch.

who were murdered by security forces of the Trujillo dictatorship on that day in 1960.[45] Subsequently many Latin American women's organizations began to have annual commemorations, which in part led to the global campaign "16 Days of Activism against Gender Violence," a key campaign for raising global awareness on the issue.

In 1983, inspired by the sense of possibility at the Copenhagen workshops, Charlotte Bunch and Kathleen Barry put together a global feminist workshop to organize against traffic in women. Thirty-four women from twenty-four countries, half from the developing world, gathered for a week in Rotterdam to document and strategize about problems of female sexual slavery.[46] Although the workshop publication refers extensively to networking, no real network emerged from the meeting, for a number of reasons. First, the issue of traffic in women provoked debate between those who argued that all prostitution should be abolished and those who advocated less drastic positions. Second, third world women did not want the network to be based in the north, but no organizations in the south could shoulder the financial and infrastructural burden of coordinating it. This problem would plague women's efforts to organize internationally for years.[47]

Yet the Rotterdam workshop was important in a number of ways. It explicitly argued that the issue of sexual slavery needed to be situated in a broader debate about women's human rights, and it rejected a campaign which would promote "one-way benevolence and the continued designation of certain exploited groups as the other." In this sense the movement transcended the historical patterns evident in the earlier campaigns against footbinding and female genital mutilation. Kathleen Barry made the point forcefully.

> What this means is that Western women must be as concerned with the exploitation and enslavement of women in their own countries and cultures as they are with that of women in other parts of the world. It is only in this context that feminists can begin to work with a full definition of women's human rights by beginning with the self, the subject, and therefore extending into international work not through concern for the objectified other but as woman to woman, subject to subject. It is there that authenticity of international feminist work is established.[48]

This quotation captures the potential of networking. Networks are usually not one-way streets whereby activists in one country "help" victims

---

[45] See "Por que el 25 de noviembre?: Un dia de denuncia de la violencia hacia las mujeres," Mujer/Fempress (January 1988), p. 2.

[46] *International Feminism*, pp. 119–21.

[47] Interview with Charlotte Bunch.

[48] Kathleen Barry, "The Opening Paper: International Politics of Female Sexual Slavery," in *International Feminism*, p. 31.

in another, but part of an interactive process by which people in far-flung places communicate and exchange beliefs, information, testimony, strategy, and sometimes services. In the process of exchange they may change each other. Lori Heise, a U.S. activist who had worked on domestic violence at home, was exposed to violence against women as an international concern while doing research on women's environmental movements in India. "The big 'ah-hah' for me came around 1985 in northern Garwhal, where I was interviewing women connected to the Chipko movement, a well-known women's movement. So I would ask the women, 'If something could change in your life to make it better, what would it be?' I was fishing for 'not having to walk five miles for firewood,' but over and over they would raise issues of alcohol abuse and domestic abuse."[49]

The issue of violence against women was not squarely on the UN agenda until the Nairobi conference in 1985, at the end of the Decade for Women. Nairobi was the first step in securing agenda attention to the issue, for initiating the change in discursive positions of governments, and for strengthening linkages among women's groups working on the issue. Local activists at the NGO tribunal at the Nairobi conference formed the International Network against Violence against Women (INAVAW), a communication network for activists; still, the issue had yet to attract substantial international attention.[50]

By 1987 sufficient interest and pressure had built, that the UN organized a meeting on violence in the family and commissioned a study, *Violence against Women in the Family*, the first comprehensive survey of research on the subject.[51] From this point on there was growing attention to the issue, with an "explosion of organizing" in NGOs.[52]

Key groups in the north included the International Women's Rights Action Watch (IWRAW), the Institute for Women, Law, and Development, and a Canadian-based group, MATCH International. All three groups worked with their own networks of counterpart organizations in the developing world. An international survey which MATCH had carried out to identify the primary concerns of women's organizations around the world indicated that "violence against women was the overwhelming priority of all groups surveyed."[53]

Latin Americans were among the most active participants in the new global conversation. Activists set up the Southern Cone Network against

[49] Interview with Lori Heise, Washington, D.C., 27 September 1995.
[50] Chapman, "Violence against Women," 57–58.
[51] UN, *Violence against Women in the Family* (New York: United Nations, 1989) Sales No. E.89.IV.5.
[52] Fraser, "International Organizing."
[53] Helen Kinsella, "Transnational Networks on Violence against Women," unpublished paper, December 1994.

Domestic and Sexual Violence in 1989, and the Latin American and Caribbean Network against Domestic and Sexual Violence in 1990, with subregional coordinators in Peru, Brazil, Puerto Rico, Argentina, and Costa Rica.[54]

Women's groups began to form regional networks in Asia as well. By the 1990s an Asia-wide movement had emerged on the issue of comfort women which involved groups in the Philippines, Okinawa, Indonesia, Korea, and Japan, and was formalized as the Asia Solidarity Network on the Forced Military Comfort Women Problem at a conference in 1992. One of the key goals of the network was "to enlist the cooperation of world human rights organizations such as the UN for the solution to the military comfort woman problem."[55]

Partly as a result of these pressures from women's networks, the late 1980s and early 1990s saw the beginning of normative development on the issue of violence against women in the UN and in the inter-American system. Women moved away from the well-institutionalized frame of discrimination, already embodied in the 1979 women's convention, toward the "rights" frame implicit in the language of violence against women. Even though rights issues were firmly embedded in the UN system, the human rights bodies and treaties paid little attention specifically to women's rights. Furthermore, the public-private divide within human rights discourse posed a significant problem for women's organizations that hoped to claim that domestic violence, dowry death, and female genital mutilation, though all carried out in the household, were nevertheless violations of women's rights for which states could and should be held responsible.

The international women's movement in the late 1980s took on this challenge with surprisingly successful results. The first step was to modify existing conventions to reflect the new concern. In response to network pressures, the Committee on the Elimination of Discrimination against Women (CEDAW), which oversees the implementation of the 1979 convention, "read into" the convention an obligation to take steps in relation to violence against women (the convention itself does not explicitly refer to it).[56]

In the context of this increasing global consciousness and mobilization around women's human rights, four phenomena that heightened attention and stimulated action around the issue of violence against women converged in the early 1990s: (1) preparations for the World Conference on Human Rights to be held in Vienna in 1993; (2) international news

---

[54] Red Feminista Latinamericana y del Caribe Contra La Violencia Doméstica y Sexual, *Boletín* 6 (November 1994): 1.

[55] Hicks, *Comfort Women*, p. 254.

[56] Andrew Byrnes, "Women, Feminism and International Human Rights Law: Methodological Myopia, Fundamental Flaws or Meaningful Marginalisation: Some Current Issues," mimeo, p. 32; UN CEDAW 11th sess., New York, 20–31 January 1992, General Recommendation no. 19.

coverage about the use of rape in wartime as an instrument of the ethnic cleansing campaign in the former Yugoslavia;[57] (3) proactive funding of work on the issue by the Ford Foundation and progressive European foundations, supported by the intermediary work of the Global Fund for Women; and (4) the crucial catalyst role played by the Global Campaign on Women's Human Rights organized by the Center for Women's Global Leadership (CWGL) at Rutgers University.

Development of the issue of violence against women resembles the pattern we see in other global networks. An emerging, dispersed network of groups begins to create global awareness about the issue. These efforts intensify and unite with the emergence of a "target" (in this case the World Conference on Human Rights, and later the Beijing conference) and a "condensation symbol" which "evoke[s] the emotions associated with the situation"[58] and provokes mass responses because it condenses threats or reassurances into one symbolic moment. In the case of the woman's movement the routine use of rape in the former Yugoslavia as a tool of ethnic cleansing condensed into a single set of events the fears and threats many women feel in their daily lives—that they will be the targets of special violence by virtue of their gender. Other events likewise heightened the symbolic power of the issue. In the United States the rape and beating of a woman jogging in Central Park dramatized the danger that women confronted in their daily lives. In India two cases focused public attention on the issue of violence against women: in the late 1970s police raped a young woman in custody, and the court found the police innocent because she was of "loose morals"; and in 1979 the deathbed statement of a young Delhi woman said her in-laws had killed her because her parents could not meet their dowry demands.[59] The "catalyst campaign" of the CWGL pulled together the awareness created by these symbolic events into a visible political campaign with concrete outcomes. This pattern—DISPERSED NETWORK→TARGET ›CONDENSATION SYMBOL→ CATALYST CAMPAIGN→STRONG NETWORK AND HEIGHTENED GLOBAL AWARENESS—is one that appears many times in the stories of successful networks.

FUNDING OF THE NETWORK

A handful of key foundations facilitated the growth of the network around women's human rights. After the UN International Women's

[57] Arvonne Fraser, "The Feminization of Human Rights," *Foreign Service Journal* 70:12 (December 1993): 31; interview with Dorothy Thomas (director, Women's Rights Project, Human Rights Watch), New York City, 20 October 1995.

[58] Murray Edelman, *The Symbolic Uses of Politics* (Urbana: University of Illinois Press, 1985), p. 6.

[59] Kumar, "From Chipko to Sati," p. 67.

Year Conference in Mexico City in 1975, the Ford Foundation's board of
trustees set aside reserve funds that field offices could claim for funding
projects on women's issues, leading to significant Ford funding on the issue of violence against women in the late 1980s. Major U.S. foundation
grants on projects on women's rights and violence against women increased from eleven grants totaling $241,000 in 1988 to sixty-eight grants
totaling $3,247,800 in 1993. Ford Foundation grants account for almost
one-half of the total dollars from large U.S. foundations on the issue during this period.[60] Exact amounts are not available for European foundations, but interviews indicate that many European semipublic and
private foundations increased their funding on women's rights in the
same period.

The increase in foundation funding in 1990, after the explosion of NGO
activity in the late 1980s, suggests that foundations did not lead, but did
greatly facilitate the growth of work on women's human rights in the period 1989–93. Some important funders of traditional human rights activity increased funding to women's rights and violence against women in
the late 1980s. Sometimes these funding patterns can be traced to staff
changes within foundations. The Shaler Adams Fund financed many of
the groups that work on violence against women in large part because
the director felt "passionately" about the issue of violence against
women, and the MacArthur Foundation got involved when Carmen Bar-
rosa joined the staff, bringing with her the premise that you can't deal
with population issues unless you deal with women's rights.[61] The overall trend suggests a broader pattern at work, where foundation staff respond to new and exciting issues in the NGO realm. Foundations were
key supporters of the organizing efforts that made women's groups a
powerful presence at the Vienna World Conference on Human Rights, as
well as the Cairo Population Conference and the Beijing Women's Conference.

Foundation funding introduces significant asymmetries into networks.
Almost all the money for network activities comes from foundations in
the United States and Western Europe. These foundations have criteria
for funding, such as "absorptive capacity" or "financial accountability,"
that may preclude participation of many NGOs based in the developing
world. Few staff members in small NGOs have the time or experience to
write demanding funding proposals to large foundations, and foundations are often unwilling to evaluate small seed or start-up grants that
new NGOs need most. As a result, the bulk of foundation funding goes to
the larger and more professional of the northern NGOs. Some "pass-

[60] Data calculated from Dialogue Database File #27, based on the *Foundation Grants Index
1988–93* (New York: Foundation Center).
[61] Interview with Marsha Freeman, Minneapolis, Minn., 1 March 1996.

through" programs like the Global Fund for Women have been developed to deliver money to smaller NGOs in the developing world, but these account for only a portion of total funding. Grants to the Global Fund for Women from U.S. foundations accounted for one-third of the total grants on women's rights from major U.S. foundations, and slightly more than one-fifth of the total dollars.[62]

One network activist from Nigeria complained that northern NGOs claim to represent southern groups when all groups are desperately seeking funding. She asked: "Why should we link hands? Local NGOs cannot get support for their work so we have to affiliate with international NGOs. Then we all hold up our hands to the 'gates of heaven.' When the international NGOs arrive at the gate, they drop us and do the talking on our behalf."[63]

The Human Rights Frame

The preparations for the 1993 World Conference on Human Rights spurred organizing efforts. Women's rights did not figure in the advance preparatory documents for the conference, something that "got people angry and also gave them a target to be organized around."[64] Many activists saw the conference as a pulpit from which to gather support for their positions.

The preparations for this conference strengthened connections between the international human rights network and the women's network.[65] The result was the application of the "human rights methodology" to the cause of women's rights, and a fuller appreciation within mainstream human rights organizations of the problems with the public-private divide that had characterized their work. The human rights methodology has been summed up as "promoting change by reporting facts." Aimed at holding governments accountable for abuses, it requires that NGOs: "a) carefully document abuses; b) clearly demonstrate state accountability for those abuses under international law; c) develop a mechanism for effectively exposing documented abuse nationally and internationally."[66] These aims are the essence of the "information politics" strategy discussed in Chapter 1 that is one of the principal tools of networks.[67]

---

[62] Figures calculated from data from *Foundation Grants Index.*

[63] Joanna Kerr, "Strategies for Action," in *Ours by Right: Women's Rights as Human Rights,* ed. Joanna Kerr (London: Zed Books, 1993), p. 166.

[64] Interview with Dorothy Thomas.

[65] Fraser, "The Feminization of Human Rights," p. 33.

[66] Dorothy Q. Thomas, "Holding Governments Accountable by Public Pressure," in *Ours by Right,* p. 83.

[67] Ibid., p. 84.

Thus women's issues were incorporated into a "rights" frame, or master frame, supplementing the "discrimination" frame of the 1979 women's convention and the "development" frame in the women in development debate. But not everyone agrees that the human rights frame, model, and methodology are always appropriate for the women's network. Marsha Freeman argues that the human rights methodology works well where you can do fact-finding, but breaks down when you are talking about systematic oppression in patriarchal societies. "Women are rarely prisoners of conscience but they are always prisoners of culture."[68] Other activists, especially from the developing world, believe that the rights frame privileges certain political and civil rights to the exclusion of economic, social, or cultural rights, and that its excessive focus on individuals obscures structural inequalities among classes and states. Even some of its advocates consider the rights frame just a starting point for organizing networks that could take on more controversial issues such as social justice or sexuality.

When mainstream human rights organizations began to take on the issue of women and human rights in the late 1980s and early 1990s, most restricted themselves to instances where states, rather than private individuals, had perpetrated the abuses. Women activists, professional staff, and contributors pressured the mainstream groups to work on women's rights. Although women's rights projects are now permanent parts of the mainstream organizations, they are often marginalized, underfunded, and understaffed.

THE GLOBAL CAMPAIGN FOR WOMEN'S HUMAN RIGHTS

The issue finally coalesced in the early 1990s around the Global Campaign for Women's Human Rights coordinated by the Center for Women's Global Leadership at Rutgers. When the Center took up the issue of women's human rights, the ground had already been prepared by the activities of international networks discussed above and of local groups in many countries. But the work of CWGL played a crucial catalytic role, cementing the consciousness created by the existing groups into a single symbolic, visible campaign.

The Center chose the theme of women, violence, and human rights "because it crosses national, class, racial, age, and ethnic lines" and because working on it offers "unique opportunities to build bridges across cultures, to learn from similarities and differences, and to link strategies globally." In 1990 the new director of CWGL, Charlotte Bunch, wrote an

---

[68] Interview with Marsha Freeman, Minneapolis, Minn., 5 May 1994.

influential article which made the theoretical and practical linkages be-tween violence against women and international human rights norms.[69] Bunch had first sensed at the Copenhagen Conference in 1980 that con-cerns about violence could bring women together. By 1983 she became convinced that human rights language offered a vehicle to approach the violence issue from a feminist perspective.[70] The article was short, pow-erful, and struck a responsive chord; it was reprinted, circulated widely, and had a profound influence on many individuals and groups.

The Center for Women's Global Leadership held an international plan-ning meeting in May 1990, at which twenty-one women from diverse re-gions and projects reviewed ongoing work and offered suggestions for priorities.[71] The preparation of the campaign offers an unusually clear ex-ample of global moral entrepreneurs consciously strategizing on how to frame issues in a way likely to attract the broadest possible global coali-tion. The planning session generated what Bunch later referred to as "network thinking" that informed the continuing work of the center.

CWGL held its first Women's Global Leadership Institute in 1991, with grassroots activists from twenty countries. Participants helped develop strategies for linking women's rights to human rights; these included the "16 Days of Activism against Gender Violence" campaign of local actions from November 25 (International Day against Violence against Women, around which Latin American feminists had been organizing since 1981) to December 10 (Human Rights Day). The "16 days" campaign was car-ried out by groups in 25 countries in 1991, 50 countries in 1992, and 120 countries in 1993.[72] Its very conception symbolically made the connection between violence against women and human rights. The campaign ac-commodated varied local activities that generally involved a combina-tion of symbolic and information politics.[73] During the sixteen-day campaign in 1991, for example, a women's group in Fiji organized ra-dio discussions, street theater, and film events. Korean women's organi-zations held a memorial service for victims of gender violence, and British women held a demonstration in Trafalgar Square.

In February 1993, CWGL held the International Women's Strategic Planning Meeting to bring together women from around the world to prepare for the Vienna Meeting. The Center for Women's Global Leader-

---

[69] Charlotte Bunch, "Women's Rights as Human Rights: Toward a Revision of Human Rights," *Human Rights Quarterly* 12 (1990): 486–98.

[70] Interview with Charlotte Bunch.

[71] Center for Women's Global Leadership, *Women, Violence, and Human Rights: 1991 Women's Leadership Institute Report* (New Brunswick, N.J.: Rutgers University, 1992), p. 8–10.

[72] Bunch, "Women's Rights as Human Rights," 146–47; Red Feminista Latinoamericana y Del Caribe Contra la Violencia Doméstica y Sexual, *Boletín* 6 (November 1994), p. 12.

[73] Interview with Charlotte Bunch.

ship joined the International Women's Tribunal Center (IWTC) and the International YWCA to initiate a worldwide petition "calling on the 1993 Conference to comprehensively address women's human rights at every level of the proceedings and demanding that gender violence be recognized as a violation of human rights requiring immediate action." The drive eventually gathered more than 300,000 signatures in 123 countries and twenty languages. Over eight hundred groups joined as cosponsors of the petition.[74] The drive continued after the Vienna conference, and by November 1994 had gathered more than 500,000 signatures and 2,000 cosponsoring groups.

In other efforts to prepare for the meeting, the Dutch cofinancing agency, NOVIB, convened a "reference group" of regional networks of women's groups from Asia, Latin America, Africa, Europe, and North America to discuss strategies for both Vienna and the 1995 Beijing conference.[75] At the same time, the International Women's Rights Action Watch advised its members on how to get input into the Vienna, Cairo, and Beijing conferences and the regional preparatory conferences, either directly by sending recommendations to the groups preparing background documents, indirectly by participating in the regional preparatory conferences, or by gaining a seat on or influencing official delegations to the conferences.[76] Women's networking efforts got support from mainstream human rights organizations, especially Amnesty International and Human Rights Watch, both of which had initiated major programs on women's rights in the late 1980s.

Vienna and Beijing

The role these networks of women's organizations eventually played at the World Conference on Human Rights in Vienna in 1993 is an example of a network's ability to draw attention to issues, set agendas, and influence the discursive positions of both states and international organizations. Most conference participants agree that the one major advance at Vienna in the international protection of human rights was integrating women's concerns into the human rights agenda, which was the direct result of lobbying by the women's rights network. The main demand of

[74] Elisabeth Friedman, "Women's Human Rights," pp. 18–35 in *Women's Rights, Human Rights*; and Charlotte Bunch, "Organizing for Women's Human Rights Globally," pp. 141–49 in *Ours by Right*. The list of international sponsoring groups to this petition includes the key groups within the network, and can be found in *Demanding Accountability*, pp. 122–23.

[75] Interview with Mario Weima (NOVIB), The Hague, Netherlands, 3 November 1993.

[76] "World Human Rights Conference in 1993," *The Women's Rights Action Watch* 5:4 (April 1992): 1.

the network petition campaign was that the UN "comprehensively address women's human rights at every level of its proceedings" and recognize gender violence as a human rights violation. The final document from Vienna explicitly recognized gender-based violence, including rape and sexual slavery, and all forms of sexual harassment and exploitation as human rights issues. Governments at the Vienna conference urged the UN General Assembly to adopt a draft declaration on violence against women. One of the more specific accomplishments of the women's rights network was the appointment of a special rapporteur on violence against women and its causes, an idea endorsed by the Vienna conference and mandated by the Commission on Human Rights. In 1992 the U.S. State Department added the category of violence against women to its annual human rights reports.

These norm-setting activities on women's rights are mainly the result of the concerted work of the international network. More than 3,000 participants representing over 1,500 NGOs from all regions of the world participated in the Vienna conference, and 49 percent of the participants were women. Grants from European and North American governments and foundations provided travel and accommodation funds for many NGO participants, especially from the south.[77]

The most dramatic network activity at the Vienna conference was that of the Tribunal for Women's Human Rights. Inspired by various people's tribunals, and by the International Tribunal on Crimes against Women in 1976, the Vienna tribunal originated in the CWGL strategic planning meeting in 1993 and was carried out by an international coordinating committee. Thirty-three women from twenty-five countries testified before three judges and an audience about their own experiences with violence or as advocates for others. The Tribunal heard specific stories of what violence means for women's lives and how human rights instruments could begin to address it. The testimonies attracted the attention of conference delegates and the media.

Preparations for the Vienna conference increased the synergy of diverse national and international efforts on violence against women,[78] and the momentum continued to build afterwards as movement activists prepared for the population conference in Cairo and then the women's conference in Beijing. The UN Special Rapporteur on Violence against Women, Radhika Coomaraswamy of Sri Lanka, presented her preliminary report to the Human Rights Commission in 1995, which summarized and highlighted much of the information that academics and women's rights activists had put forward over the pre-

[77] Ludwig Boltzmann Institute of Human Rights, "World Conference on Human Rights, Vienna, Austria, 14–25 June 1993," *NGO Newsletter* 4 (July 1993): 1.
[78] Interview with Dorothy Thomas.

vious five years. On the controversial issues of family, culture, and religion the report was forceful: though a source of positive values, the family was a main site for violence against women and for socialization processes that can lead to its justification. Coomaraswamy argued that negative cultures and traditions involving violence against women "must be challenged and eliminated." Follow-up reports would examine the three major sites of violence against women—the family, the community, and the state—as well as specific issues.[79] The first of these issue reports, on military sexual slavery in Japan and Korea during the Second World War, provoked a hostile reaction from the Japanese government.[80]

The initial program document for the Beijing conference was full of bracketed language indicating areas of disagreement. One activist remarked that such disagreement illustrated just how fragile the global consensus around women's human rights was going into the Beijing meeting.[81] But the international women's movement had developed sophisticated strategies for lobbying governments. By monitoring the status of bracketed issues and suggesting language to government delegations, representatives of NGOs and networks had real input into the final document.[82] In some cases government delegations incorporated language suggested by NGOs directly; in others governments consulted with NGOs to shape their positions on issues.[83] The final documents of Beijing and all UN world conferences are only policy statements; they are not binding on governments. Nevertheless, many activists believe that the debates at world conferences and the final documents produced are useful for raising the awareness of governments and for holding them accountable for their practices.

The downside of the network's intensive preparations for the Vienna and Beijing conferences is that many organizations were so focused on these that they neglected their own communities. The conferences stimulated global awareness and networking, but there was still a considerable distance between the new resolutions and changing actual practices.

[79] "Towards a New World Order in Human Rights: Analytical Report of the 51st Session of the Commission on Human Rights," *Human Rights Monitor* 28 (May 1995): 26.

[80] See Special Rapporteur on Violence against Women, Its Causes and Consequences, Radhika Coomaraswamy, "Report on the Mission to the Democratic People's Republic of Korea, the Republic of Korea and Japan on the Issue of Military Sexual Slavery in Wartime," UN Economic and Social Council, Commission on Human Rights, 52d sess., 4 January 1996.

[81] Interview with Dorothy Thomas.

[82] Marissa Navarro, plenary session "Report from the 5th World Congress on the Status of Women, Beijing," 19th International Congress, Latin American Studies Association, Washington, D.C., 28 September 1995.

[83] Interview with Marsha Freeman.

OTHER ADVOCACY NETWORKS

It may be useful to contrast the work of the transnational network on women's rights with that of another advocacy network with which the women's rights activists clashed at the Cairo and Beijing conferences. A transnational network of pro-life or antiabortion activists has gathered strength in recent years; one list of international NGOs contains fifteen international right-to-life organizations.[84] Two key organizational players in the network are the International Right to Life Committee (IRLC), and Human Life International, which works with affiliate organizations in thirty-seven countries. Both groups sponsor regional and international gatherings of activists and try to influence international organizations as well as their own governments. Over forty countries sent delegations from IRLC affiliates to the Cairo population conference.[85] These NGOs found powerful allies in the Vatican and the governments of a number of Middle Eastern countries. The resulting antiabortion, profamily coalition attempted to block what it considered the Western feminist thrust at the Cairo meeting and later at Beijing as well.[86]

The Vatican made several strategic discursive moves in their Cairo campaign. First, they framed their position in terms of universal human rights—not only the right of the unborn child, but also the right to have a large family. But the Vatican also invoked the counterclaim of cultural imperialism, charging that Westerners were attempting to impose immoral and inappropriate ideologies including "abortion on demand, sexual promiscuity, and [a] distorted notion of the family."[87] The Vatican also referred to another theme frequently stressed by third world countries and some transnational environmentalists: the problem is not overpopulation but overconsumption, particularly in the West.[88]

Nonetheless, analysis of the media coverage of the Cairo meeting suggests that although the antiabortion activists captured rapt media attention and stalled negotiations over the wording of key phrases, they failed to impose their vision either on the overall work of the conference or on the final document. The antiabortion network succeeded in changing a

[84] *Encyclopedia of Associations: International Organizations 1995*, 29th edition, ed. Jacqueline Barrett (Washington, D.C.: Gale Research, 1995), p. 2972.

[85] "Prolife Movement Worldwide," *Christianity Today*, 19 February 1990, p. 31; brief telephone interviews with staff of Human Life International and National Right to Life Committee, 30 January and 27 February 1995.

[86] This section draws heavily on Michael Riley, "Transnational Networks, the Media, and the Battle over Meaning: A Case Study in Cairo," unpublished paper, 9 November 1994.

[87] Cardinal John O'Connor, quoted in the *New York Times*, 15 June 1994, cited in Riley, "Transnational Networks," p. 20.

[88] *Washington Post*, 5 September 1994, cited in Riley, "Transnational Networks," p. 10.

reference to abortion in one paragraph of a 113-page plan, but it had little effect on the conference's other policy recommendations.[89]

The explanation for the relative lack of influence of the antiabortion forces is not completely clear, but several factors stand out. First, although the Vatican overshadowed the NGO participants, its legitimacy at the Cairo and Beijing conferences was undermined by certain contradictions inherent in the situation. One of its critics questioned the authority of the Holy See, a "so-called country" with a "citizenry that excludes women and children . . . to attract the most attention in talking about public policy that deals with women and children."[90] Second, the Vatican's population control message at the Cairo meeting was that abstinence and rhythm were the only appropriate birth control methods. To a conference of experts, pragmatic politicians, and advocates, the impracticality of these proposals may have limited the Vatican's influence on the broader policy agenda. While other actors within the antiabortion network may have had a more pragmatic and positive population control agenda, their views were outweighed by the Vatican's.

Women's rights networks anticipated the approach that antiabortion forces would take and tried to develop a counterattack. They argued, for example, that the Vatican's position was merely a "smokescreen" for its efforts to limit women's equality and control over their own lives.[91] Realizing the power of the religious message behind the antiabortion network, the Ford and Pew Foundations had funded and convened a gathering of religious thinkers in Belgium before the Cairo conference to prepare a religious response to the antiabortion network.[92] Progressive foundations also provided extensive funding for a transnational religious pro-choice organization, Catholics for a Free Choice, especially for their Latin American programs.[93]

The battle at Cairo was a skirmish in an ongoing struggle. Regardless of the weight of an actor like the Catholic church, the antiabortion network is clearly a transnational advocacy network fueled by powerful and emotionally charged principles. The antiabortion campaign fits our definition of one of the kinds of issues around which transnational networks can organize successfully—because it invokes images of bodily harm to vulnerable individuals. Only 40 percent of the world's population lives in countries where abortion is available on demand. The trend of most legislative reform on this issue, however, is toward liberalizing abortion

[89] Riley, "Transnational Networks," pp. 1–2, 25.
[90] Francis Kissling (president of the U.S.-based Catholics for a Free Choice), quoted in *Los Angeles Times*, 8 September 1994, cited in Riley, "Transnational Networks," p. 23.
[91] Joan Dunlop (president of the International Women's Health Coalition), quoted in *New York Times*, 15 June 1994, cited in Riley, "Transnational Networks," p. 13.
[92] Riley, "Transnational Networks," p. 13.
[93] Dialog Database File #27, *Foundation Grants Index 1988–1993*.

laws.[94] Pro-life groups have emerged in the wake of liberalization,[95] so antiabortion networks will no doubt increase in the future unless technological advances on the so-called "morning-after pill" effectively take the issue out of the public realm.

An illuminating example of an issue around which a strong women's network campaign has not developed is the issue of veiling or purdah. Purdah does not reflect a single cultural pattern but rather a core set of values about the importance of sheltering and separating women, which are expressed variously in different cultures. Its common elements are that women will wear veils covering their faces and bodies while outside their houses, and will not talk to men as a rule.[96] Justifications for purdah are similar to those given for footbinding among the Chinese: it is a sign of social standing and prestige and it emphasizes the primacy of the domestic realm in women's lives.[97]

There is a significant movement of advocates of Muslim women's rights, including the Women Living under Muslim Laws network, formed in 1985–86, but these groups have not made veiling or purdah one of their core foci. Instead they focus on the rights to education and to own and inherit property, and on the reform of Muslim family law on issues such as divorce and custody of children.[98] Particularly interesting is that Muslim women recognize that a struggle over the interpretation of texts, especially the Qur'an, is central to their enterprise. The call for education for women, including religious higher education, is important because it would give women "credibility in interpreting the texts" in a way that is more favorable for the rights of women.[99] One important activity of groups such as Women Living under Muslim Laws has been to publish excerpts to allow women to start interpreting the Qur'an for themselves.[100]

Veiling has not been the object of an external campaign in part because of its multiple and contested meanings for women themselves. For young women in Algeria, or in Iran under the Shah, veiling became an act of personal liberation and a statement of national sentiment. For many Islamic women the veil offers a form of dignity, protection, and

[94] Rebecca Cook and Bernard Dickens, "International Developments in Abortion Laws: 1977–1988," *American Journal of Public Health* 78:10 (1988): 1305–11.

[95] J. Christopher Soper, "Political Structures and Interest Group Activism: A Comparison of the British and American Pro-Life Movements," *Social Science Journal* 31:3 (1994): 322.

[96] Sylvia M. Hale, "Male Culture and Purdah for Women: The Social Construction of What Women Think Women Think," *Canadian Review of Sociology and Anthropology* 23:2, (1988): 280.

[97] Ibid., p. 279–80.

[98] "Women's Rights Gaining Attention within Islam," *New York Times*, 12 May 1996, p. A3.

[99] Boutheina Cheriet, as quoted in "Women's Rights," *New York Times*.

[100] Women Living under Muslim Laws, "Women in the Qur'an," from a meeting on Qur'anic interpretation by women, Karachi, 8–13 July 1990.

even empowerment. It offers "freedom from the oppression of an over-bearing western world, which they see as morally degenerate; freedom from unwanted male advances and insults."[101]

In Chapter 1 we argue that issues involving bodily harm to vulnerable individuals or issues about legal equality of opportunity are most likely to result in successful transnational networks. Veiling invokes neither of these concerns. Only in Iran and Afganistan, where veiling is legally mandated, does the issue of legal equality of opportunity arise. Elsewhere it is a matter of personal choice within contexts of varying degrees of social coercion. Many of the strongest proponents of the veil are women themselves. In this sense it differs from apartheid, (with which some have compared it), which involved the legal separation of and discrimination against people based on race. Despite many interpretive disputes about issues relating to violence against women (especially female genital mutilation), a greater consensus has emerged around the idea that violence against women is unacceptable and should be ended, than has emerged in opposition to the veil.

Effectiveness of the Network on Violence against Women

Let us now consider the effectiveness of the network activity around the issue of violence against women, using the five stages of effectiveness discussed in Chapter 1: (1) issue attention, agenda setting, and information generation; (2) discursive change, or establishing prescriptive status of norms; (3) procedural changes, such as treaty ratification or cooperation within international organizations; (4) changes in policies; and (5) influence on behavior of state and nonstate actors.

Before the campaign, the issue of violence against women was not on the policy agendas of international organizations. It was absent both from the conclusions of the 1975 International Women's Year Conference in Mexico City and from the 1979 Convention on the Elimination of All Forms of Discrimination against Women. At the Beijing conference, however, it was a centerpiece of the final document. In twenty years the issue had moved from no international attention to a high level of awareness.

To show that discursive change has occurred, or that a norm has gained prescriptive status, we need to show that actors "refer regularly to the rules both in characterizing their own behavior and in commenting on the behavior of others."[102] An example of lack of prescriptive status on this issue

[101] Lama Abu-Odeh, "Post-Colonial Feminism and the Veil: Considering the Differences," *New England Law Review* 26 (1992): 1530; see also "The Kinder, Gentler Face of Islamic Fundamentalism," *Sunday Times* (Singapore), 17 January 1993.

[102] Volker Rittberger, "Research on International Regimes in Germany," in *Regime Theory and International Relations*, ed. Volker Rittberger (Oxford: Oxford University Press, 1993), pp. 10–11.

would be, for example, the statement by a parliamentarian during floor debates on wife battering in Papua New Guinea: "Wife beating is an accepted custom . . . we are wasting our time debating the issue"; or the response by the assistant to the public prosecutor in Peru when a woman reported being sexually molested by police officers while in custody: "Are you a virgin? If you are not a virgin, why do you complain? This is normal."[103]

Important discursive change has occurred at both national and international levels, as reflected in the positions governments took condemning violence against women at the UN conferences at Nairobi, Vienna, and Beijing. By 1994 the UN General Assembly had adopted a Declaration on the Elimination of Violence against Women, and the Organization of American States (OAS) adopted the Inter-American Convention on the Prevention, Punishment, and Eradication of Violence against Women.

It could be that states have made rapid discursive change because they perceive the women's rights campaign as less threatening than the mainstream human rights campaigns that focus on human rights abuses carried out by the state. Yet many feminists believe the documents from these conferences and the UN and OAS declarations and conventions indeed give them leverage with their governments. They hope to engage in accountability politics, demanding that their governments uphold the positions they supported.

Some procedural change has occurred as well. One innovation of the OAS convention was its inclusion of stronger enforcement mechanisms than those of any existing convention on women's issues. This convention sets out a specific section on the duties of states to refrain from engaging in violence against women and to prevent, investigate and impose penalties for violence against women in the public and private sphere. The convention permits any person or group of persons, or any NGO legally recognized in one or more states of the OAS to lodge petitions with the Inter-American Commission on Human Rights containing denunciations or complaints of violations of Article 7 of the convention (which lists the duties of the states) by a state party. As of September 1995, fifteen months after it was adopted, twelve member states have ratified the convention and another ten have signed but not yet ratified it.

Change in discursive positions, procedural innovations, and policies are also occurring at national levels. Bolivia, for example, participated actively in the elaboration of the convention, ratified it promptly, and proposed a National Plan for the Prevention and Eradication of Violence against Women.[104] It set up a subsecretariat for gender issues as part of

[103] Heise et al., *Violence against Women*, p. iii.

[104] Ministerio de Desarrollo Humano, Secretaría Nacional de Asuntos Etnicos, de Género y Generacionales, Subsecretaría de Asuntos de Género, "Plan Nacional de Prevención y Erradicación de la Violencia Contra la Mujer," Documento de Trajajo, La Paz, Bolivia, October 1994.

the Ministry of Human Development, and opened the Office of Battered Women, which runs a shelter. The Bahamas, Barbados, Belize, and Malaysia have criminalized domestic violence, and a number of others have similar laws under consideration. Some countries in Latin America have created women-only police stations to facilitate the reporting of domestic abuse. Other recent government initiatives against gender-based violence include national programs, committees, and / or special constitutional provisions to combat violence against women in Canada, Chile, Australia, Brazil, Colombia, and Ecuador. At the same time, reform and training projects have been carried out in the United States, Zimbabwe, Costa Rica, and Malaysia to sensitize the judiciary and the police to issues of rape and violence against women. Most governments took these initiatives in the period 1988–92 after networks helped put the issue of violence against women on the international agenda.[105]

THE INFORMATION PARADOX

One of the most important (and often overlooked) functions of networks is the generation of information, either through their own activities or through pressures on other institutions. This function sometimes creates a paradoxical situation for evaluating effectiveness. Prior to the campaign on violence against women very little data was available on the incidence of domestic abuse, female genital mutilation, or other kinds of gender-based violence. As a tool in the campaign, and as a by-product of it, networks began to help generate more reliable data. But by doing so they sometimes create the impression that the incidence of violence against women has increased, because there is now better reporting of the practice. When women or police stop viewing a practice like wife battering as ordinary behavior and begin seeing it as violence or domestic abuse, they begin reporting the practice in larger numbers. For example, in Brazil, in response to pressures from the woman's movement, special police stations for women were created beginning in 1985. "Everywhere they have been instituted, the number of complaints has grown, and they have made visible the physical, sexual, and emotional aggression women experience."[106]

We might call it a success of the movement that such violence is more visible, and that complaints are up. Such a definition of "success," however, makes it difficult to document the effectiveness of networks. Ideally, effective networks should lead to a decline in the number of cases of vio-

---

[105] Heise et al., *Violence against Women*, pp. 31–33.
[106] Vera Soares et al., "Brazilian Feminism and Women's Movements: A Two-Way Street," in *The Challenge of Local Feminisms*, p. 317.

lence against women. But because of the cycle of issue creation and issue attention as the necessary antecedents to discursive and behavior change, the problem may at least appear to get worse before it gets better. It is also possible that trends such as urbanization or situations such as economic stagnation may be leading to an actual increase in domestic violence. In the absence of accurate baseline studies, it will be very difficult for a number of years to say whether the practice is declining or increasing.[107] Still, the presence of the network appears to be the precondition for drawing enough attention to the issue so that accurate studies begin to be conducted.

CONCLUSIONS

With remarkable speed, violence against women emerged as a "common advocacy position" around which women's organizations in many parts of the world could agree and collaborate. Why did this way of framing the problem of women's inequality resonate across cultural divides so much more powerfully than either the Western feminist "discrimination" frame or the "women in development" frame?

We believe that part of the answer is intrinsic to the issue itself. Opposition to practices that result in bodily harm to vulnerable individuals are most likely to mobilize transnational networks, especially where the causal chain between the perpetrator and the victim is short. The preservation of human dignity, including protection from physical abuse, appears to be a transcultural value. Some political theorists have argued for essentialist understandings of a set of basic capacities that permit "human flourishing."[108] The most basic of these are life and bodily integrity.

Concern with bodily harm appears to avoid both the indifference resulting from cultural relativism and the arrogance of cultural imperialism. Participants from more than twenty different countries in the first Women's Leadership Institute on Women, Violence, and Human Rights struggled with developing international standards that could be applied across cultures. They were trying to avoid both "culture bashing" and the opposite tendency to accept all customs simply because they are grounded in culture. "The phrase 'practices that are physically harmful

[107] For example, a 1993 survey on interfamily violence in Costa Rica (funded by the Rockefeller Foundation and the Swedish Agency for Research and Cooperation with Developing Countries) found that there were relatively few existing studies on the issue of violence against women in Costa Rica. Leonardo Mata, "Encuesta Nacional Sobre Violencia Intra-Familiar, Costa Rica Urbana, 1992" (San Jose: Asociación para la Investigación de la Salud y PRISMA Consultoría, 1993), p. 18.

[108] Martha C. Nussbaum, "Human Functioning and Social Justice: In Defense of Aristotelian Essentialism," *Political Theory* 20:2 (May 1992): 202–46.

to women or girls' held some appeal as a first approximation of such a standard. The group added the qualifier 'physically' to the phrase widely used by the World Health Organization because a standard based on physical injury seemed easier to apply cross-culturally than notions of emotional or psychological harm."[109]

The frame of violence against woman resonated with this transcultural consensus and innovated within it, thus exemplifying an important test of usefulness raised in Chapter 1. It helped women's groups attract new allies by situating them within the larger "master frames" or "metanarratives" of violence and rights. At the same time, this frame forced human rights groups to rethink their agendas. Women's rights activists, by appealing to the human rights discourse, succeeded in convincing publics of what Charles Tilly has suggested might be called an "adjacency principle." Because states have accepted their obligations to protect certain forms of human rights, if activists can convince publics and policymakers that women's rights are human rights, then they can make the case that states also have obligations to protect women from violence. What made the adjacency argument convincing was that both central human rights norms and violence against women involved severe physical harm. The issue gained attention because of the intrinsic power of the idea, but it was the activists themselves who created the category, and who, through their organizing, placed it on the international agenda.

The women's rights campaign is a story of self-conscious activists who are simultaneously principled and strategic. They are principled in their motivation for action: international feminist activists believed deeply in equality and rights for women everywhere. But they chose their organizing foci and campaign tactics strategically. They hoped to build alliances with women worldwide, knowing it would be difficult. The issue of violence against women came most forcefully from women's groups in the third world, but it found an echo among groups working on battered women in the north. Strategic networkers identified it as an issue that could build bridges internationally, and initiated global campaigns. Women's global interactions served as a microcosm of international resonance, and the issue's bridge-building potential was borne out in the broader arena. As in many transnational advocacy networks the primary motivation is normative, but the means used to carry out campaigns are strategic. Principled goals and strategic means sometimes come into conflict with each other, as in the pro-ERA campaign in the United States, but as activists learn from past campaigns their strategies will develop accordingly.

The campaign on violence against women picked up on issues that were not initially the dominant strands in the mainstream national

---

[109] CWGL, *Women, Violence, and Human Rights*, p. 44.

women's movement in the United States and Europe in the 1970s. Concerns about rape and domestic abuse were more common in local women's groups, and among more radical feminists. The impact of transnational linkages on the U.S. feminist movement is similar to that of the transnational network in the British suffrage debate when it supported the radicals' demand for the vote for married as well as single women. International linkages appeared to amplify and extend the concerns of domestic groups in the United States, producing a more radical critique of the social order. In this sense the influence of transnational networks is important for the politics of domestic movements as well; as it selects those issues with transcultural resonance, it also may boost the legitimacy of marginalized opinions within a domestic movement.

Although the discrimination frame remains important in the debate over women's rights, the frame of violence against women has gained more prominence and led to more rapid institutional change. However closely related, they still represent significantly different ways to frame women's predicament, and the choice of frames influences how the issue resonates with different audiences and which institutional arenas women have access to for redress.

Critics sometimes argue that transnational networks are vehicles for imposing concerns of Western states, foundations, or NGOs upon social movements in the third world. The violence frame helped women overcome this often sterile north-south debate by creating a new category: when wife battering or rape in the United States, female genital mutilation in Africa, and dowry death in India were all classified as forms of violence against women, women could interpret these as common situations and seek similar root causes. In one form or another violence affects large numbers of women in all countries—developed and less developed. For example, the initial campaign on female genital mutilation (FGM) had become an explosive topic for the women's movement by the Copenhagen conference in 1980. Some women and men from countries where it was practiced argued that for Western feminists to criticize genital mutilation was inappropriate and even a form of "cultural imperialism" and racism. Other African women's organizations recognized the problems associated with the practice but wondered why it got so much more attention than other pressing problems of health and development. At the same time, some Western feminists worried that the uproar over FGM might come more from a certain lurid fascination with the practice rather than from a real concern with women's rights. When the opposition to FGM was resituated within a broader campaign against violence against women, it was defused and legitimized. At that point opposition to FGM was embraced by a wider number of groups, including especially groups of African women.

The violence against women issue sometimes plays a similar "bridging" role within national women's movements as well. In countries as diverse as Mexico, Turkey, and Namibia, activists have mobilized around violence against women across numerous divisions (politics, race, ethnicity, class, rural vs. urban).[110] Still, it is important to remember that at the same time that a given frame facilitates some kinds of relationships, it may constrain others. Some women's rights activists now admit that they jumped into the rights frame without fully thinking through the consequences for their movement.[111] What the human rights discourse implied was that if women's organizations were going to use international and regional human rights bodies and machinery, they would have to enhance their knowledge of international law. This requires privileging lawyers and legal expertise in a way that the movement had not previously done nor desired to do. The wisdom of this approach is still being debated within the transnational network, and some activists are now trying to reframe violence against women as a health issue. They note that the human rights frame has been important for raising consciousness about the issue, but they fear that it won't be as effective for prevention and treatment. By framing violence against women as a health issue, especially with reference to health care practitioners and international health organizations, they hope to draw additional attention to the issue and help victims receive treatment.

Clearly, asymmetries continue to exist within the network, created by funding flows and the resulting strategic dominance of U.S. and European organizations and individuals. But the emergence of a common advocacy position around violence against women is the result of much more complicated interplay than is suggested by the "human rights is cultural imperialism" model. Like the new understandings of the diversity of relationships between human beings and nature that evolved within environmental networks during the 1980s, the commonalities discovered in advocacy around violence illustrate the important role that networks play as political spaces.

[110] Dianne Hubbard and Colette Solomon, "The Many Faces of Feminism in Namibia," p. 180, and Marta Lamas et al., "Building Bridges: The Growth of Popular Feminism in Mexico," p. 343, in *The Challenge of Local Feminisms*.
[111] Interview with Lori Heise.

CHAPTER 6

Conclusions: Advocacy Networks and
International Society

Scholars theorizing about transnational relations must grapple with the multiple interactions of domestic and international politics as sources of change in the international system.[1] The blurring of boundaries between international and domestic arenas has long been evident in international and comparative political economy, but its relevance for other forms of politics is less well theorized. Our work on transnational advocacy networks highlights a subset of international issues, characterized by the prominence of principled ideas and a central role for nongovernmental organizations. In this subset of issues, complex global networks carry and re-frame ideas, insert them in policy debates, pressure for regime formation, and enforce existing international norms and rules, at the same time that they try to influence particular domestic political issues. Throughout this book we have tried to achieve greater theoretical clarity in a number of areas. First, we specify how, why, among whom, and to

[1] For example, see Robert Putnam, "Diplomacy and Domestic Politics: The Logic of Two-Level Games," *International Organization* 42 (Summer 1988): 427–60; David H. Lumsdaine, *Moral Vision in International Politics: The Foreign Aid Regime, 1949–1989* (Princeton: Princeton University Press, 1993); Peter Haas, ed., *Knowledge, Power, and International Policy Coordination* special issue, *International Organization* 46 (Winter 1992); James Rosenau, *Turbulence in World Politics: Non-State Actors, Domestic Structures, and International Institutions* (Cambridge: Cambridge University Press, 1995); Thomas Risse-Kappen, ed., *Bringing Transnational Relations Back In* (Princeton: Princeton University Press, 1990); Douglas Chalmers, "Internationalized Domestic Politics in Latin America," Studies, Princeton University, April 1993; Ronnie Lipschutz, "Reconstructing World Politics: The Emergence of Global Civil Society," *Millennium* 21:3 (1992): 389–420; and on transnational social movement organizations see Jackie G. Smith, Charles Chatfield, and Ron Pagnucco, *Transnational Social Movements and World Politics: Solidarity beyond the State* (New York: Syracuse University Press, forthcoming 1997).

what end transnational relations occur. Second, we discuss the characteristic content of such relations—what kinds of ideas and issues seem to require or be amenable to these linkages—and the strategies and tactics
networks use. Finally, we consider the implications for world politics of
forms of organization that are neither hierarchical nor reducible to market relations.

We suggest that scholars of international relations should pay more attention to network forms of organization—characterized by voluntary,
reciprocal, and horizontal exchanges of information and services. Theorists have highlighted the role of networks in the domestic polity and
economy. What is distinctive about the networks we describe here is their
transnational nature, and the way they are organized around shared values and discourses. Networks are difficult to organize transnationally,
and have emerged around a particular set of issues with high value content and transcultural resonance. But the agility and fluidity of networked forms of organization make them particularly appropriate to
historical periods characterized by rapid shifts in problem definition.
Thus we expect the role of networks in international politics to grow.

Both technological and cultural change have contributed to the emergence of transnational advocacy networks. Faster, cheaper, and more reliable international information and transportation technologies have
speeded their growth and helped to break government monopolies over
information. New public receptivity arose partly from the cultural legacy
of the 1960s and drew upon the shared normative basis provided by the
international human rights instruments created after the Second World
War. Transnational value-based advocacy networks are particularly useful where one state is relatively immune to direct local pressure and
linked activists elsewhere have better access to their own governments or
to international organizations. Linking local activists with media and activists abroad can then create a characteristic "boomerang" effect, which
curves around local state indifference and repression to put foreign pressure on local policy elites. Activists may "shop" the entire global scene
for the best venues to present their issues, and seek points of leverage at
which to apply pressure. Thus international contacts amplify voices to
which domestic governments are deaf, while the local work of target
country activists legitimizes efforts of activists abroad.

Transnational networks have developed a range of increasingly sophisticated strategies and techniques. We highlight four: *information politics;*
symbolic politics; leverage politics; and *accountability politics.* Networks
stress gathering and reporting reliable information, but also dramatize
facts by using testimonies of specific individuals to evoke commitment
and broader understanding. Activists use important symbolic events and
conferences to publicize issues and build networks. In addition to trying

to persuade through information and symbolic politics, networks also try to pressure targets to change policies by making an implied or explicit threat of sanctions or leverage if the gap between norms and practices remains too large. Material leverage comes from linking the issue of concern to money, trade, or prestige, as more powerful institutions or governments are pushed to apply pressure. Moral leverage pushes actors to change their practices by holding their behavior up to international scrutiny, or by holding governments or institutions accountable to previous commitments and principles they have endorsed.

Issues involving core values—ideas about right and wrong—arouse strong feelings and stimulate network formation among activists, who see their task as meaningful. Activists capture attention where their issues resonate with existing ideas and ideologies. To motivate action, however, network activists must also innovate, by identifying particular social issues as problematic, attributing blame, proposing a solution, and providing a rationale for action, or by making new connections within accepted value frames.

We have claimed that network actors try to frame issues in ways that make them fit into particular institutional venues and that make them resonate with broader publics, use information and symbols to reinforce their claims, identify appropriate targets, seek leverage over more powerful actors to influence their targets, and try to make institutions accountable in their practices to the norms they claim to uphold. What can we say about what works and what doesn't?

EVALUATING NETWORK SUCCESS OR FAILURE

Networks influence politics at different levels because the actors in these networks are simultaneously helping to define an issue area, convince policymakers and publics that the problems thus defined are soluble, prescribe solutions, and monitor their implementation. We can think of networks being effective in various stages: (1) by framing debates and getting issues on the agenda; (2) by encouraging discursive commitments from states and other policy actors; (3) by causing procedural change at the international and domestic level; (4) by affecting policy; and (5) by influencing behavior changes in target actors.

The structure of domestic institutions is relevant here, some institutions being more open to leverage than others.[2] The closed political structure in societies where participatory channels are blocked or limited may

[2] On the influence of domestic structures on transnational relations, see Thomas Risse-Kappen, "Ideas Do Not Float Freely: Transnational Coalitions, Domestic Structures, and the End of the Cold War," *International Organization* 48 (Spring 1994): 185–214.

lead citizens to seek international linkages to press their claims more effectively. The combination of closed domestic structure in one country
with open structures in other countries and with international organizations is what activates the boomerang pattern characteristic of networks.

Still, domestic structures are only a starting point for understanding
why and how actors form networks, rather than an explanation of the
conditions under which networks can be effective. They cannot tell us
why some transnational networks operating in the same context succeed
and others do not. That similar institutional venues accommodate strik-
ingly different outcomes owes more, we believe, to the nature of the issues and the networks than to domestic or international structures *per se*.

Institutional openness to leverage varies significantly across issue areas
within a single institution or state structure. The environmental movement has leveraged the World Bank, getting stronger environmental conditions in loans, but has not always been able to get these conditions
enforced. The human rights movement has tried to gain similar leverage
in the bank and has failed. The human rights movement has had much
greater success in convincing the United States and European countries
to consider human rights in their military and economic aid policies.
Much of the success of the human rights movement can be attributed to
its ability to leverage state aid policies. The U.S. environmental movement has had much more difficulty in establishing a similarly routinized
form of linkage; efforts to influence the NAFTA negotiations were only
partially successful, and the discussion of trade linkages has exacerbated
network divisions within the United States and internationally.

Our case studies suggested that understanding dynamic elements in
domestic politics is at least as important to success as understanding domestic structures. Under some circumstances, political oppositions may
mediate the influence of transnational actors as much as or more than institutional incumbents. The clearest cases of this in our research were the
footbinding and female circumcision cases. The campaign against footbinding resonated within the modernizing discourse of an emergent re-
formist opposition; the campaign against female circumcision became a
symbol for nationalists of colonialism's effort to destroy deeply held cultural values. For almost all transnational campaigns, how the issue of nationalism is engaged is crucial to achieving issue resonance.

Evaluating the influence of networks is similar to evaluating the influence of sanctions, about which there has been considerable study and
much disagreement.[3] As in the sanctions literature, we must look at characteristics of the "target" and of the "sender" or "source," and at relations

---

[3] See David Baldwin, *Economic Statecraft* (Princeton: Princeton University Press, 1985);
and Stefanie Ann Lenway, "Between War and Commerce: Economic Sanctions as a Tool of
Statecraft," *International Organization* 42:2 (Spring 1988): 397–426.

between the two. Because a network as a sender is not a single actor like a state, but a multiple actor, its influence is even more difficult to trace.

Issue Characteristics

Advocacy networks develop around issues where international relations theorists and theorists of collective action would not predict international cooperation. Except where repressive regimes (as in Haiti) caused serious refugee flows, policymakers could easily ignore human rights, and the doctrine of sovereignty and nonintervention instructed them to do so. The new social knowledge that democracies don't go to war with other democracies may change the stakes in the human rights game; if security (a collective good) is enhanced by the worldwide existence of democracy, then promoting democracy could become a self-interested policy, not just a principled one. Yet the transformation of human rights policies and regimes came well before the emergence of the new social knowledge. As with human rights, states have not traditionally seen women's or indigenous issues as posing collective goods problems. Some environmental issues do pose serious externalities, but these are not necessarily the issues around which advocacy networks form. The environmental networks discussed here, for example, bring pressure on issues that are recognized as posing problems of collective goods, but whose resolution is politically very costly; both sovereignty and property issues are on the table in tropical forest negotiations.

States have few incentives to cooperate on these issues, and because many of the network campaigns challenge traditional notions of state sovereignty, we might expect states to cooperate to block network activities. Active intervention by a committed actor is necessary to get these issues onto political agendas. Human rights violations must be deliberately brought to the foreign policy agenda of a third party or an international organization before influence can be brought to bear. Deforestation and misuse of infant formula became issues rather than mere problems when network activists gave them identifiable causes and proposed remedies.

Actors within government can also raise the salience of an issue, but for states to act, either the values in question must plausibly coincide with the "national interest" or the government acting must believe (correctly or not) that the action is not costly (or at least that it is less costly than not acting). Part of what networks do is to try to transform state understandings of their national interests, and alter their calculations of the costs or benefits of particular policies. Moreover, the activists promoting the issue must seek state actors who are either network members themselves (in terms of their willingness to take costly action to promote issues they care deeply about) or who have other incentives to act. Environmentalists in the multilateral bank campaign got crucial support from Wisconsin senator Robert Kasten, chair of the Foreign Operations Subcommittee of the Senate Appropriations Committee, more because of his general hostility to the multilateral banks than because of his principled support for their particular aims.

The second characteristic of network issues worth highlighting is that they are all *in their general form* issues around which sustained mass mobilization is unlikely. The problem is transforming diffuse agreement (protect the environment, defend human rights) into willingness to take action.[4] The difficulty of constituent mobilization is one explanation for the predominance of advocacy pressure tactics over mass mobilization campaigns in these issue areas. There are exceptions. Amnesty International's organizational model involves large numbers of people in regular activities; boycott strategies, such as those used in the infant formula campaign and the tropical timber campaign, have similar characteristics.

New ideas are more likely to be influential if they fit well with existing ideas and ideologies in a particular historical setting.[5] Since networks are carriers of new ideas, they must find ways to frame them to resonate or fit with the larger belief systems and real life contexts within which the debates occur.[6] The ability of transnational advocacy networks to frame issues successfully is especially problematic because, unlike domestic social movements, different parts of advocacy networks need to fit with belief systems, life experiences, and stories, myths, and folk tales in many different countries and cultures. We argue that the two types of issues most characteristic of these networks—issues involving bodily harm to vulnerable individuals, and legal equality of opportunity—speak to aspects of belief systems or life experiences that transcend a specific cultural or political context.

There are various explanations about why such issues appear most prominently in international campaigns. Although issues of bodily harm

[4] This is similar to the problem of mobilization around consensus issues, discussed in social movement theories. For differing views, see Michael Schwartz and Shuva Paul, "Resource Mobilization versus the Mobilization of People: Why Consensus Movements Cannot Be Instruments of Social Change," pp. 205–23, and John D. McCarthy and Mark Wolfson, "Consensus Movements, Conflict Movements, and the Cooptation of Civic and State Infrastructures," pp. 273–300, in *Frontiers in Social Movement Theory*, ed. Aldon Morris and Carol McClurg Mueller (New Haven: Yale University Press, 1992).

[5] Peter Hall, *The Political Power of Economic Ideas* (Princeton: Princeton University Press, 1989), pp. 383–84; Kathryn Sikkink, *Ideas and Institutions* (Ithaca: Cornell University Press, 1991), p. 26.

[6] David Snow and Robert Benford suggest that four sets of factors account for successful framing: the "robustness, completeness, and thoroughness of the framing effort"; the internal structure of the larger belief system the framers want to affect; the relevance of the frame to the real world of the participants; and the relationship of the frame to the cycle of protest. Snow and Benford, "Ideology, Frame Resonance, and Participant Mobilization," in *Frontiers in Social Movement Theory*, p. 199.

resonate with the ideological traditions in Western liberal countries like the United States and Western Europe, they also resonate with basic ideas of human dignity common to most cultures. Not all cultures have beliefs about human rights (as individualistic, universal, and indivisible), but most value human dignity.[7] Gross violations of human rights run contrary to these divergent conceptions of human dignity. Issues of bodily harm also lend themselves to dramatic portrayal and personal testimony that are such an important part of network tactics.

Another transcultural belief with wide resonance is the concern with protecting the most vulnerable parts of the population—especially infants and children. The contrast between the Nestlé boycott and other issues that did not lead to international boycotts may capture the importance of the ability to resonate transnationally. Although more deaths are attributed to tobacco use than to the misuse of infant formula, there has been no successful, sustained international consumer boycott of tobacco companies. The perceived harm to vulnerable infants and their mothers who believe they are using a quality product generates more concern than does harm to adults who choose to smoke. A campaign against "Joe Camel" cigarette advertisements is the exception that proves the rule: organizers achieved some success because they claimed that the ads attempted to market cigarettes to children.

The Nestlé boycott also illustrates the importance of framing issues to resonate with existing belief systems. Both the company and the boycott tried to capitalize on the transcultural desire to do the best thing for one's baby. The baby food companies tried to convince mothers that infant formula was a modern healthy way to feed their babies, but the baby food network mobilized information and testimony strategically to convert the bottle from a symbol of modernity and health into a potentially dangerous threat to infant health in the third world.

Campaigns involving legal equality of opportunity also appear to lend themselves to transnational campaigns. Why this issue should have transcultural resonance is not completely clear. Most of the societies where such campaigns are carried out have adopted liberal institutions of democracy and rule of law, yet exclude some signficant part of the population from participation in these institutions. This disjuncture between the neutral discourse of equality implicit in liberalism and the unequal access to liberal institutions opens a space for symbolic political action and the accountability politics of networks. In other words, liberalism carries within it not the seeds of its destruction, but the seeds of its expansion. Liberalism, with all its historical shortcomings, contains a subversive element that plays into the hands of activists. We agree with the work of John Meyer and his col-

[7] See Jack Donnelly, *Human Rights in Theory and Practice* (Ithaca: Cornell University Press, 1989), pp. 49–50.

leagues that there is a global cultural process of expansion of liberal values; where we differ is how this leads to political transformation.[8] We argue that liberal discourse can provide opportunities for activists to expose the gap between discourse and practice, and that this has been an effective organizing tool. For example, the organizers of the first conference on women's rights at Seneca Falls in 1848 eloquently and effectively stated their grievances using the words of the U.S. Declaration of Independence but substituting the word "woman" for "man," and "men" for "King George."

Why would we expect concern about the gap between discourse and practice, especially in the authoritarian regimes that are often the target of network pressures? Scholars have long recognized that even repressive regimes depend on a combination of coercion and consent to stay in power. Network campaigns have been most successful in countries that have internalized the discourse of liberalism to such a degree that there exists a disjuncture to plumb and expose. Liberal discourse and institutions also place limits and constraints, which is another reason why issues involving equality of opportunity are easier to organize around than these involving equity of outcome.

Cross-cultural resonance of issues does not necessarily eliminate all of the tensions implicit in the encounter. This is particularly true of issues that address poverty and inequality within an intentionalist frame. Within all networks that involve activists from both developing and developed countries, awareness of vastly unequal access to resources underlies conversation about issue framing, and also about the relationships among network members.

Actor Characteristics: Networks and Targets

Not surprisingly, networks are more effective where they are strong and dense. Network strength and density involves the total number and size of organizations in the network, and the regularity of their exchanges.[9] Strong and dense networks also include many "nodes" within the target state of the campaign. Network campaigns against human rights violations were more successful in Argentina and Chile than in Guatemala in the mid- to late 1970s partly because well-organized domestic human rights organizations existed in those countries. Although rights violations in Guatemala were even more severe than in Argentina and Chile, no effective local human rights NGOs existed in Guatemala until the mid-1980s; the presence of such organizations as part of the net-

[8] George M. Thomas, John W. Meyer, Francisco O. Ramirez, and John Boli, eds., *Institutional Structure: Constituting State, Society, and the Individual* (Newbury Park, Calif.: Sage, 1987).
[9] Analysts of networks within cities or countries are able to measure network density, but the task is far more difficult for a far-flung transnational network.

work increased the success of human rights pressures on Guatemala in the early 1990s. Local network members contribute information and bestow increased legitimacy on the activities of the network as a whole.

The density and strength of networks comes both from their identity as defined by principles, goals, and targets, and from the structural relationships among the networked organizations and individuals. In other words, the network-as-actor derives a great deal of its effectiveness from the network-as-structure, within which ideas are formulated, reformulated, tested, and negotiated. However much an individual or representative of a particular organization may speak and act in the name of a network without necessarily consulting its other members regularly, the synergy of networking nonetheless transforms the timbre of his or her voice. The "voice" of the network is not the sum of the network component voices, but the product of an interaction of voices (and different from any single voice of a network member).

This is not to suggest that advocacy networks are egalitarian structures. We recognize the asymmetrical or lopsided nature of most network interactions. Power is exercised within networks, and power often follows from resources, of which a preponderance exists within northern network nodes. Stronger actors in the network do often drown out the weaker ones, but because of the nature of the network form of organization, many actors (including powerful northern ones) are transformed through their participation in the network. However amorphous or weak the structure, it is still true that the nature of the agency we are talking about derives from that structure—just as the structure is itself a creation of the singular agents embedded within it. Networks cannot be undermined simply by characterizing them (the structures) as "agents" of a particular actor or position. Undermining a dense network rather requires destructuring it—that is, eroding the relations of trust or mutual dependence that exist among networked actors. The Malaysian government attempted to do this in 1993, for example, by circulating a story claiming misuse of funds by NGOs doing fundraising in the Sarawak case, and accusing Randy Hayes of the Rainforest Action Network of fabricating a story about abuse of Penan tribesmen. Network communications were sufficiently strong to weather this set of accusations.

Crucial determinants of the effectiveness of international networks are the characteristics of the targets, especially their vulnerability to both material and moral leverage.[10] The target may be vulnerable to particular

[10] Our notion of vulnerability includes but is not limited to the idea of "vulnerability interdependence" developed by Keohane and Nye. For them, when a country is faced with costs imposed by outside action, vulnerability rests on the "relative availability and costliness of alternatives." Robert Keohane and Joseph Nye, *Power and Interdependence*, 2d ed. (Glenview, Ill.: Scott, Foresman, 1989), p. 13.

kinds of issue linkage, for example when external aid is dependent on human rights performance. Vulnerability may come from prior normative commitments, as when the World Bank, already committed in many statements to sound environmental performance, was criticized for loans that arguably worsened the environmental situation. Targets may experience greater vulnerability at particular junctures, as was the case with Mexico during the negotiations for the North American Free Trade Agreement; Mexico's need to safeguard its prestige in that context provided openings for both human rights and environmental networks to press claims. Finally, vulnerability may simply represent a desire to maintain good standing in valued international groupings.[11]

Large military and economic aid flows to Latin American countries in the 1970s and 1980s gave the human rights network leverage against repressive countries in the region. Pressuring a country like China or Burma was more difficult because neither was receiving large economic and military assistance from Western countries. The only available leverage was trade privileges—most favored nation status or the generalized system of preferences—the use of which is more controversial, as it hurts the exporters in Western countries. Ecological groups achieved influence in the bank campaign by providing information that convinced members of Congress and the Treasury Department to instruct U.S. executive directors of multilateral development banks to monitor closely the environmental impact of loans; similar processes took place in European countries.

Even if leverage is available, the target country must be sensitive to the pressures. As the failure of economic sanctions against Haiti in 1993–94 made clear, some governments can resist pressures successfully for long periods. Countries most sensitive to pressure are those that care about their international image. For issue linkage to work, the target country must value the carrot being extended (or good withheld) more than it values the policy being targeted. But as the cases of human rights in Haiti or tropical deforestation in Sarawak illustrate, linkage with money, trade, or prestige is not a sufficient condition for effectiveness. Haiti's military rulers chose to hang onto power in the face of universal moral censure and economic collapse. Only the threat of military invasion led to a last-minute agreement to relinquish power. In Sarawak, local politicians become immensely wealthy by granting logging concessions, and the state government depends on logging for a good part of its revenues. Although the Malaysian federal government was sensitive to attacks on its international status, it was even more vulnerable to threats by Sarawak's politicians to defect from the government coalition.

[11] Audie Klotz, *Norms in International Relations: The Struggle against Apartheid* (Ithaca: Cornell University Press, 1995).

The Nestlé Corporation was vulnerable to the pressures of a consumer boycott because a large range of its consumer food items were identified by the company name (Nestlé Quik, Nestlé Crunch) and because it had invested heavily in a corporate image of quality goods ("Nestlé makes the very best") which could be easily undermined by the accusation that Nestlé goods led to infant deaths in the third world. Attempts to organize a similar boycott against other producers of infant formula in the United States have failed because they have targeted less familiar corporations—American Home Products, Abbott Laboratories—whose products rarely carry the company name.

IMPLICATIONS FOR INTERNATIONAL SOCIETY

Central to this project is an understanding of the international system not as anarchy but as international society. We share with Hedley Bull and the English school of international relations scholars the idea that we live in an international society when on the basis of common interest and values states "conceive themselves to be bound by a common set of rules in their relations with one another and share in the working of common institutions."[12] We disagree, however, with Bull's emphasis always on a society of *states*. Even in 1977 when he wrote his classic work, Bull recognized that international society was evolving, and that the human rights issue offered a particularly potent challenge to the logic of a society of sovereign states.

> Carried to its logical extreme, the doctrine of human rights and duties under international law is subversive of the whole principle that mankind should be organized as a society of sovereign states. For, if the rights of each man can be asserted on the world political stage over and against the claims of his state, and his duties proclaimed irrespective of his position as a servant or a citizen of that state, then the position of the state as a body sovereign over its citizens, and entitled to command their obedience, has been subject to challenge, and the structure of the society of sovereign states has been placed in jeopardy. The way is left open for the subversion of the society of sovereign states on behalf of the alternative organizing principle of a cosmopolitan community.[13]

Our vision is closer to what Bull called "neo-medievalism," where non-state actors begin to undermine state sovereignty. The term doesn't adequately portray the dynamism and novelty of the new global actors we

<hr/>

[12] Hedley Bull, *The Anarchical Society: A Study of Order in World Politics* (New York: Columbia University Press, 1977), p. 13.
[13] Ibid., p. 146.

discuss, but Bull's central insight of a new system with "overlapping authority and multiple loyalty" does capture part of the change we describe.[14] Bull issued two serious challenges, one empirical—the task of documenting the extent and nature of changes—and the other theoretical—to specify what kind of alternative vision of international politics might modify or supplant the centrality of interactions among sovereign states.

Recent empirical work in sociology has gone a long way toward demonstrating the extent of changes "above" and "below" the state. The "world polity" theory associated with John Meyer, John Boli, George Thomas, and their colleagues conceives of an international society in a radically different way. For these scholars, international society is the site of diffusion of world culture—a process that itself constitutes the characteristics of states. The vehicles for diffusion become global intergovernmental and nongovernmental organizations, but neither the sources of global cultural norms nor the processes through which those norms evolve are adequately specified.[15]

Proponents of world polity theory have documented the rise and diffusion of a wide range of cultural norms and practices and the related emergence of international nongovernmental organizations (INGOs) and intergovernmental organizations (IOs). These are presented as enactors of basic principles of the world culture: universalism, individualism, rational voluntaristic authority, human purposes, and world citizenship; there is thus no meaningful distinction between those transnational actors espousing norms that reinforce existing institutional power relationships and those that challenge them.[16]

We argue that different transnational actors have profoundly divergent purposes and goals. To understand how change occurs in the world polity we have to understand the quite different logic and process among the different categories of transnational actors. The logic of transnational advocacy networks, which are often in conflict with states over basic principles, is quite different from the logic of other transnational actors, such as the International Olympic Committee or, the International Electrotechnical Commission, who provide symbols or services or models for states. In essence, world polity theorists eliminate the struggles over power and meaning that for us are central to normative change. Martha Finnemore makes a similar point when she argues that despite its im-

[14] Ibid., p. 245.
[15] See Martha Finnemore's excellent review essay on the world polity school, "Norms, Culture, and World Politics: Insights from Sociology's Institutionalism," *International Organization* 50:2 (Spring 1996): 339.
[16] John Boli and George M. Thomas, "Introduction," in *World Polity Formation since 1875: World Culture and International Non-Governmental Organizations*, ed. Boli and Thomas (Stanford: Stanford University Press, forthcoming), p. 7 (manuscript).

pressive achievements, world polity theory marginalizes politics, obscures power, and "omits conflicts, violence, and leadership." She challenges political scientists to engage in a dialogue with the world polity theorists because "political process, coercion and violence, value conflict and normative contestation are our business."[17]

Nevertheless, the world polity theorists have an important insight. At some point, they suggest, what was once unthinkable becomes obvious, and from then on change starts to occur much more rapidly. The early battles to gain the vote for women were fought tooth and nail country by country, and success came very slowly. This history does not look at all like the natural process of cultural change suggested by the polity theorists. But after a critical mass of countries adopted woman suffrage, it was naturalized as an essential attribute of the modern state, and many countries granted women the vote even without the pressure of domestic women's movements. Perhaps some understanding of "thresholds" might help integrate our work with that of world polity theorists. These sociologists have focused theoretically on the second part of the process of change, when norms acquire a "taken for granted quality" and states adopt them without any political pressures from domestic polities. Thus they privilege explanations for normative change that highlight the influence of world culture. We explore the earlier stages of norm emergence and adoption, characterized by intense domestic and international struggles over meaning and policy, and thus tend to privilege explanations that highlight human agency and indeterminacy. Rather than seeing these as opposing theoretical explanations for causes of normative change, an understanding of stages suggests that the process of creating and institutionalizing new norms may be quite different from the process of adhering to norms that have already been widely accepted.

World polity theories treat IOs and INGOs as conveyor belts carrying Western liberal norms elsewhere. Once again, our research suggests that much modern network activity does not conform to this pattern. Many networks have been sites of cultural and political negotiation rather than mere enactors of dominant Western norms. Western human rights norms have indeed been the defining framework for many networks, but how these norms are articulated is transformed in the process of network activity. For example, indigenous rights issues and cultural survival issues, at the forefront of modern network activity, run counter to the cultural model put forward by the world polity theorists.

In other words, as modern anthropologists realize, culture is not a totalizing influence, but a field that is constantly in transformation. Certain discourses such as that of human rights provide a language for negotiation.

---

[17] Finnemore, "Norms, Culture, and World Politics," pp. 327, 339, 340, 344.

Within this language certain moves are privileged over others; without doubt, human rights is a very disciplining discourse. But it is also a permissive discourse. The success of the campaign in making the point that women's rights are human rights reveals the possibilities within the discourse of human rights. Because international human rights policies came simultaneously from universalist, individualist, and voluntarist ideas *and* from a profound critique of how Western institutions had organized their contacts with the developing world, they allowed broader scope for contradictory understandings than might be expected. These critiques led in a very undetermined fashion to the emergence of human rights policy; theorists in the late twentieth century should not assume that the trajectory was predetermined by homogenizing global cultural forces.

Reconceptualizing international society does not require abandoning a focus on actors and institutions to seek underlying forces that make states and other forms of association epiphenomenal. We do find, however, that enough evidence of change in the relationships among actors, institutions, norms, and ideas exists to make the world political system rather than an international society of states the appropriate level of analysis. We also believe that studying networks is extraordinarily valuable for tracking and ultimately theorizing about these evolving relationships.

In the world political system today, states remain the predominant actors. But even for theoretical purposes it is hard to imagine conceiving of the state as "a closed, impermeable, and sovereign unit, completely separated from all other states."[18] Although the notion of the unitary state remains a convenient convention for certain kinds of international interactions, central to most interstate relations (as well as relationships between states and other individuals or associations) is the recognition of internally differentiated states and societies.[19] But sovereignty is eroded only in clearly delimited circumstances. The doctrine of the exhaustion of domestic remedies that is embedded in human rights law, for example, captures the nature of the relationship between the society of states and the emerging cosmopolitan community: individuals who hope for recourse for the alleged violation of their rights must have exhausted domestic remedies or shown that attempts to do so are futile. Then, and only then, if they still believe that they have been unjustly treated, may they have recourse to the international arena. The cosmopolitan community can bring pressure to bear at stages of the domestic process, but the state is still in charge.

---

[18] Arnold Wolfers, *Discord and Collaboration: Essays on International Politics* (Baltimore: John Hopkins University Press, 1962), p. 19.

[19] Robert Putnam captures part of this reality with his two-level games metaphor. See "Diplomacy and Domestic Politics: The Logic of Two-Level Games," *International Organization* 42:3 (Summer 1988): 427–60.

There are few theorists of international relations to whom we can turn for help in giving voice to this vision of the global potential and limitations of a cosmopolitan community of individuals. Anything that hinted of idealism was so thoroughly discredited by the perceived failures of idealism in the interwar period that no self-respecting international relations theorist dared admit a role of individual human agency motivated by principles in transforming the global scene. Yet it was precisely the obvious failure of states to protect human dignity during the interwar period and the Second World War that for political philosophers, such as Hannah Arendt, made such agency necessary. Arendt, argues Jeffrey Isaac, was not a theorist of human rights, but a "theorist of the politics made necessary by a world that despoils human rights," a politics that "might encourage new forms of regional and international identity and moral responsibility."[20]

The international system we present is made up not only of states engaged in self-help or even rule-governed behavior, but of dense webs of interactions and interrelations among citizens of different states which both reflect and help sustain shared values, beliefs, and projects. We distinguish our view from what Sidney Tarrow has called the "strong globalization thesis" which sees structural forces inevitably pulling the world into even more tightly knit global process.[21] The globalization process we observe is not an inevitable steamroller but a specific set of interactions among purposeful individuals. Although in the aggregate these interactions may seem earthshaking, they can also be dissected and mapped in a way that reveals great indeterminacy at most points of the process. There is nothing inevitable about this story: it is the composite of thousands of decisions which could have been decided otherwise.

The problem with much of the theory in international relations is that it does not have a motor of change, or that the motor of change—such as state self-interest, or changing power capabilities—is impoverished, and cannot explain the sources or nature of the international change we study here. Classic realist theory in international relations has not been useful for explaining profound changes, such as the breakdown of the Soviet Union and the satellites states in Eastern Europe, the end of slavery, or the granting of women the right to vote throughout the world.

Liberal international relations theory has a more compelling explanation of change because it is based on the proposition that individuals and groups in domestic and transnational society are the primary actors, that these groups in turn determine the preferences of states, and that the nature

[20] Jeffrey C. Isaac, "A New Guarantee on Earth: Hannah Arendt on Human Dignity and the Politics of Human Rights," *American Political Science Review* 90:1 (March 1996): 67, 69.

[21] Sidney Tarrow, *Power in Movement: Social Movements and Contentious Politics*, rev. ed. (Cambridge: Cambridge University Press, 1998), chapter 11.

and intensity of state preferences determine the outcomes in international politics. Liberalism places significant emphasis, then, on domestic regime type, because whether or not a state is democratic determines which groups and individuals it represents.[22] Regime type is also important because authoritarian governments can "stunt the growth of domestic and transnational civil society."[23] Structural liberalism also argues that there has been a "collapse of the foreign/domestic distinction," and that foreign policy is no longer insulated from domestic politics in the way that it was once perceived to be, an argument that finds substantial support in the cases discussed in this book.[24]

Our approach differs from liberalism in a number of important respects. Liberalism assumes self-interested and risk-averse actors, and therefore its theory of how individuals and groups change their preferences must be based on changes in context leading to changing calculations of interest or risk.[25] We study individuals and groups who are motivated primarily by principled ideas and who, if not always risk-takers, at least are not risk-averse. We share the liberal assumption that governments represent (imperfectly) a subset of domestic society, and that individuals influence governments through political institutions and social practices linking state and society. But liberalism, as currently formulated, lacks the tools to understand how individuals and groups, through their interactions, might constitute new actors and transform understandings of interests and identities. We argue that individuals and groups may influence not only the preferences of their own states via representation, but also the preferences of individuals and groups elsewhere, and even of states elsewhere, through a combination of persuasion, socialization, and pressure.

Network theory can thus provide a model for transnational change that is not just one of "diffusion" of liberal institutions and practices, but one through which the preferences and identities of actors engaged in transnational society are sometimes mutually transformed through their interactions with each other. Because networks are voluntary and horizontal, actors participate in them to the degree that they anticipate mutual learning, respect, and benefits. Modern networks are not conveyor belts of liberal ideals but vehicles for communicative and political exchange, with the potential for mutual transformation of participants.

In this sense, network theory links the constructivist belief that international identities are constructed to empirical research tracing the

---

[22] This discussion of structural liberalism relies upon Andrew Moravcsik, "Liberalism and International Relations Theory," and Anne-Marie Slaughter, "International Law in a World of Liberal States," *European Journal of International Law* 6 (1995): 503–38.
[23] Slaughter, "International Law," p. 509.
[24] Ibid., p. 514.
[25] Moravcsik, "Liberalism and International Relations Theory," p. 3.

paths through which this process occurs, and identifying the material and ideological limits to such construction in particular historical and political settings.

The importance of this process of mutual constitution is particularly relevant for considering the issue of sovereignty, about which significant differences may exist among network members. For the most part, activists in the north tend to see the erosion of sovereignty as a positive thing. For human rights activists it gives individuals suffering abuse recourse against the actions of their own state; for environmental activists it allows ecological values to be placed above narrow definitions of national interest. Given the innumerable glaring violations of sovereignty perpetrated by states and economic actors, why should measures that protect individuals from harm raise such concern? Northerners within networks usually see third world leaders' claims about sovereignty as the self-serving positions of authoritarian or, in any case, elite actors. They consider that a weaker sovereignty might actually improve the political clout of the most marginalized people in developing countries.

In the south, however, many activists take quite a different view. Rather than seeing sovereignty as a stone wall blocking the spread of desired principles and norms, they recognize its fragility and worry about weakening it further. The doctrines of sovereignty and nonintervention remain the main line of defense against foreign efforts to limit domestic and international choices that third world states (and their citizens) can make. Self-determination, because it has so rarely been practiced in a satisfactory manner, remains a desired, if fading, utopia. Sovereignty over resources, a fundamental part of the discussions about a new international economic order, appears particularly to be threatened by international action on the environment. Even where third world activists may oppose the policies of their own governments, they have no reason to believe that international actors would do better, and considerable reason to suspect the contrary. In developing countries it is as much the idea of the state, as it is the state itself, that warrants loyalty.

For many third world activists involved in advocacy networks, the individuated and intentional model of action that networks imply—the focus on "rights talk"—begs the question of structural inequality. At conference after conference, this question has at some point moved to center stage. The issue of sovereignty, for third world activists, is deeply embedded in the issue of structural inequality.

It is over such issues that networks are valuable as a space for the negotiation of meanings. In the emergence of the focus on violence for the international women's networks, in the evolution of the multilateral bank campaign and the tropical timber campaigns, the political learning that took place within the networks involved not only strategies and tactics but normative shifts in understanding of shared identities and responsibilities. The tropical timber campaign's focus on consumers of tropical hardwoods as much as on producers is the result of such a shift. Because parts of states and international organizations also participate in these networks, this process of negotiation within the emergent cosmopolitan community is not "outside" the state. Instead it involves state actors in active reflection on state interests as well.

Recognizing this dual character of networks provides correction for the continuing inability of structuralist theory to motivate change in the international system.[26] If transnational advocacy networks involve patterned interaction among states and nonstate actors whose agency is expressed in the international system, then by derivation states are bringing more than their relations with other states into their systemic relations. They are bringing more even than the domestic political baggage implied by Putnam's two-level game formulation (which, nonetheless, has the virtue of bridging the domestic international divide in a mutually determining fashion).[27] State actors as network components bring to international relations identities and goals that are not purely derived from their structural position in a world of states—and that may even be constituted by relationships established with citizens of other states. These identities and goals, furthermore, may contain elements in profound contradiction to the usual systemic roles of these states. Resolving these contradictions may require shifts in interstate relations that are not driven either by national interest or by "self-help" as traditionally understood.

The conflicting identities and goals that states qua network components take into the international system are increasingly enmeshed in the structural interaction between state and nonstate actors that is the network. The agency of a network usually cannot be reduced to the agency even of its leading members. This is true even if the network's access to the international arena is dependent upon a state's representative role in relation to other states. However, if the network's agency cannot be reduced to that of its most powerful node, then the appearance of states to each other is described—and circumscribed—by the multiple relationships and identities they carry around always. From the negotiation of this multiplicity of agencies and structures in which states are embedded comes the possibility of change—not so much the negation of self-help as a richer rendering of the constitution of self, and of the substance of the helping.

The concept of a transnational advocacy network is an important element in conceptualizing the changing nature of the international polity

[26] But see also, for a different but similarly motivated argument, David Dessler, "What's at Stake in the Agent-Structure Debate?" *International Organization* 43:3 (Summer 1989): 441–73.
[27] Putnam, "Diplomacy and Domestic Politics."

and particularly in understanding the interaction between societies and states in the formulation of international policies. It suggests a view of multiple pathways into the international arena, a view that attributes to domestic actors a degree of agency that a more state-centric approach would not admit. States remain the major players internationally, but advocacy networks provide domestic actors with allies outside their own states. This approach suggests answers to some of the questions about how issues get on the international agenda, how they are framed as they are, and why certain kinds of international campaigns or pressures are effective in some cases but not in others. Our initial research has suggested that networks have considerable importance in bringing transformative and mobilizing ideas into the international system, and it offers promising new directions for further research.

Abbreviations

AAAS: American Assocation for the Advancement of Science
AI: Amnesty International
BIC: Bank Information Center
CEBRAP: Brazilian Center for Analysis and Planning (Centro Brasileiro de
  Analise e Planejamento)
CEDAW: Committee on the Elimination of Discrimination against Women
  (United Nations)
CEDI: Ecumenical Center for Documentation and Information (Brazil)
CSM: Church of Scotland Missionary Society
CWGL: Center for Women's Global Leadership
ECOSOC: Economic and Social Council (United Nations)
EDF: Environmental Defense Fund
EZLN: Zapatista National Liberation Army (Mexico)
FAO: Food and Agriculture Organization (United Nations)
FOE: Friends of the Earth
FUNAI: National Indian Foundation (Brazil)
IACHR: Inter-American Commission on Human Rights
ICW: International Council of Women
IDA: International Development Agency
IFN: International Feminist Network
INESC: Institute of Socio-Economic Studies (Brazil)
INGO: international nongovernmental organization
IO: international organization
IPHAE: Institute for Pre-History, Anthropology, and Ecology (Brazil)
IRLC: International Right to Life Committee

ITTO: International Tropical Timber Organization
IUCN: International Union for the Conservation of Nature and Natural
    Resources
IWRAW: International Women's Rights Action Watch
IWSA: International Women's Suffrage Assocation
IWTC: International Women's Tribune Center
JATAN: Japan Tropical Forest Action Network
KCA: Kikuyu Central Association
NGO: nongovernmental organization
NOVIB: Netherlands Organization for International Development Cooper-
    ation.
NRDC: Natural Resources Defense Council
OAS: Organization of American States
PAN: National Action Party (Mexico)
PRI: Institutionalized Revolutionary Party (Mexico)
SAM: Sahabat Alam Malaysia
UNCTAD: United Nations Conference on Trade and Development
UNDP: United Nations Development Program
UNEP: United Nations Environmental Program
UNESCO: United Nations Educational, Scientific, and Cultural Organiza-
    tion
UNHCR: United Nationas High Commissioner on Refugees
U.S.-AID: United States Agency for International Development
WOLA: Washington Office on Latin America
WRM: World Rainforest Movement
WWF: World Wildlife Fund

Index

Indigenous Peoples, Year of, 22, 25
Indonesia, 136, 158, 180
Infant formula, 14, 20–21, 28–29, 131, 209.
  See also Nestlé boycott
Information, 14, 16, 30, 36, 96, 132; and
  effectiveness of networks, 194–195;
  strategic use of, 147–149
Information politics, 16, 18–22, 45, 53; and
  environmental networks, 156, 161; and
  human rights networks, 107, 115, 117;
  and women's rights, 183, 185
Institutionalized Revolutionary Party
  (PRI), 110, 112–113, 115
Inter-American Commission on Human
  Rights (IACHR), x, 17, 80, 93, 97, 106–107,
  109, 113–114, 193. *See also* Organization
  of American States
Inter-american Convention on the
  Prevention, Punishment, and
  Eradication of Violence against women,
  172–173, 193
Interest groups, 30–31
International Council of women (ICW),
  55–56
International Development Agency, 139, 147
International Feminist Network, 167, 175
Internationalism, 15–16, 81. *See also* Liberal
  internationalism; Solidarity tradition
International Monetary Fund, 28, 140, 156
International organizations, 95–97,
  126–127, 210, 211. *See also* Organization
  of American States; United Nations;
  World Bank
International society, 209–211
International Tribunal on Crimes against
  Women, 175, 187
International Tropical Timber
  Organization (ITTO), 127, 150, 152–154,
  156, 158–160, 162
International Union for the Conservation of
  Nature and Natural Resources (IUCN),
  122, 125–126, 129–130, 133–15, 154
International Whaling Commission (IWC),
  127, 154
International Woman Suffrage Assocation
  (IWSA), 53, 55–58
International Women's Rights Action
  Watch (IWRAW), 179
International Women's Tribune Center,
  169, 186
International Women's Year Conference in
  Mexico City, 168–170, 175, 181–182, 192,
  208
International Year of the Forest, 135, 153
Iran, 191–192
ISIS International, 170, 175

Issue characteristics, 26–28, 203–206
Italy, 104, 145

J

Japan, 57, 62; and environmental issues,
  129, 133, 139, 153, 154, 158; and violence
  against women, 175–176, 180, 188
Java, 57, 136

K

Kasten, Robert, 139, 204
Katzenstein, Peter, 3n, 34n
Kayan. *See* Dayak
Kenya, 39–40, 60, 67–77
Kenyatta, Jomo, 70–71, 75
Keohane, Robert, 1n, 4n, 5n, 29, 207
Kikuyu, 39, 67–75, 77
Klotz, Audie, 3n, 16n, 34n, 57n, 208n
Korea, 175–176, 180, 185, 188
Kratochwil, Friedrich, 3n

L

Latin America, 15, 22, 58, 129; and human
  rights, 80, 84–87, 90–95, 98, 106, 109,
  118–119, 208; and women's rights,
  170–172, 175, 177–179, 185–186, 190, 194.
  See also individual country listings,
  Inter-American Commission on Human
  Rights; Organization of American States
Latin American and Caribbean Feminist
  Network against Domestic and Sexual
  Violence, 167, 180
Law, 24–25, 109; and human rights, 212;
  international, 11, 34, 36, 81, 84–85, 87
League of Nations, 55, 81, 82, 84
Lemkin, Raphael, 81–82, 87–88
Leverage politics, 2, 12, 16, 23–24, 54, 118,
  202, 207–208; and environmental
  networks, 135, 146, 155–156, 161
Liberal internationalism, 15–16, 81–82, 88
Liberalism, 119, 205–206, 213–214
Lincoln, Abraham, 49–51
Little, Mrs. Archibald, 62–63, 73, 75
Lumsdaine, David, 3n
Lutzenberger, José, 143, 146

M

Maasai, 40, 68
Mahathir Mohamad, Prime Minister,
  150–152, 157, 159

About the Authors

Margaret E. Keck is Professor of Political Science at the Johns Hopkins University. She is the author of *The Workers' Party and Democratization in Brazil*.

Kathryn Sikkink is Professor of Political Science at the University of Minnesota. She is the author of *Ideas and Institutions: Developmentalism in Brazil and Argentina*, also from Cornell.